Daughters of the Dra

Other books by Christine Hall

How to Books Ltd
How to Get a Job in Germany
How to Live & Work in Germany
How to be a Freelance Journalist
How to Work in Retail (with Sylvia Lichfield)
Living and Working in Britain
Living and Working in China

In Print Publishing Ltd
Teaching English in China (in preparation)

Daughters of the Dragon
Women's lives in contemporary China

Christine Hall

Scarlet Press

Published in 1997 by Scarlet Press
5 Montague Road, London E8 2HN

British Library Cataloguing-in-Publication Data
A catalogue record for this book is available from
the British Library

ISBN   1 85727 068 1 pb

Designed and produced for Scarlet Press by
Chase Production Services, Chadlington, OX7 3LN
Typeset from the author's disk by
Stanford DTP Services, Milton Keynes
Printed in Great Britain

Contents

Acknowledgements

Many thanks to all the people who contributed to the book, including all my case study interviewees, although it is doubtful if they will ever be able to read my work.

Sarah Lowis from Scotland, who worked as a VSO teacher in China, helped greatly by taking photos 'to order' and by interviewing her students to fill gaps in this book.

Li Lian from the correspondence and liaison department of the magazine *China Pictorial* in Beijing helped by answering questions, clarifying contents of the editorial magazine and by sending additional material. The Chinese Embassy in London sent a wealth of practical information and statistics, and the Great Britain-China Centre in London allowed me the use of their library by post. Anna de Cleene, Far East Projects Manager of the University of Central Lancashire in Beijing, contributed information which I found difficult to obtain in Britain.

Nicholas D. Kristof and Sheryl WuDunn contributed information beyond quotes from their joint book *China Wakes*, which I find the best available book on life in China today. Both assisted me generously with their own observations.

Su Xiaohuan, author of *The First Step Towards Equality*, and Wu Naitao, author of *Mother Wife Daughter*, as well as their publisher, China Intercontinental Press, have given the much appreciated permission to use extracts from these books.

Author David Rice, and his agents, Peters Fraser & Dunlop, allowed me to use quotes from his book (unfortunately currently out of print), *The Dragon's Brood*, which contains fascinating interviews with contemporary young Chinese.

Gina Corrigan and the Guidebook Company gave permission to use extracts from the *Odyssey Illustrated Guide to Guizhou*, a book which offers colourful photography and cultural information beyond what one would expect of a guidebook. The *Independent* newspaper allowed the use of quotes from an article by Teresa Poole.

Thanks also to Zhang Haixiang, a middle-school teacher in Beijing, and the western medical expert (who will recognize herself although she insisted on remaining unnamed) who contributed enlightening information and frank, courageous views on the education and health system.

Thanks also to Wang who introduced me to the art of Manchurian fan dancing in Tonghua, to Carol who taught me Chinese, to Li, Xiao, Ruth, and Joan for their guidance and invaluable help. Also to authors Norman Toulson, Claire Gill, Diana Lloyd Taylor and Mary V. Webb who assisted with the proofreading of, and comments on, several chapters, and to Kate Chitham who produced the map.

I would welcome readers' comments on this book, whether their observations of women's lives in China agree or disagree with mine. Please write to me c/o Scarlet Press.

May 1996   Christine Hall

Foreword

**Katie Lee, Director of the
Great Britain-China Centre, London**

Christine Hall has written a thorough and timely survey describing where women stand in Chinese society today. It is important to remember just how much the position has changed since 1949 and how liberated Chinese women are now in comparison with their grandmothers. Many of the barriers and hindrances that a Chinese woman faces in society are similar to the ones we face in the 'liberated' West. But in the case of China much of the challenge is still new ground and Chinese women are finding their own way of changing their situation.

We must be careful when applying formulas to Chinese women as to all women. To understand their position we need a very good understanding of China's cultural history. Christine Hall goes some way towards providing that understanding and her book is a useful introduction to the situation, although as with much of our knowledge of China, we can never delve deep enough. Ironically a policy with which most women, and men, might have a problem, that of the one-child family, has proved in the urban centres to be liberating for daughters. With only one child there is no choice but to put all your efforts, concern and ambition into that child even if it is a daughter. This is making a new generation of confident and demanding women!

I had not been to China for nearly ten years before a trip to Beijing in February 1996. I was astounded by the visual changes in the cityscape, the high rise buildings, the karoake bars, and not least by the way people dress. Whilst change is most apparent in women, with some extraordinary (to a Western eye) combinations of dress styles, it is no less obvious in the case of men with their Western suits, shiny leather shoes, and ties. The change is not only on the surface. Two of my closest Chinese friends, both women, got married and divorced during the time that I was away. The move for the divorce came from them, and was resisted by their husbands, and yet they have kept their jobs and position. They are certainly breaking new ground, albeit in the highly sophisticated environment of Beijing and Shanghai. The same acceptance may not have been possible in a rural setting.

The Great Britain-China Centre in its exchange programme with China has focused, amongst other projects, on developing capacity among Chinese women's NGOs as they prepared for the Fourth World Conference on Women, and continues to work in this area. There is undoubtedly a lot of room for support in this area, and Ms Hall's book will give anyone new to the China scene a good introduction to the situation as it is today.

Preface

There is more than one truth about everything, and this is probably more the case in China than anywhere else. I found I was constantly confronted by three truths: the official view, backed by facts, statistics and the law; the view of the independent observer from the outside, who applies different criteria, and compares what she sees with what she has experienced elsewhere; the view of the women themselves, how they perceive their situation. Sometimes these three views complement one another, sometimes there is a sharp contrast.

No truth is 'truer' than the other. My book is a mixture of all three, but the main focus is on the truth as seen by the women themselves. There are other, notable books available which analyse official sources (such as the series of booklets published by China Intercontinental Press) or record a Western observer's view.

Wherever possible, I have allowed the women to speak out in this book, even if their view cannot be supported by official sources or if it disagrees with my opinion. I have used official information and my own notes mostly to put the women's experience into perspective.

I concentrated on the lives of women today, as there seems to be a shortage of information. I did not go in any depth into the fate of women in China's past, simply because there are some excellent books on the subject already on the market, notably the books by Elisabeth Croll which cover the earlier twentieth century.

The lives, ambitions and problems of the individual women I interviewed reflect and provide an insight into those of Chinese women in general, but Chinese culture and life is so diverse that it is not possible to present a 'typical' or 'representative' woman. Many matters vary greatly, depending on climate, religion, ethnic group and level of education. Even crucial points such as the enforcement of the one-child policy are in the hands of provincial authorities and therefore handled differently. The women I have chosen represent one or several aspects of Chinese life.

I worked for a Chinese publisher in 1994, which gave me the marvellous opportunity to make friends with Chinese women and to work side by side with them, gaining insights from which the journalist or scholar on an official research visit is barred. She is shown only what she should see. Perhaps this has made me more 'streetwise' than I would have been after officially sanctioned research.

I had expected the Chinese to be reluctant about being interviewed. After all, a few years ago they might still have been arrested for talking to a foreigner. To my surprise, most women were eager to cooperate, to tell their life stories, to discuss their problems, feelings and ambitions, and to pose for photographs. The only subjects on which they were not forthcoming were their participation in the Cultural Revolution and their religious beliefs.

Many interviewees were surprisingly frank and have given me permission to use their real names. Others have asked that their names and circumstances should be changed to protect their identity. I have used fictitious names for these, but marked them (pseudonym).

I interviewed about 100 women from different walks of life and chatted to many more informally. Most of this book is based on these conversations, and I have supplemented them with other people's interviews and research in other geographical areas. The majority of interviewees are from the northeast of China, where I lived and worked.

Most quotations are taken from notes as I wrote them down in my diaries and in numerous notebooks during the interviews in 1994. In very few instances I have recounted the quotes from memory. This was in cases when I did not have a notebook at hand, or when I did not expect I would ever use the material. I did not know I was going to write this particular book until after I had returned from China and did not always realize how significant a comment could be: for example, the woman who told me that she had adopted a girl, or the one who mentioned during a casual conversation that she suspected slave dealers in the labour market. Of course I have quoted from memory only where my memory is clear and where the quote contributes to the chapter. When I quoted from memory, I've pointed this out in the annotations.

One of the difficulties was the language, especially where the interviewees were peasants or workers and spoke no English. The interviews were conducted either with a mutual friend acting as an interpreter, or in English (of which many interviewees had only a very basic command), or in Chinese (of which I had only a basic command). In these cases I used the gist of the quotes, rather than a word-by-word account.

Whenever I use information that is not derived from personal interviews, but from other people's interviews and observations, I have made this clear by using annotations.

Although I have tried to give up-to-date information, please remember that everything in China is changing rapidly. Especially where wages and prices are mentioned, the rapid inflation can distort comparisons. When I did make comparisons, I used examples from the same month. Most of these refer to the period of January to July 1994, but even within this limited period prices changed drastically. Amounts mentioned in one chapter should not be compared directly with amounts mentioned in another chapter. Even amounts referring to the same period but differing areas can be misleading, as living costs vary enormously. Attempts to measure the value of Chinese money against Western currencies would give wrong impressions. The basic currency is the *yuan* (popularly called *'kwai'*). 1 *yuan* = 10 *jiao* (*'mao'*) = 100 *fen*.

Spellings of place names can be confusing, as the official spelling of many provinces and cities has been changed repeatedly this century. For example, *Peking* became first *Peiping* and then *Beijing*. I have always used the spelling which is currently used in the *pinyin* (latinised writing) of the People's Republic of China. Where a former place name is better known in the West than the current one, I have added it in brackets. For example: *Guangzhou (Canton)*.

To avoid confusion, I used the current *pinyin* spelling of people's names in all cases, regardless of when they lived; for example: *Mao Zedong*, not *Mao Tse Tung*. Where Western readers might not recognize the Chinese spelling, I've put the better known version in brackets; for example: Kung Fuzi (Confucius). There is no consistency in *pinyin* whether or not to write the second and third syllable of a person's name in one word or in two. Even my Chinese friends changed the way they wrote their own name from time to time. I've decided to write them in one word throughout the book, so that every Chinese name consists of two words, the family name and the individual's name; for example, *Xi Gaoli*, not *Xi Gao Li*.

I have applied the word *Liberation* to the Communist Revolution of 1949, even though the term smacks of political ideology. Calling it Liberation helps to differentiate the 1949 revolution from the other Chinese revolutions mentioned in the book. Liberation is also the word the Chinese use. Last but not least, the 1949 revolution literally liberated the women of China by giving them equal rights for the first time in their history.

All information, unless otherwise specified, refers to the People's Republic of China, also known as 'red China', 'communist China' or 'mainland China', as opposed to Taiwan, which is also known as the 'Republic of China'.

Which areas belong to the People's Republic (PR) is debatable and depends on political viewpoint. Is Taiwan part of communist China, or is it a separate country? Do forty-five years of Chinese occupation make Tibet a Chinese province?

It is with considerable hesitation that I have decided to use the PR Chinese government's definition of the PR China. However, all official figures and statistics relate to the People's Republic as defined by the People's Republic's government, and other information is simply not available.

There are three types of administrative divisions: provinces, autonomous regions and centrally administered municipalities. As this can be quite a mouthful, and as this is a book about lifestyles not administration policies, I'm referring to them all as 'provinces' for ease of reading.

1 Women in China – their history

One quarter of the world's women live in China. Before 1949, their lives were among the most restricted and oppressed on earth. In 1950, with the beginning of communist China, they gained social and political equality with men. Today in the 1990s, many Chinese women are ready to cede their social equality in order to gain the freedom of fashion and style, to achieve higher living standards and to become desirable in the eyes of men. Are the women reverting to their traditional role in Chinese society, trading feminism for feminity?

The country: damp jungles and sandy deserts

China is one of the largest countries in the world, with 9,597,000 square kilometres. From north to south, the country measures about 5,500 kilometres, and from east to west, about 5,200 kilometres[1] embracing over 50 ethnic peoples with their differing cultures, histories, attitudes, and lifestyles, a variety of climates which range from subtropical to frigid, and landscapes which include damp jungles, snow-covered mountains and expanses of sandy desert.

Because of the sheer size of the country and its different cultures, the condition of women is, of course, far from uniform.

The Western idea of China as a country full of lush green paddy fields is vastly inaccurate. Instead, think of China as a country of mountains: two-thirds of the landscape are taken up by hills, mountains and plateaus. One hundred mountains in China exceed 7,000 metres in height, including the Qomolangma (Mount Everest).[2]

China's surface slopes down from the west to the east in three steps. At the top in the west, there is the Tibetan Plateau which, with an average height of more than 4,000 metres, is often called the 'Roof of the World'. Mountain ranges within this step are the Himalayas, the Kunlun, and the Gangdise. The second level is at an altitude of between 1,000 and 2,000 metres and consists of the Inner Mongolian, Loess and Yunnan-Guizhou Plateaus, and the Sichuan, Tarim and Junggar basins. Further east, the third step is about 500 to 1,000 metres high; it includes the Greater Hinggan, Taihang, Wushan and Xuefeng Mountains, the Northeast Plain, the North China Plain, and the Middle-Lower Changjiang (Yangtze) Plain. The plains are interspersed with picturesque hills.[3]

Most people live in the east, where the economy is dictated by the great drainage basins of the Huanghe and Changjiang (Yangtze) rivers. Intensive irrigation in the warm and humid southeast helps to produce one third of the world's rice – in up to three harvests per year – as well as maize, sugar and oil seeds.

In the cold northeast – the former Manchuria there are still sufficient water supplies to farm the land, but the cold climate and frequent droughts cause problems. There are some rice fields, but they allow only one harvest per year, while wheat, maize, barley and soybeans are grown in large quantities.

The Chinese coast, which ranges over 18,000 kilometres from the Vietnam border in the south to the Korean border in the east, comprises cities such as Guangzhou (formerly Canton), the capital Beijing and Shanghai, and is the wealthiest and most densely populated part of China.

Many Chinese dream of living in one of the coastal cities, and many rural people flock to the south. Shanghai is the largest city in China, with a population of 13.37 million.[4] Goods 'made in Shanghai' are regarded as superior to those made anywhere else in China.

The central north and the west are, on the whole, poor areas and are far less densely populated. Cultivation is restricted to sheltered valleys and oases. In the southwest, the Tibetan Plateau supports scattered sheep herding and in the the north, there are vast dry desert areas. Many ethnic minority tribes live in the north and west.

Ethnic minorities

China is not a single nation, but a multinational country with many ethnic groups, each with their own history, culture, and attitudes.

When outsiders talk about 'the Chinese' and 'Chinese culture', they usually refer to the biggest ethnic group, the Han people, who dominate large parts of China, including the capital, Beijing (formerly Peking), and the wealthy coastal areas in China's south and southeast.

How many ethnic groups there are depends on the political viewpoint. The government of the People's Republic of China insists that there are 55 ethnic minorities. This figure does not include the Han majority, or some ethnic groups (such as the 20,000 Kucongs) who are not officially recognized as a separate nationality;[5] but it includes the Gaoshan nationality of Taiwan and the Tibetans.

Ethnic minorities account for less than 10 per cent of China's population. Their combined population of 90.567 million is 8.01 per cent of the national total and almost 49 per cent of them are female.[6]

The minorities inhabit more than half (64 per cent) of the land. However, this land is mostly deep in the mountains or in remote and border areas, where communication is poor and natural conditions are unfavourable. The economy is usually underdeveloped and livelihood can be tough. They are mainly concentrated in five autonomous regions and other autonomous administrative units. Most of their land surrounds China like an outer semi-circle from the southwest to the northeast, starting in the rainy mountains of the Yunnan and Guangxi Provinces in the southeast, through the ice plateau of Quinghai and Xiyang (Tibet) Provinces and the deserts of Xinjiang Province to the broad steppes of Inner Mongolia and finally the plains and mountains of Manchuria (Heilongjiang, Jilin and Liaoning Provinces).

The largest nationalities are the 14 million Zhuang in the Guangxi Province, and the 7.5 million Hui in the Ningxia Province who are an Islamic sub-group of the Han. Other important nationalities include the Miao, Bouyei, Dong, Hani, Yao, Yi, and Manchu. Some have a specific way of life, such as the nomadic Ewenki hunter tribe in the northeast and the Kirghiz herders in the northwest.

Most have strict patriarchal societies, such as the Islamic Hui in the Ningxia Province in the north, and the Uygur in the Xinjiang Province in the northwest, which many Chinese regard as the worst place for a woman to live.[7] Another ethnic group among whom life for women is particularly difficult is the Hani nationality. When women of other ethnic groups discuss the status of women and complain about discrimination and lack of opportunities, they will often add, 'At least we're better off than Hani women'. The Hani area in the Yunnan Province in the southwest of China is economically backward and extremely conservative. Living standards there are the lowest among the large (more than 1 million population) ethnic groups, and women are regarded as the far inferior sex. Traditionally, if a couple had no boys they were punished and were forced to live in houses where parts of the walls were removed to expose them to strong winds. Luckily, such customs are decreasing.[8]

A few minorities, including the Jinuo and the Naxi (also in the Yunnan Province), have essentially matriarchal societies. This is discussed in Chapter 5.

Whenever I asked Chinese people in which part of China women enjoy the greatest freedom, respect and power, they agreed that this was in the south, southeast and southwest, regardless of Han or minority domination.

There is an amazing racial variety among the minority groups. Tribe wanderings in historical times, political upheavals earlier this century and work placements in recent years have led to members of ethnic minorities living all over China. There is not a typical 'Chinese face', because every nationality has its own facial characteristics.

Women account for 47 per cent of ethnic minority employees and for 26.6 per cent of ethnic minority cadres (senior officials). It appears that women of ethnic minorities are particularly active in politics. Among the deputies to the Eighth National People's Congress, 106 were ethnic minority women, accounting for 17 per cent of the total of women deputies. Three ethnic minority women have been elected members of the Standing Committee of the National People's Congress.

In Western countries, we are used to thinking of ethnic minorities as groups which are discriminated against. This is not the case in China, where members of ethnic minorities are, on the whole, accepted and respected. China is proud of its nationalities and the Chinese like to display the wealth of cultures at festivals and events. People from minority nationalities in traditional dress are often depicted in series of postage stamps and they are the only women whose pictures appear on banknotes.

Members of ethnic minorities not only have the same citizens' rights as the Han people, but they enjoy special protection and have several privileges. For example, in family planning they have considerably more rights than the majority and they are not usually bound by the one-child rule. Ethnic minorities are encouraged to continue their traditional way of life, but at the same time the government strives to introduce modern methods of healthcare, midwifery, education and agriculture. Between 1990 and 1993, the government allocated 212.86 million *yuan* (a huge amount, as a rural worker's annual income was often below 2,000 *yuan*) for 'funds targeting the food and clothing problems of poor ethnic minority areas'.

Standards of hygiene, healthcare and literacy are often poor in ethnic minority areas, and the 1990s have seen massive programmes to improve quality of provision in those areas. These tasks are difficult, not only because of deep-rooted traditions and attitudes, but because of the sheer expanse of the area and the lack of transport, and also because some minorities have their own spoken and written languages. Once they've been trained in the cities, teachers and skilled health workers resist being sent back into the poverty-stricken countryside.

Women in pre-communist China: sexy crippled feet

Pre-communist society was based on the teaching of Kung Fuzi (Confucius, 550-478 BC), whose main doctrine was that inequality of everything, and specifically the inequality of the sexes in society, was natural and necessary. He taught that everyone had their place – and a woman's place was at the bottom of the hierarchy. Kung Fuzi stated: 'Women are human but lower than men' and 'It is the law of nature that woman should not be allowed any will of her own.'

Many sayings and proverbs confirm the woman's role in society: 'Women have no voice, and their words carry no weight'. 'The woman's right place is within and the man's right place is without.' 'To be a woman means to submit.' 'Man is like sun and woman is like moon who shines only in his light.' 'If you rear a son, he belongs to you; if you rear a daughter, she belongs to another family.' 'A woman without talent is virtuous.' 'An educated woman is bound to cause trouble.'

Until 1949, women possessed no political rights. Among most ethnic groups, including the Han majority, they were excluded from social and political rights. Economically dependent on the males of their family, they could not own property, had no inheritance rights and possessed no source of income. They were forced to obey their fathers before marriage and their husbands after marriage. If they survived their husbands they had to obey their sons, although in practice widows often ruled their families. Society allowed them little personal dignity or independent status, and they had little or no say in their choice of marriage partner. The only way of rising to a higher status was to have a married son. This led to a position of 'lower management' within the extended family, because the wives of sons had to serve their mothers-in-law. They were harassed by systems of polygamy – a man could have as many concubines as he wished – and of prostitution.

Historically, the husband's word was the law: he was the head of the family and the wife remained subservient. Divorce was impossible to obtain for women, while men could discard their wives for a variety of reasons, including 'being talkative', 'being disrespectful to her parents-in-law' or 'refusing to accept the husband's concubine'. The laws changed little throughout the centuries.

The teachings of Kung Fuzi were firm on the inequality of the sexes and allowed a man to take a concubine if his wife was infertile or bore only daughters. Many Chinese men went further and took as many concubines as they wished.[9] Poor farmers and farm labourers accounted for 70 per cent of the rural population, owned only 10 per cent of the land, and women had no right to own land at all.

Becoming a concubine was often the only escape from starvation for village women. In many areas peasant men were too poor to support a wife, and as women were not allowed to possess property and had no income, they turned to well-off men who could afford concubines. In the 1930s, especially in the northeast, women found it hard to find men who could afford a single wife, but there were men willing to take them as concubines, often in return for hard work. Just to survive, these women were willing to do anything required of them, from washing to weeding, from chopping wood to collecting dry dung. Taking a concubine was regarded as equal to buying a cow – something that provided work and babies.[10]

In many cases, it was the parents who arranged for their daughter to become a concubine, often at an early age and in exchange for money. Parents betrothed their daughters as early as possible to avoid the risk of their becoming spinsters. If they waited too long before arranging a betrothal, the landlords sometimes claimed first rights (that is, the right to deflower a girl) and after that, it was nearly impossible to marry her off. To sell girls as concubines was better than to have them end up as prostitutes, and the money from the sale was often used to buy sons out of the army. Girls had no say in the choice of their husband.[11]

The situation was even worse for the so-called 'child-wives': girls aged between three and eighteen were a popular commodity. They were sold either into prostitution or a combination of sexual and domestic slavery. While the men who kept concubines were usually well off and could afford to feed their extended family, the owners of child-wives were frequently poor themselves and child-wives subsisted at near-starvation level. They often had to go to bed with empty stomachs or with a meal made from rice that higher-status members of the family had left over. Child-wives found stealing food were beaten. In her book *Women of China* Bobby Siu mentions the case of a seven-year-old child-wife who was found stealing some left-over rice intended for the chicken: her grandmother-in-law beat her with a thick bamboo stick.[12]

Peasants did not rear daughters for sale, but in times of famine they did not hesitate to offer their daughters for sale either in the market or to the landlord. Periods of drought and famine happened often and affected large areas. One such famine occurred in northern China from autumn 1876 until 1879. It appears from contemporary reports that the sale of women and children began during the first few months of the disaster. Timothy Richard, a baptist missionary, reported that when the last of the grain was gone in 1876 people ate turnip leaves and grass seeds, then pulled down their houses to sell their timber, and finally resorted to selling their clothes and their children. In winter 1877, women as well as children were sold for pennies in the markets.[13] In 1920 and 1921, much of the Hebei Province, as well as parts of Shandong, Henan, Shanxi and Shaanxi, were affected by several droughts and caught in a cycle of famine. Houses were stripped of doors and beams, either to sell the wood or to burn it for warmth. Tens of thousands of children were sold as servants, prostitutes or secondary wives.[14]

There are few reports of boy children being sold; either because parents were more reluctant to part with sons or because they had less value in domestic or sexual service. However, when Mao Zedong conducted a meticulous survey in Xunwu area in the

Jiangxi Province about matters such as prostitution and sale of children, he found several cases in which peasants had sold their boy children aged three to 14, but none of the girls. Jonathan D. Spence, in *The Search For Modern China*, suggests that this is because hard labour was top priority in the area, rather than domestic work or sexual services.[15] I believe there is another possible explanation: peasants cared less about the loss of a daughter and they may not have bothered to report the sale because they did not wish to take back a daughter who had already been 'used' by the buyer and had more than likely lost her virginity.

For many centuries, peasant women had helped supplement their families' incomes with their spinning, weaving and needlework. Although the income was not usually theirs to dispose of, at least it gave them a small amount of independence and status. But the influx of foreign cotton goods at the beginning of the century brought the collapse of these women-run cottage industries; by 1930, it had become cheaper to buy foreign cloth than to make it. The decline of the handicraft industry meant that peasant women lost their only source of income and their status declined further.[16]

Women were often subject of physical abuse, the most severe of which was the binding of the feet. Small feet were considered attractive and were also a way of preventing women from moving about or escaping. From an early age – starting between five and ten – girls had their feet bound in tight bandages, toes pointing downwards and inwards until they broke, and nails growing into the flesh. Ultimately, most toes simply fell off. Small girls were exposed to excruciating pain for many years and remained crippled for the rest of their lives. There were several grades of the so-called 'lily feet': the smaller the feet, the more attractive and desirable was the woman. Court ladies had the smallest feet. There is no doubt that tiny crippled feet were considered sexy by virtually all men in northeast China. Men who suggested that footbinding should be abolished didn't do it because the sight of painful crippled feet repelled them, but because sexy small feet could lead men astray. 'Persons with bound feet' became a synonym for the female gender in China.

However, not all women underwent the footbinding; bound feet were essentially a custom of the upper class in parts of northeast China. Unfortunately, the middle classes strove to imitate the court customs, and even some traders, peasants and workers bound their daughters' feet to enhance the girls' marriage prospects. In the south, most women escaped this barbaric custom because women had a stronger position in some southern societies, while in others, men probably regarded women as valuable working equipment which it would be foolish to damage.

I never saw women with crippled feet during my stay in northeast China, not even among the older generation of Han, but some of my Chinese friends remembered that their grandmothers had had 'lily feet'. They told me that when they were children, they regarded small crippled feet as normal, 'something grandmothers had'.

In the nineteenth century, missionaries saw schools as an instrument to civilize and convert the Chinese, and at the end of the century schools for women were introduced. However, education remained the fashionable privilege of a few thousand women from rich and intellectual families in the cities. Giving in to pressure for reform, the Manchu government established a school for women in Shanghai in 1898, and a few more in 1900.[17] The situation improved only slowly and it is estimated that at the time of the Communist Revolution up to 90 per cent of women were still illiterate.

There were strong movements long before the Communist Revolution to protect women from footbinding and to give them education. In 1898 members of the court led by Kang Youwei called for reforms which included schools for women, and the emperor agreed to them. Kang Youwei also asked that footbinding should be prohibited and that anti-footbinding associations everywhere in China should be encouraged. However, these reforms lasted for only 100 days – too short to protect girls from mutilation.

In the first decade of the century there were some organized protests by peasant women who drew attention to starvation, demanded better living conditions, protested against the maltreatment of children and against the wrecking of houses as a form of punishment. For example, a group of women pillaged the private granaries of certain well-to-do farmers in the market town Suzhou in 1907,[18] but such pillages were not a typically female action. There were several rice riots taking place in the same year, when the starving masses ransacked rice shops and granaries, for example in Gaoyou (Jiangsou), Yuyao (Zhejiang), Shaoxing (Zhejiang), Hangzhou (Zhejiang) and Taiping (Anhui).[19] At any rate, such female peasant uprisings occurred only on a local level and were dispersed by military force.

The 1911 revolution kindled a feminist movement which focused on equal rights for women and men, and for the participation of women in politics. But the feminist movement had only a restricted impact, because it was limited to groups of intellectual women in the cities and to Chinese women in Japan.[20] The revolution failed to fulfil the hopes of the women, or indeed of the people in general. Instead of the hoped-for wonderful world of egalitarian rule, independence from foreign countries and wealth for all, the country ended up in the hands of warlords who were local dictators engaged in fighting one another.

Yuan Shikai, the new Republican president, passed a series of laws which restricted the freedom of press, speech, association and assembly. This meant that women were not even allowed to join political groups or to attend political meetings, a big blow to the feminist movement. The period between 1911 and 1949 was one of great suffering and unrest which included increasing corruption, civil war between nationalists and communists, and Japanese occupation during which monstrous atrocities were committed, mostly against women.

Between 1917 and 1927 there were several organized strikes by women workers who demanded better working conditions, but many of these were brutally subdued, in some cases with the execution of the strike leaders.[21] The largest one took place in Shanghai in 1922, when several thousand female workers in silk factories went on strike for higher wages and better conditions.[22] The same year also saw the foundation of a major women's rights league. From then on until 1949, many women's organizations were started which then grew in strength.

After the 'Liberation'

In 1949 the communist party came into power – mostly because of the support they had among the poor, especially the women – and in that same year women gained equal rights. There is no doubt that the Communist Revolution was the single most important event in the history of Chinese women, and that women benefited more than any other social group from the changes. The Chinese refer to the Communist Revolution as 'the Liberation'. I am using this term in this book to differentiate the event from other Chinese revolutions, and also because the word 'liberation' has a literal meaning especially for Chinese women.

The First Plenary Session of the Chinese People's Political Consultative Conference in Beijing had 10 per cent female delegates. This may seem low for a party which had gender equality in politics written on its banner, but it was an incredible step forward for women who previously had never had any political rights whatsoever. A woman, Song Qingling, was elected vice-chair of the People's Central Government.

The common programme had the status of a provisional constitution and stipulated that women and men had equal rights in all spheres of life, mentioning in particular political, economic, cultural, social and family life. Immediately after the founding of the People's Republic, the All-China Women's Federation was established.

In 1950, the Marriage Law was promulgated and implemented. It abrogated completely the forced arranged marriages and also the feudal marriage system that regarded men as superior. It put into practice a new system of equality, monogyny and equality and safeguarded the legal rights and interests of women and also of children.[23]

A widespread and profound land reform distributed land on the basis of the number of members in a family. The allocation for female family members became equal to that of male family members, and if a family consisted of women only, women were for the first time masters of their own soil. This fundamentally altered the economical status of women, but the distribution of land to individuals was subsequently changed into a system of collectives. At first, this system of agricultural work units functioned well, but when productivity dropped it left the Chinese in poverty again.

The electoral law of 1953 stipulated that women had the same rights to vote and to stand for election as men. The elections in December 1953 were the first ever large-scale general ballot in Chinese history. More than 90 per cent of women cast their vote. Seventeen per cent of people's deputies elected were women.[24] In 1954 the first constitution of the People's Republic confirmed the women's rights of the provisional constitution.

The communists changed existing sayings and propagated new women-friendly ones, the most famous and successful of which was Mao Zedong's 'Women hold up half the sky'. Although women did not always achieve full equality in practice, especially in patriarchal rural societies, life offered far more freedom and opportunities for them than before.

Chiang, from Honan (central China), was the daughter of poor tenant peasants; her father was illiterate, her mother had learnt some basic reading skills after the Liberation. Chiang had one sister and two brothers. She had spent her childhood working as a scullery maid in the local landlord's house, wearing rags, and had received next to no education before the Liberation. By the time journalist Edgar Snow interviewed her in about 1960, she had graduated from school and was a 22-year-old sophomore at an engineering college and owned two dresses.[25]

The cheated generation: survivors of the Cultural Revolution

In 1966, Mao Zedong started the Cultural Revolution, which was meant to cleanse China of its old ideas, cultural customs and habits, and to make the revolutionary idea shine in a new light.

It went disastrously wrong. Mao put the power into the hands of the 'red guards', the organisation of young people of China who, though uneducated, controlled everything from railway stations and schools to hospitals. Senior staff and intellectuals were, at best, dismissed from their jobs but more likely, were sent to the countryside to do forced hard labour. At worst, they were beaten up, imprisoned, tortured, executed. Victims included doctors, politicians, teachers, people who spoke a foreign language, people who had been to university, people who had had a good income or power, foreigners living in China, Chinese people who had been abroad, religious leaders, lawyers and everyone who was related or married to, or had contact with, a member of any of these groups.

One of the victims of the Cultural Revolution is Qin, whose parents – both professors – were beaten and imprisoned by the red guards. Because of her parents' status, the 15-year old girl was taken away from her family and sent to do hard labour in the countryside. She remembers sleeping in a mud hut, the walls of which had ice on the inside, and after a day's work in the field the skin sometimes came off her fingers when she took off her gloves.[26]

People were discriminated against for having the wrong 'class background'. The red guards destroyed books, places of religious worship works of art and ancient buildings. Most classic operas and other works of art and culture were forbidden and replaced with 'revolutionary' works. Schools, colleges and universities were either closed or taught only political studies. A whole generation graduated from school with hardly any academic knowledge; many remained illiterate. The only people who could get some form of higher education were those with the right class background, that is those who came from peasant, worker and soldier families. This frenzy involved many executions and murders and lasted for ten years. Even today, no one can estimate how many people were killed.

Today, most Chinese are reluctant to talk about that period. The older people I asked just shook their heads sadly and were still afraid of repercussions if they spoke freely. The students were too young to have conscious memories of the violent wave. People in the middle age group had mostly been red guards themselves and were possibly ashamed of their own contribution to the violent 'cleansing'. Only two women, both from the northeast, were willing to talk about their memories.

Liang Zhi Quiao, a 41-year-old accountant in Tonghua (Jilin Province) told me:

> I was a pupil during the Cultural Revolution. I had already learnt to read and write a little when it started. They taught us a little English at middle school – but that was only singing the communist *International Song*. I can still sing it by heart, but I don't understand a word of it and I never did. When I was a pupil, political studies had priority before academic studies. Working was very important too. We had to study 'working', that was our main subject. The curriculum didn't leave much space for anything else. [27]

Tang Qing (a pseudonym), a 51-year-old teacher in Beijing, said:

> Before the Cultural Revolution I was an energetic young woman. I taught Russian at school. I also spoke some French and some English. I had great plans for my future. Then suddenly I was branded as an 'intellectual' and an 'enemy of the people'. When I did or said something of which my students disapproved of, for example criticize their homework, they would beat me up. I think it was worse for me than for the other teachers at school, because languages were a dangerous skill to possess in those days. They sent me to the countryside for 're-education'. The reality was, I was being kicked about by peasants while doing all their dirty work. I was ill and hungry most of the time.

Then someone suggested, "Why don't you marry a peasant to prove that you have reformed?" I agreed, because this was the only way to escape the abuse. They chose a man who was more or less the village idiot, but I did not know that when I agreed. He was kind to me, and my life became much better. I continued to be a peasant for many years. Then language teachers were needed again. I started teaching at rural school but my husband became violent and started beating me. Now I work in Beijing and visit him only twice a year. He and his parents demand that I bring them a lot of money every time. I do not have the courage to obtain a divorce. I would not find another man now at my age. To be a woman without a husband would be to be covered in shame. I do not have the spirit to fight for happiness any longer. All my spirit and strength went when I was a young woman. They kicked it out of me.[28]

David Rice, in his book *The Dragon's Brood*, says he also found it difficult to get people to talk about the Cultural Revolution. He interviewed 37-year-old Xiaohong who tries to make up for the loss of her education by studying English from the television. She remembers her time as a red guard:

We believed in the theory of Mao, continuous revolution under the dictatorship of the proletariat ... Now, looking back, we feel ridiculous about those happy times we had. We attacked our teachers. And it's a thing we feel bad about now. One of them died.

Another woman, Song Lan, also talked about her experiences:

During those ten years they set out to make people stupid ... Every day you had to face Mao's portrait and recite some slogan, so you could become an approved revolutionary expert ... I wasn't allowed to join the red guards, because they said my parents were 'capitalist roaders'. [Her grandfather had been a landlord.] My father was beaten up and locked up for several years in the cellar of the polytechnic where he was principal. He eventually died from the long-term prosecution ... My mother's left ear is permanently deaf and she can't straighten her left arm because of what the red guards did to her.[29]

China today

China is probably the fastest developing country of the developing world. A more market-oriented economy, which has become freer every year since 1978, has increased living standards beyond what most Chinese dared to dream of. Unfortunately, this leads to an ever-widening gap between rich (mostly in the cities) and poor (mostly in the ethnic minority-inhabited countryside).

Simultaneous with the advent of the market economy there was a relaxation of central control and state interference into private lives. It appears that this has brought about a resurgence of traditional values, many of which are detrimental to the status of women in society.

China possesses vast resources of natural minerals, such as tin, copper and zinc in the Yunnan Plateau in the southeast, and coal and iron ore in the northeast. Oil is extracted from beneath the Yellow Sea.

Manufacturing industries include the production of iron and steel, cement, light engineering and textile manufacturing. The textile industries, where many women are employed, are growing. They include cotton-weaving, printing and dyeing, wool- and linen-weaving, silk, synthetic fibres, knitting and clothing manufacture. In 1994, export earnings generated by China's textile industry alone exceeded US$30 billion.

Agriculture remains important and is the foundation of China's national economy. Rice accounts for 38.9 per cent of China's grain production, followed by wheat and maize, each with 22.3 per cent. China is self-sufficient not only in cereals but also in livestock and fish, although it becomes increasingly difficult to produce enough food for the growing population. Cash crops include cotton, peanuts, rape, sesame, sugar cane, silk cocoon, fruit, tea and tobacco.[30]

China's number one problem is how to feed its growing population. During the 1950s, the Chinese government encouraged people to have as many children as possible – babies were regarded as future workers and soldiers. In the 1960s, some politicians became aware of the increasing problem of overpopulation, but it was not until the 1970s that energetic measures for population control were introduced. Under Deng Xiaoping's leadership, the government made family planning a basic state policy but despite that, the population continued to grow. In 1949, there were 542 million people in China. By 1964, the number had grown to 705 million, by 1982 to 1.017 billion and by 1993 to 1.185 billion. The official estimate for 1995 is 1.212 billion. Experts reckon that even with the strictest population control measures and enforced contraception, there will be 1.272 billion Chinese by the year 2000. It is true that the annual population growth rate has fallen sharply since the implementation of the family planning policy in the early 1970s, from 2.9 per cent in 1970 to 1.1 per cent in 1993. But because of the large absolute size of China's population, the annual net addition to the population has been constant at nearly 15 million.[31]

Since 1950, the government has made several attempts to increase the productivity of agriculture as well as industry. But they rarely showed the desired results, and some of them backfired and harvests were lost almost completely. The most disastrous of these was the 'Great Leap Forward' launched in 1958 which led to the starvation of at least three million people.[32]

Progress has been made: in 1994 China's output of grain reached 445.1 million tons, an increase of 46 per cent over 1978.[33] However, large areas of China's surface are not suitable for agriculture. Almost very inch of arable land, even along road verges and in graveyards, is being farmed, and there is simply not enough scope to improve productivity at the same rate as the population growth.

Strict population control is the only method which can prevent starvation. Although it means salvation for society, it can bring hardship, pain and humiliation to individuals, especially to women, whose value is often still measured by the number of their sons. This also results in frightening developments such as the 'disappearance' or 'death at birth' of female children. Chapter 6, on 'Motherhood', will look at these issues in more depth.

Another area of great concern is the increasing migration of families and individuals from poor rural areas in central China, the north and the west, in order to seek their fortune in the wealthy cities along the coast. While some find employment in the growing textile industries, many others remain unemployed and live in utter poverty. For women, attempts to migrate to the cities can result in abduction, domestic slavery, enforced prostitution or sale into marriage. We will look at these issues, along with the restrictions the Chinese face when choosing a career or trying to change their jobs in Chapter 3 on 'Careers'.

A third major problem is illiteracy and low educational standards. This is an old problem, concerning especially ethnic minorities and women. (See Chapter 2, 'Education and training')

Old customs die hard, but where women are prepared to fight over a long period, they usually achieve their aim. To me, the dragon boat of the Dai people is a symbol for women fighting for equality. The dragon boat race is a traditional festival of the Dai people in which women were previously not allowed to participate. When a woman's shadow fell on the sawdust while the boat was built, this was a bad omen unless the sawdust could be discarded immediately. The Dai believed that if a woman touched a boat, it would capsize, and pregnant women were not even allowed to walk past a boat. In 1958, some courageous women had the idea of organizing an alternative boat race for women only. The local Women's Federation branch offered to sponsor it, but they could not get enough women to brave public opinion and the idea had to be dropped.

In 1974, the matter came up again. More women were interested, but they were still worried about public opinion. They asked the chair of the Women's Federation branch, who offered to join in to give the event respectability. With her in the lead, several women participated in the big dragon boat festival, and some experienced boatmen even volunteered to be their coxwains. Since then, the number of women in the boats has grown and in 1985 there were enough female participants to fill four dragon boats.[34]

2 Too many and too few teachers: education and training

Invisible locks on school gates

The levels of education vary greatly in China. On average, rural people are less educated than city-dwellers, ethnic minorities less than members of the Han nationality, and women less than men. The differences are drastic, although in theory everyone has the right to the same education and is encouraged to gain as much education as possible.

The difference between women's and men's educational levels has historical roots. A system which guaranteed equal rights to education for all was only introduced in 1950. This change came as a shock for many who had been brought up in the belief that a woman's virtue lay in her ignorance. In 1949, just before the Liberation, only 20 per cent of girls entered school and nine out of ten women were illiterate. Not every woman realized the importance of her and her daughters' rights to education. The old perceptions were like an invisible lock that blocked women from the school gates and, although the education of Chinese women has achieved great successes over the last 46 years, these invisible locks still exist for many as far as higher education is concerned.

Spies in the classroom

The aims of the Chinese educational policy are expressed in a statement from the State Education Commission:

> China lays special emphasis on making students develop morally, intellectually and physically, on cultivating in them a devoted and hardworking spirit for the welfare of the country and people, on having ideals, morality, culture, discipline, love for the socialist motherland and

construction, and on having a scientific attitude and unswerving will of pursuing new knowledge and bravely creating new things on the basis of seeking truth from facts and independent thinking.[1]

Like many aspects of Chinese life, education is centrally organized. The State Education Commission (SEC) reports directly to the State Council, an arrangement which reflects the importance China currently places on education. There is a national curriculum, but it is left to the administrative units (provinces, autonomous regions and municipalities) to enforce educational policies, to find workable compromises and to adapt it to existing facilities. Sometimes one or two provinces pioneer a new approach, and only when they have implemented the changes successfully do the other provinces follow. One recent example is the introduction of English in the curriculum for primary schools in the Jilin Province. The autonomous regions (such as Xinjiang, Inner Mongolia, Ningxia) in particular have considerable freedom in their curriculum planning.

A compulsory education law was promulgated in April 1984. Article 5 of the law stipulates:

> All children who have reached the age of six shall enrol in school and receive compulsory education for the prescribed number of years, regardless of sex, nationality or race.[2]

The prescribed number of years is interpreted as anything between six and nine years, although in some areas the authorities regard it as a success if they get pupils to attend for four years.

In theory, a pupil's progress through the education system is as follows: from three to five she attends a kindergarten if one is available at her parents' work unit. From six to twelve she goes to primary school, which is compulsory, and from twelve to 15 to middle school. At 16 she passes the regional exam and goes on to a high school, or a secondary professional or vocational school. At 18 or 19, she passes the college entrance exam and enrols for a university or college (tertiary professional or vocational school) course for two to five years.

However, practice and theory differ widely as far as the ages are concerned. There are regional differences in the structure of the school system as well as in the contents of the curriculum and duration of compulsory schooling. Most students begin their primary schooling at a later age. Many fail the exams necessary to pass on to the next education level and repeat a particular year several times until passing the exam. This means that many students are 23 or older by the time they enter university. Students' learning is geared towards exam requirements and exams are strict, requiring students to memorize large amounts of text material, with assessment usually in the form of written assignments.

The educational system is riddled with bureaucracy, with a party secretary whose job it is to implement and monitor communist education and morality. When the party secretary and the department head lock horns, little gets done within the department. There is tension and a struggle for power between the political and the academic hierarchy at many educational institutions.

Similarly, each class has student monitors – some of whom have administrative or representative tasks, but there is also one monitor for political liaison. She or he brings all classroom materials in for departmental review, reports on any untoward classroom discussions and even indiscretions of teachers and pupils. These 'classroom spies' have always been a fundamental part of the Chinese system, even before the Communist Revolution.

The educational system is particularly underdeveloped in some of the regions where ethnic minorities live, including Inner Mongolia. The situation is a vicious circle: because the living standard in those areas is so low, qualified teachers cannot be persuaded to stay there to improve the schools for any longer period than their obligatory six or eight years.

Rural schools remain sub-standard, due to a lack of teachers and especially a lack of resources and teaching materials. The students don't acquire the skills to help increase the wealth and improve the living standards in the area, nor are they learning much under these conditions. Many parents conclude that schools are obviously useless and take their children out of school before they have completed their compulsory education. These frustrated pupils add to the already high number of pupils who drop out because of material reasons.

Heilongjiang in the northeast is a reasonably wealthy province with urban as well as rural areas. It is far better off than most provinces in the north, northwest or in inner China, although it is not as rich as the southern coastal provinces. Even here, full attendance at compulsory education was only achieved in 1993.

Shau Bin, of the Heilongjiang Education Authority, said at a conference in Harbin in 1994, which I attended:

> Many difficulties in education have been caused by economic shortcomings, especially in rural areas. We have enforced compulsory schooling for primary schools for everyone in the whole province. As far as school buildings are concerned, we have made good progress. We have restored old buildings which had been unusable and erected new ones. The problem hasn't been solved yet, but the situation is looking better.

Shau Bin hopes to address the problem of teachers' salaries or at least partially solve it, but she fears that any effort will falter because there is not enough money.[3]

Co-education

Girls and boys are educated together, sharing classrooms and facilities on an equal basis. Their progress through schools and colleges is the same, although female students are less likely to progress to higher levels than their male counterparts. To the Chinese, a separation by gender would seem unnecessary and costly: officially, any gender bias has been eradicated.

In practice, this has been to the detriment of girls. Especially in the Muslim provinces of Xinjiang and Ningxia, parents will not allow their daughters to go to the village school where they would be taught by a male teacher and share lessons with boys. The low rate of girl pupils in turn means that there are even less female teachers in the area. In effect, co-education often means no education at all for the girls.

In the Muslim Ningxia Province in the northeast, traditionally only the boys were sent to school. People felt that boys were the pillars of the family, whereas girls were destined to bear children for another (their husband's) family. From a young age, girls had to work hard with housekeeping chores and they were married young. The population increased and girls were also needed to look after a growing number of younger siblings. Uneducated mothers could not argue their daughters' case, places at school were limited, and female teachers often unavailable. Before 1985, the enrolment rate of girls in Tongxin (a county in the Ningxia Province) was only 42 per cent.

In 1985, the first primary school for girls only was established with a woman as the head teacher. To persuade parents to send their daughters to school, the curriculum focused on acknowledged 'female' skills such as drawing, handicrafts, embroidery, calligraphy, tree planting, sewing and cooking, as well as Chinese and a little arithmetics. The enrolment and retention rate for girls in the school's area reached 98 per cent in 1994. Similar projects have since been started in other areas of the Ningxia, Gansu and Quinghai Provinces.[4]

In the 1990s, additional primary schools for girls and some women's colleges have been introduced, mostly to help women's education in the ethnic minority areas, but also encourage women to train for management and cadre positions. There are women cadres' colleges in several provinces, training female cadres especially in how to help other women. Subjects include 'the rights of women working in foreign-funded enterprises', 'dealing with sexual harassment of secretaries', 'rural women being bullied', 'family violence' and 'psychological pressure of competition at work'.

Recently established women's colleges train women in what are perceived as female domains, like domestic science and secretarial skills, rather than management skills. Feminists will probably regard this as a step backwards. But these 'feminine' courses are popular with women, who increasingly put feminity before feminism. There are even women-only evening classes which aim to give executive women more femininity. Xiao, who holds a responsible position in a Shanghai company, attends a 'Domestic Science and Etiquette Course for Professional Women'. She says: 'I'm newly married and I want to learn the arts and skills that will add harmony to our family.'[5] Professor Zhao Hijian from the Pathology Department of a Shanghai hospital studies domestic science 'to make up for the blank space in my life that I shouldn't have had'.[6]

Primary schools

In 1994, there were 128.23 million pupils enrolled in 683,000 primary schools.[7] The key problem is to get all children to attend primary schools. Shau Bin reported at the conference: 'We are proud that we have now achieved compulsory primary schooling for everyone in practice and not just on paper in Heilongjiang – that's more than can be said of some other provinces.'

In provinces where not all children attend primary school, it is usually the girls who miss out on education. According to statistics released by educational departments, 98.3 per cent of all children aged 7–11 were enrolled at a school, but only 96.9 per cent of girls were enrolled. However, the statistics show a definite improvement. The enrolment figure for girls is 76 per cent higher than in 1949, and 3.4 per cent higher than in 1985.[8] These figures refer to enrolment, not to attendance, and the number of girls attending school regularly is probably lower.

In theory, pupils start their school life at the age of six. But when I visited primary schools in the countryside, it turned out that many of the first-year pupils were between eight and ten, some even twelve years old. Sometimes the parents are simply not ready and willing to let their children go, either because they don't want to pay the school fees or because they need the children as unpaid labourers, and it can take some coaxing or pressure from the authorities to persuade them to do so.

In cities and more affluent areas many children begin their education at the age of three or four – I found that many kindergartens, run by work units, doubled up as pre-schools or nurseries and took on babies and toddlers.

The second problem is that, although there is a national curriculum which stipulates that the children must study moral character, Chinese, mathematics, nature, history, geography, drawing, music and physical culture, many schools simply don't have the teachers or the materials to teach these subjects. In some rural areas, children learn only what their teacher happens to be able to teach.

Sun Lian Fen is headmistress of the Petroleum Primary School near Tonghua (Jilin Province). Her school is modern: three white single- and two-storey buildings arranged around a playing field, bright rooms with large windows, a ping-pong room. The students at her school don't wear a uniform, apart from the red scarf around their neck which identifies them as 'Young Pioneers' – the equivalent of the scout movement for young children – having to perform frequent good deeds. Sun says:

> Most pupils come here when they are eight years old. They study for 48 hours per week. They also participate in school activities – learning to do good deeds. We place importance

on moral values. We encourage them to bring food to a hospice for the homeless, and to give little performances of song and dance to bring joy to others.

Last year, some pupils found a purse containing 1,000 *yuan* [in that area and period, this amount was the approximate equivalent of what a senior teacher earned in two months]. They went to some trouble to find out who the owner was and to restore it to him. I was pleased about this, it shows that our moral education works.

The main subjects are Chinese, English and maths, and these are taken seriously because the pupils have to pass an exam to go on to middle school. English is new for primary schools. The Jilin Province was one of the first to take it on, we are very progressive. Two of our teachers retrained within two years to become English teachers. Side subjects are history, politics, geography, and physical education. There are about 40 pupils per class. In their spare time the pupils love sports, ping pong, singing and dancing. We have 37 teachers for 598 pupils. Of course the school is co-educational.[9]

Secondary, further and vocational education

Six years at primary school are followed by three years at middle school. In 1994, there were 82,000 middle schools, with 49.817 million students enrolled. The subjects normally include Chinese, mathematics, English, politics, history, geography, physics, chemistry, biology, physical culture, music, physiology and fine arts.[10] For most students, middle school ends with a national examination in the final year, although some exceptional students may be exempt from it. Most students in the countryside finish their education at this stage to become workers or peasants. In cities, they are likely to continue their studies at general high schools or specialized colleges, depending on their exam results in the relevant subjects.

Those who want to learn skilled jobs, such as car mechanics or electricians, apply for a place at secondary vocational colleges. There are also specialized secondary colleges which train young people to become paralegals, technicians and nurses. Students can attend these as soon as they have passed their regional exam, from about the age of 15 or 16, but many students at colleges are in their late teens or early twenties.

Those who choose the high school route may then be tracked into tertiary vocational schools or go on to university. Admission to colleges and universities is based on exam results, on the perceived need for people with the relevant skills and on the ability of one's parents to pay tuition fees.

During the Cultural Revolution, academic degrees were considered to be against the spirit of socialism and were abolished. The academic degree system was not resumed until 1982.

The annual statistical report of the State Education Commission shows the gender distribution of students at specialized secondary schools in 1993: many more women studied health-related subjects, teacher training or arts; men were more attracted to physical culture, forestry, industry, agriculture, politics and law. Finance and economics were equally popular with women and men.[11]

In 1994 there were 3,987 secondary schools and colleges, with 3.198 million students, and 1,080 institutions of higher learning (such as universities) with 2.799 million students.[12]

Many secondary schools provide vocational training. These schools are part of a complex system of vocational education and have different names and status, depending not only on the level of education they require and provide, but also on how they are funded (for example, by private enterprises, by the municipality, and so on). In Beijing, these include 104 called 'ordinary secondary specialized schools', 165 'technical schools', 200 'vocational high schools', 100 'vocational schools', 24 'vocational secondary schools', 14 'provincial-level key vocational schools', 60 'independent vocational schools', as well as unspecified numbers of 'adult technical colleges' and 'comprehensive schools which combine vocational schools and ordinary senior middle schools'.[13]

At present, 964,000 women students attend university or college in China, that is 34.5 per cent of total university and college students. Although there is no official restriction on women in traditional men's professions, women account for only 27 per cent of students at science and engineering universities. At Masters and doctoral degree level, there are less women. In 1993, women accounted for 26 per cent of all MA degrees and for 11 per cent of all doctoral degrees awarded.

However, women can achieve the highest level of education. One example is Lai Luhua, who, aged only 29, was promoted to professor in 1992 and works in the Chemistry Department of Beijing University, one of the most prestigious universities in China.[14]

Good learning is painful

The faces in class are eager and earnest: learning is not meant to be fun. Girls and boys sit at wooden desks; there is no segregation of sexes in the classroom, although girls usually choose to sit next to another girl and boys next to another boy. Most girls and some boys wear sleeve protectors made from colourful, printed fabric, covering their arms from the wrists to the elbows. They stand up whenever a teacher enters or leaves the classroom, and when they are called to answer a question.

Forty to 60 students per class is the norm. At many schools and colleges, there are no more than 15 textbooks per 150 students – and no photocopying facilities.

Physical education is an important aspect of student life. For most students, the early morning call to exercise in the open air is compulsory. A voice roaring from a loudspeaker gives the instructions and hundreds of students carry them out simultaneously. These exercises are gentle and non-competitive, sometimes based on tai chi or other martial arts movements, and are performed at all educational institutions from kindergartens to universities. At colleges and universities they may be voluntary; students are also encouraged to play netball, tennis or participate in other sports.

During art classes – even at art college – the emphasis is on reproductive skills. Students learn to copy Chinese and Western masters rather than develop their own creative ideas; the most successful art students in this system are those with the least imagination.

The strengths of Chinese students are that they can memorize huge amounts of vocabulary in a structural way, expect learning to be hard work and are remarkably disciplined. But they memorize new words and structures without always knowing how to use them and often don't develop an instinct for suitable usage. They can spend a long time exploring and studying minor details of complicated grammar, but are careless about basic errors.

Students expect learning to be hard, even painful. The more difficult a course of study, the more the learning is appreciated.

Studying is a respected pastime. Teenage students find it easiest to escape from parental or teachers' supervision by claiming they must 'study'. 'Studying together' and 'borrowing books' are popular excuses for girls to meet with boys.

The traditional Chinese approach to teaching and learning – strict discipline and memorizing – is well suited to conditions like large class sizes and lack of resources. But now more student-centred methods have been introduced especially in linguistic subjects. Most teachers and students are set against these changes, especially where they have neither the experience nor the resources to introduce and follow them.

Shau Bin hopes that the quality of language teaching will improve substantially. At present, students learn English with a view to getting high marks in examinations which will secure a place at college and university and possibly a grant.

> They are not interested in using the language. Strictly exam-oriented grammar lessons are the norm. Because speaking and listening don't always form part of the final examinations, teachers and students regard them as secondary skills, not worth bothering about. For many years, pupils knew the words but could not open their mouths. Now it is different, new methods have been introduced; but teachers must change their attitudes, their teaching methods and their approach. They must also judge and support students according to their talents and abilities. They must research teaching methodology. The focus of the new textbook, *Junior English for China*, is on students who should open their mouth and speak. But this means, that the teachers must have these skills first.

Zhang Haixiang, English teacher at a middle school in Beijing, agrees: 'In this country, the methodology is traditional, not modern. Lessons are strictly teacher-based. Students are often not good at listening and speaking.'

He points out another obstacle:

> Our teachers are not very well qualified. Our country is poor and we have no money to train our teachers. Teachers like me need higher, continued education. The training teachers are receiving is not enough. Even qualified teachers should have at least four years' teacher training: psychology, educational theory, methodology. They learn some of these

at the colleges now, but not enough. They don't pay enough attention to psychology.

However, longer and better training for teachers will remain a theory for years to come. There simply are not enough teachers, for English as well as for other subjects including music. The Chinese government has to recruit and train as many teachers as possible.

Several provinces, including Heilongjiang and Jilin, are able to offer new programmes which enable teachers to continue their studies and update their knowledge during their holidays. They are subject-oriented but can include methodology and are often structured as modular courses. Unfortunately the teachers themselves have to pay for the courses.

Mild contempt for the teachers

Teaching is a low paid job. A teacher is supposed to work mainly to fulfil a vocation and was traditionally paid with goods (for example farm produce) rather than money. The average teacher's salary is far below that of the average worker.

But trainee teacher Xiao Wen Jun, 21, thinks it is not all bad being a teacher in China: 'At least, for teachers it is easy to find a job. Each of us will have a job when we graduate from teachers' college; we need not fear unemployment.'

But having a job does not automatically mean earning money. Many schools are chronically underfunded and unable to pay outstanding salaries. Some teachers are owed wages for a year or more. Small wonder that many teachers take to 'moonlighting' to improve their income: for some, this means running a small business, for others, giving private tuition.

A survey among ten Beijing schools showed that 20 per cent of the teachers transferred to other posts. Forty per cent had second jobs, mostly as private English or music teachers.[15]

Accelerated inflation is the main reason why schools, colleges and education authorities are often underfunded. But there is another cause. Bao Tianren, a former English teacher who now runs a successful publishing business for educational materials, says:

Despite lack of active teachers, there are often 600 teachers employed for 1,000 students at a college. Only 150 of them teach actively and regularly (which can mean as little as six or eight hours per week), others occasionally or not at all. But they all receive a salary.

The contradiction between a desperate lack of teachers on the one side and overstaffed institutions on the other is one of motivation. Most teachers aim to work in the big, glamorous cities, and few are willing to go to the poor countryside. Teaching is a white collar job, and many young people from peasant families aspire to becoming teachers to avoid hard work. Educational institutions also harbour many *guanxi* employees. *Guanxi* is a complex system of dealing in contacts, favours and bribes; for example, a work unit manager might say to an education official: 'I'll give your daughter the prestigious title of secretary if you arrange a job for my son as a teacher in a large town, on the understanding that neither is actually required to do any work.'

Another problem is the image of teaching. Before the Cultural Revolution the teacher was a highly respected, revered person. But during the turbulent years from 1966 to about 1976, teaching, learning, conventional and academic knowledge were despised and destroyed. Students often beat up and humiliated their teachers in every possible way. Many teachers either died as the result of physical injuries or committed suicide.

In the minds of today's Chinese, the image of the teacher is a confused one: the deep ancient respect for learning and wisdom is in conflict with the memory of the teacher as a hated scapegoat. The majority of teachers are still men, although at primary school the numbers are about equal. Middle schools, universities and colleges have more male than female teachers. However, this is bound to change since about twice as many women as men study to become teachers.

This drop in status may be one of the reasons why teaching has become mostly a women's profession. Another reason is that 'nurturing' and 'looking after children' are supposed to be women's special strengths, just like in most countries in the world.

On average, city people may have mild contempt for the teaching profession whereas country people are more likely to show greater respect. Many regard it as an excellent career for educated, intelligent young women, but believe that educated, intelligent young men are wasted as teachers. Officially this gender bias does not exist.

Wanted: anyone who can teach English or music

China suffers from a lack of teachers, especially English teachers in secondary schools. The causes go back to the time of the Cultural Revolution when there was virtually no language training in China. Before and after that time, the foreign language taught was Russian, because of the close political, military and trade links with the Soviet Union during the Cold War period.

In 1972, English was re-introduced as a side subject at some educational institutions. In the 1980s it was decided that everyone should learn English, and gradually it became a compulsory school subject in middle schools. In some provinces, English is already compulsory in primary schools. Today, you cannot gain access to a college or university in China without having achieved a certain grade of proficiency in English. Many parents invest heavily in private tuition to secure a place at a good university for their (usually only) child. However, there are not enough people whose knowledge of English is sufficient to be able to teach. Middle school teacher Zhang remembers:

> English is a comparatively new subject in schools, introduced in 1972, and now compulsory. I was working as a Russian teacher, for which I was qualified. Then, suddenly, English teachers were required. In 1977, we needed lots of English teachers! I was sent, at the age of 25, to a college to learn English and within two years I 'qualified' as an English teacher and was sent out to teach English at schools.

Zhang worked for several years, then realized his skills' limitation and went to university to study foreign languages for two years, before returning to work.

Zhang speaks and writes English fluently now, but many 'English teachers' are still unable to speak or understand English, and don't even dare to greet a stranger with 'good morning' for fear that their uncertainty about pronunciation could come to light.

Bao Tianren, editor of *The English Coaching Paper*, which is widely used as a teaching aid, says: 'Many teachers speak or understand no English at all, although they may recognize written words. Others know only the words and structures which they are using year after year, because they teach only one grade.'

The Chinese government is aware of the problem and actively encourages foreign native English teachers to take up postings in China. Native English speakers with teaching qualifications can easily find jobs at secondary schools, but more importantly, the government strives to place foreigners at teachers' colleges, where students train to be English teachers.

After being ignored for two decades, Russian is gradually becoming important again. Some 50 colleges and universities in China have about 2,000 students of the Russian language. About 250,000 middle school students are learning Russian as their foreign language, most of them from northeast China near the Russian border. In the early 1990s, Russian became fashionable again and is seen as a useful skill to have in foreign trade. There is a demand for Russian language graduates and employers seek to contract students even before graduation. But as with English, there simply are not enough people to teach Russian competently, and there is not even a standardized Russian language test at higher education institutions.[16]

But these are not the only subjects for which there is an extreme shortage of teachers; according to Wei Wei, writing in *China Daily*, the 1990s will be remembered in China as 'the decade the music died'.

Most primary and junior high schools only have one music teacher. In Beijing high schools alone another 60,000 teachers are needed to give regular music lectures. In country and village schools students are often dismissed from music class because there are no teachers available.

The national curriculum stipulates two music lessons per week for most types of schools. After primary school, pupils should be able to read music and sing some songs by reading music notes. After junior secondary school, students should have a general understanding of traditional Chinese music and some Western classics. But very few school leavers meet these requirements.

Li Weinan, a second year junior high school student in Beijing, said in an interview with *China Daily*: 'I like singing and hope to learn music notes in school, but I have not attended music lectures for nearly three months.'

Fan Shui, an official in the Art Education Department of the State Education Commission, is quoted in the same article, saying: 'A steady teaching force is the basic promise to improve the music education in school ... There will be an army of art illiteracy if we do not pay attention to the basic art training for children.'

He added that the SEC had set up 120 schools especially to train music teachers. Two thousand teachers graduate every year from such schools and are assigned to teach throughout the country, yet many turn to other professions, or take on a second, more profitable job. 'How can I be stimulated by teaching with a salary much lower than my friends working in companies or teaching private students?' challenged Guo Zifen, a music teacher in a Beijing primary school. To encourage more people to train as music teachers, the SEC is now allowing music teachers to train in top musical academies like the Central Conservatory of Music and the Music Institute of China.[17]

When parents cannot afford the school fees

Although primary and middle school is compulsory for everyone, parents have to pay fees to send their children to school – a strange situation in a communist country.

Primary head teacher Sun Lian Fen says: 'The school fee per child and term is three *yuan*. That's not expensive. Everyone here can afford it. I don't know of any parents who have difficulty in paying it.'

The fee is indeed low. The three *yuan* per child per term would buy five apples in the street market. However, the rural area around Sun's school is comparatively wealthy, with high employment because of the chemical and petroleum industries. Parents can afford the fee without suffering. In cities, the school fee is regarded as nothing more than a token payment.

By contrast, for peasant families in some of China's poorest areas in the centre, north and west, the fees are an unaffordable expense. If the family belongs to an ethnic minority, they are still likely to have several children. Many parents cannot pay for all their children to go to school at the same time and will certainly stop their children's schooling after primary school. If only one child can be educated, it is usually the eldest son, sometimes the eldest daughter, but even they are often taken from school after just a couple of years to help earn the family's keep or to look after their younger siblings.

Even in the towns, students rely on part-time jobs to help finance their studies. Zhin Xuelian from Tonghua is envied by many for her job as a governess:

> I work four hours per week and earn 220 *yuan* per month. This is excellent payment. If I were a qualified teacher, I would get about 400 *yuan* per month. The family for whom

I'm working are rich. They want their daughter to get very good marks at school so that she will be admitted to a good university. They are willing to spend money on her education.

May, at the same college, is less fortunate:

> I was hoping to find an evening job down in the town, maybe cleaning. I relied on the extra money to pay the tuition fee for computing lessons. These are not included in our normal college fees. My parents cannot possibly afford to pay any extra money for my tuition. But there's a rapist loose in Tonghua. The college has warned all female students not to go out in the evenings until he has been caught. He is dangerous; three students from this college have already been violently attacked. I don't dare go out. I will have to give up the computer lessons.

China Pictorial mentions the case of Tang Yongtao from the Yunnan Province who won a place at the Geophysics Department of Beijing University. He, his parents, his brother and his sister live on a monthly income of 400 *yuan*. The total cost of study is estimated to be at least 20,000 *yuan*. Tang is quoted as saying 'My father has assured me that no matter how difficult, he will provide for my studies until I graduate'.[18] The main sacrifice in cases like his is almost always the sister's education. To finance the son's university studies, parents may deprive their daughter of any secondary education.

Teenager Ye Yuwai lives in a mountainous De'ang minority village in the Yunnan Province (southwest China). The second of six children in her family, she had to leave school after the fourth year at primary school because her father died. She and her elder sister had to help their mother support the family. She would have preferred to continue school, but had no choice.[19]

Apparently there are no college graduates among the 15,462 De'ang population. He Yunan, 41, is the first De'ang woman to study at a vocational school and also the first woman doctor. She never got the chance to study at school until she was 18 years old. She used to envy her brothers who could do simple accounts and could write their names. Sometimes she followed them to school, but was stopped by her parents who needed her labour for housework.

He Yunan ran away when she was 18, to attend a work-study class in the nearest town. She went to classes in the morning and did odd jobs to earn money in the afternoon. After only eight months of schooling, she was selected to train as a doctor. This was difficult for her because she had less educational background and a more limited vocabulary than her fellow students. Since 1974, she has practised gynaecology and obstetrics.[20]

Many rural children – two-thirds of them are girls – are deprived of education mainly because of their families' poverty. A foundation called 'The Hope Project' was established by the China Youth Development Foundation in 1989. It is the equivalent of a Western charitable organization, and individuals and organizations from all over China, and sometimes from abroad, donate money to help finance rural education. The Hope Project mainly aims to give children basic primary education.

Another project was also established in 1989, the 'Spring Bud Plan', with the Children's Foundation of China as the organization behind it. This plan aims at providing girls with education, including higher education, and was first carried out in eight limited geographical areas within the Guangdong, Sichuan, Hunan and Guangxi Provinces.

Pan Zhenying, a girl from the Yao minority in the Guangdong Province, is a beneficiary of the Spring Bud Plan. She could go to primary school locally for the first three years, but the local school did not provide the fourth year. Pan would have had to board in a town. Her family could not afford the boarding fees, and anyway Pan had to do her daily share of the housework and cattle herding. Two years after she had had to give up school, she heard that there was a Spring Bud boarding school for girls. She applied for a place and was accepted. The funding provided for boarding accommodation, textbooks and meals. Her family still lost Pan's labour, but at least they did not have to pay for her education. Most of the girls in Pan's class say they want to become teachers.

Today, the Spring Bud Plan has spread to 16 provinces. Eight hundred girls-only classes have been established and 40,000 girls have returned to school after funding was provided. Ninety per cent of the girls who have received support come from ethnic minorities.[21] In addition, there are company scholarships offered by work units and private enterprises for talented local students, but, although much publicized and praised, these are only a drop in the ocean.

Grants and conditions

Grants are the government's method of channelling students into careers where there is a skills shortage, as there is currently in the teaching profession. The average student and their parents cannot afford to pay the college or university fees. They may be entitled to a grant – but they accept the grant on condition that the student studies at whatever college she gets sent to and that she works in that occupation for a minimum number of years.

Students on grants are often highly motivated to gain a higher education – any sort of higher education, but they lack the vocation for the specific career.

There are three types of college students, according to their grant status (fees refer to teachers' college students in the Jilin Province in 1995).

- **Ding Xiang**. These have been admitted to college on the strength of their school grades and pay only 200 *yuan* a year. This sum is affordable for most Chinese families, except in poor rural areas. However, there are additional fees to be paid for accommodation, special tuition, worksheets and so on. Students of this group are assigned jobs by the government and have to take them. They have no choice in the matter unless they pay a huge penalty which is usually way beyond their family's resources.
- **Wei Tou**. This type of student's school grades were not good enough to earn them a full grant. She has to pay 2,200 *yuan* per year – a fee only the rich can afford. (Comparison: Depending on their qualifications and position, teachers earn between 300 and 1,200 *yuan* per month.) Some middle-class parents may take out a loan and almost starve in order to finance their only child's education. On average, these students come from well-to-do families. They are assigned jobs by the government, but are not obliged to take them and can take a better job if they find one.
- **Zi Fen**. These students pay 1,800 *yuan* a year, just to get the degree and the knowledge. They must find their own jobs without help from the government, but are not restricted in their choice of career.

The system is changing gradually towards fee-paying students. The SEC's aim is that by 1997, all colleges and universities will introduce a system in which students pay about 1,500 *yuan* _tion costs (plus accommodation and meals), but are free to choose their own jobs. Some scholarships or part-grants will be available to students who study agriculture, forestry, navigation, physical culture, water conservation, geology, public security and meteorology. These are subjects in which the SEC expects a lack of skills in the near future and in which few students currently show great interest.[22]

College and university accommodation: up to twelve students to a small room

Students have to pay extra for accommodation, which is in dormitories housing six to twelve students in each small room. I visited several college and university dormitories, and found them claustrophobic.

Tonghua Teachers' College has three dormitories: a five storey-building and a two-storey building for female students, and a four-storey building for male students. This reflects the female/male ratio at the college.

Because of the extreme cold (minus 40 degrees centigrade!) the windows are nailed shut throughout the winter. There are open-cubicle toilets and washing troughs on the two lowest floors in each building, but the water supplies are sporadic. Moreover, many of the boys can't be bothered to go downstairs at night, so they do their business in the aisles ...

The girls' dorms are equally crammed, but neat and tidy. They have made a conscious effort to respect each other's privacy, with little curtains on the bedsteads, posters and paintings on the walls. Their possessions don't take up much space: a couple of pairs of trousers, a skirt and a few tops each, a radio, a few items of make-up, and the essential thermos flask of hot drinking water and some lidded mugs.

They have to be in their dorms at nine p.m., but are not allowed to pursue any hobbies there. Hobbies are definitely discouraged by the college: the students should concentrate on studying. If they are caught knitting in their room, they may be in trouble. There is little else for the girls to do. For most of the year, Tonghua is too cold to sit outside. There's no common or hobby room; access to the classrooms is only for voluntary study; they have no money to go shopping or sit in a restaurant. Even going for a walk is dangerous; there have been brutal rapes in the recent past.

Occasionally the girls get together in groups of ten or more to go for a walk. I asked why the male students didn't join them, offering some form of protection. The boys were evasive: 'We have other things to do,' they said.

When a girl screamed in the schoolyard in the evening, the boys pointedly ignored her cries for help. 'We know her by her voice. She's a bad girl anyway,' shrugged a 21-year-old male student. The incident turned out to be an escalated quarrel with her boyfriend, but what if it had been an attack by the rapist? The same male student commented uncomfortably: 'We don't want to get into trouble, you know.'

The students don't have cooking facilities, but cheap meals are served in the refectory. Zhin reports: 'I think the college food is not always good. Sometimes there's some sand in the rice, or the steamed bun is sour. Some of the vegetables are really delicious.'

But the vegetables tend to be very salty – salt is used as a preservative – and many students cannot afford vegetables on top of the rice, so their diet is low in vitamins.

Adult education

Adult education in China is organized by radio and television programmes, workers' and farmers' colleges, correspondence courses, evening universities, vocational and technical schools, basic education and literacy programmes, and technical courses.

In 1994, there were 2.352 million people studying in adult education institutes of higher learning: 2.638 million were in adult vocational secondary schools, 47.58 million in adult technical schools and 7.615 million in adult middle and primary schools. An estimated 4.634 million adults became literate in 1994.[23]

Distance learning

A distance learning school, the Central Agricultural Broadcasting and Television School (CABTS), aimed mainly at people in rural areas who have already achieved a basic level of education but either failed the college entrance exam or live in such remote areas that they cannot attend a normal college, was established in the early 1980s. Subjects offered are mostly agricultural, such as farm production, storage and processing. The school helps farmers to improve their general education as well as their knowledge of farming techniques.

However the tuition does not reach those people who need it most. Tuition is provided by means of radio and television broadcasts, video and audio tapes. From the government's point of view, this is a low-cost method of teaching which saves teachers' salaries and books. But for the average peasant who does not own a radio and would not even dare to dream about television and video, education via the CABTS is beyond reach.

Students also need to attend supplementary classes in towns. Those who can't afford to leave their fields or to spend money on travel and accommodation, and those who can't read and write well, lose out.[24]

Fighting illiteracy

China undertook three anti-illiteracy campaigns. The first took place in 1949 when the People's Republic was founded after the Liberation and continued throughout the first five-year plan of 1953–1958, when 35 million people were lifted out of illiteracy. But an 'anti-rightist campaign' in 1957–63 and the Cultural Revolution of 1966–1976 ruined most of what had been achieved.

The second literacy campaign came after the end of the Cultural Revolution. More than 6 million illiterate people learned to read and write every year.

The third campaign started in 1991 and is still running.[25]

In 1994, 961,000 schools were opened at all levels, 2.7 times as many as there were in 1949.[26] However, this is still not enough.

According to Wang Cunming, vice-minister of the State Education Commission, about 145 million people (12 per cent of the country's population) are illiterate. Thirty-five million of them are aged between 15 and 45. In 1995, China's adult literacy rate was just 85 per cent, which means that the situation was worse than in most Latin American countries and many neighbouring Asian countries.[27]

Illiteracy is higher among women than among men in any age group. The difference becomes smaller among younger people. Almost all women and a little more than half of the men over 65 are illiterate. In the 45–54 age group, it is about half of the women and less than a quarter of the men. In the 25–34 age group, it is less than 20 per cent of the women and less than 10 per cent of the men.

This gender difference in illiteracy is significant, because it leads to gender difference in social life and status. About 70 per cent of China's illiterate people are women. Among rural women, the illiteracy rate is 37 per cent – twice that of men in urban areas. The worst situation is in Tibet, where 88 per cent of rural women and 43 per cent of urban women are illiterate.[28]

Gao, head of the women's congress of a township in the Anhui Province, was illiterate herself. She could only recognize two characters: 'Attend meeting'. One day she received the summons to attend and hurried to the meeting, only to be asked where the others were. She had not realized that the invitation was extended to other people from her area.

After that, Gao mobilized over 30 women to attend an experimental winter school. With her baby on her back, she went to attend reading and writing classes. Literacy classes usually take place in winter because peasant women's labour is needed in the summer months. At the literacy class in the following year, Gao was no longer the student, but the teacher. A winter school comprises about 164 hours of classes, during which students aim to learn to read 2,000 simplified Chinese characters.

In the late 1970s, when the collective system of agriculture was changed to a contracted management of individual households, every family counted its available manpower. Children's labour was needed to keep up the living standards. It was impossible to let all the children go to school. Some children had to quit school – and these were usually the girls.

In spring 1983, 148 illiterate young women from the Jiangsu Province dictated a letter addressed to the All-China Women's Federation: 'We are all 15–16 year-old girls. Influenced by feudal ideas, our families felt it was useless for girls to go to school. Young as we are, we are busy all day doing household chores or farm work. We have lost the chance to go to school.'

Their letter went on to describe some situations in which the girls' felt their loss of education most sharply. Some had found jobs in a village factory, but could not count production numbers. Others were active in village life and had been proposed as cadres, but illiteracy made it impossible for them to fulfil this function competently. Others found that illiteracy brought trouble to their marriages.

Their letter drew attention and the army stationed in their area, with the help of the Women's Federation, started a girls' night school.[29] But isolated projects improve the situation for very few females only and they cannot change the overall situation.

In 1989 the All-China Women's Federation started literacy programmes which involved learning times adjusted to seasonal farming requirements and which taught agricultural skills such as starting seedlings or raising fish in ponds, as well as reading and writing. These were on the whole successful with one hundred and twenty million women in the countryside participating in them.[30]

Written and spoken language: 5,000 characters in daily use

China's traditional written language is a system of ideographs based on pictures. The pictures became more stylized and simplified, a process that continues today as Chinese scholars strive to make common characters easier to read and write – and more politically correct. For example, the character for 'woman' (*nü*) was changed twice – from a kneeling figure to a bowing figure to a figure moving in large strides.[31]

When it comes to new characters for new ideas, especially in technology, the awkwardness of written Chinese becomes obvious. Only experts can recognize the complicated characters used in science, technology, computers, medicine and research. These characters are often unknown and indecipherable to most laypeople.

There are about 5,000 characters used commonly on a daily basis. There are an estimated total of 230,000 written characters and compounds, many of them used in technical, scientific or medical terms; no one person can possibly know them all. Just consider the 5,000 common characters: there are only about 400 syllables which the human voice can make to express these 5,000 ideas. So the same sound is used in different tones: high tone, low tone, rising tone, falling tone ... the way you say a sound determines what it means. Apparently, one sound can be used for 100 various written characters.

In an attempt to try and translate the characters and tones into understandable Latin characters, scholars have for centuries been battling with the baffling tones. The latinisation system now used all over China is called *pinyin*. Thus, Peking became Beijing and Canton Guangzhou. All pupils and students have to learn *pinyin* as well as the traditional Chinese characters.

Yet matters are even more complicated than that. Some ethnic minorities have their own spoken or written languages, some of which are used by only a few thousand people, others by large groups of the population, such as the Uygur language in the northwest. In the south, Cantonese is the predominant language. Even in provinces where Mandarin is the main language, the pronunciation differs; in others, different characters are used for the same words. This causes huge problems in administration and education, not to speak of computerization. The literacy campaign often has to begin by teaching women how to write in their nationality's own system, to enable them to read, for example, price signs in the market. But when these newly-literate women want to continue their education, they have to learn standard Chinese and *pinyin*. Mastering three systems of writing is beyond the ability or motivation of most people.

Obstacles on the way to women's education

Gaining a thorough education is difficult for a Chinese woman, unless she comes from a well-off, progressive, urban family.

For the average rural girl, there are many obstacles, some of which may prove unsurmountable: non-existence of schools and colleges within reach, schools which lack basic resources, too few and often unmotivated teachers, parents who cannot or don't want to afford the school fees for a girl child, and the traditional perception that much education is not beneficial for a woman. Women and girls who have overcome these difficulties and have learnt to read and write the local language and characters, may face another hurdle when they try to continue their education at an urban college or university, where the teaching language is Mandarin.

The government and other organizations have made great efforts to address the problems of illiteracy, lack of teachers and school drop-outs. The focus of their work is on helping girls and women. It looks likely that the situation will progress rapidly, and that soon almost all women will be able to read and write, and almost all girls will get at least primary schooling. The ratio of girls to boys in secondary education is also likely to improve.

I expect women will continue to be disadvantaged as far as access to institutions of higher education is concerned. Here again, things will get better – albeit slowly – not so much because of government efforts but because of the hopes and ambitions parents of daughters have for their only child.

However, many women take up the teaching profession simply because they have no choice and look forward to the day when they have completed the compulsory number of years in their unloved profession. This means that for many years to come, schools and colleges will be staffed by unmotivated, and therefore usually ineffective, teachers, making government efforts at encouraging and providing education less successful.

3 Careers: a bed in every office

Working women

Before the founding of the People's Republic of China in 1949, most Chinese women were bound to the home and largely separated from society. During the early industrial period of China women worked in the textile industries, and a few women had posts as teachers and secretaries. But it was only from 1949 onwards that women entered the workforce on a large scale. They soon broke the dividing line between 'female' and 'male' jobs and became tractor drivers, locomotive engineers, and aviators. Eighty-five per cent of all Chinese women and 92 per cent of all men are in work and women form 38 per cent of China's total labour force.[1]

They are employed by state-owned, collective-owned or private enterprises. The difference between women's and men's employment figures are partly due to women retiring at 54, earlier than men who retire at 59 (the ages are approximate and depend on the geographical region as well as other circumstances), and also to the fact that women are more likely to be made redundant than men.

Today, the Chinese regard it as normal that a woman should work, regardless of her family status and of having children. There are no jobs which are barred to women. Since the Liberation in 1949/50, the communist government has encouraged women to enter traditionally 'male' occupations, such as electronic engineering or building and construction. Chinese law mentions, but does not specify, 'special types of work or posts unsuitable to women' for which employers can refuse female candidates.[2] In practice, women can be found in every area of work, but some occupations are considered more suitable than others. A woman will not be discriminated against if she chooses a 'male' occupation; society accepts it, except in some minority areas. But she will have to work harder to succeed for promotion against male competitors.

43

Between 1979 and 1993, women accounted for 15.2 per cent of technicians winning state awards for innovative work.[3] In 1992, the country had 21,012 female judges and 4,512 women lawyers.[4] Chinese statistics show that in 1990, women accounted for 45 per cent of professional and technical personnel, 11 per cent of all heads of authorities and government organizations, enterprises and institutions, 26 per cent of office and clerical staff, 47 per cent of workers in commerce, 53 per cent of labourers in agriculture, forestry, animal husbandry and fishery, and 36 per cent of workers in industrial production and transport.

There has been a slight improvement in the ratio since 1982, when the number of women in technical and professional occupations was only 38 per cent, and only 10 per cent of heads of organizations and enterprises were women. The traditional pattern of employment for females mostly in the service industries has changed little.[5]

The 1990 population census shows the gender distribution in the 20 most common occupations. More women than men are shop assistants, workers in poultry farms, textile workers and tailors, and machine operators. More men than women worked as plasterers, truck drivers, purchasing agents, furniture carpenters, teachers in secondary education, electricians and mining workers.

According to those figures, the ratio is near equal for primary school teachers, accountants and auditors, vegetable growers and office staff.[6]

Working conditions

During the first half of this century, factory workers, especially women and children, were exploited to a horrifying extent. It was quite normal for people to die from exhaustion at work. When the communists came into power, they protected the workers, introducing limited work hours, compulsory breaks, and special protection for pregnant, breastfeeding and menstruating women. The Law of the People's Republic of China on Protection Rights and Interests of Women, adopted in 1992, states that 'women shall be under special protection during menstrual period, pregnancy, obstetrical period and nursing period', which means reduced work hours, additional breaks and no hard physical labour.

According to a survey cited in the official publication *The Situation of Chinese Women*, 85.3 per cent of pregnant workers and staff in urban areas enjoy a three-month paid maternity leave, while some units have extended the leave to six months. Female workers have their workload and work time reduced. Most state enterprises with predominantly female staff have their own gynaecological clinics, rest rooms for pregnant women, breastfeeding rooms, nurseries and kindergartens.[7] It must be pointed out, however, that this information is based on answers given to official questions, which may have influenced the result, and that it refers only to urban areas and to state-owned work units. Workers in state-run enterprises, whether male or female, are so protected that many of them rarely need to do hard work.

Guo Shufang, 18, started working at the Foreign Experts Hotel at the Youdian Daxue (University of Post and Telecommunications) in Beijing as soon as she left middle school. She is the chambermaid responsible for one floor. Her workload is minimal: every morning she makes the beds, then she sits at her desk waiting to see if hotel residents have any requests. She also makes sure that there is always hot drinking water in the boiler. During slow periods – that is, most of the time – she studies English. She has kept her textbooks from middle school.

> My job gives me plenty of time to study. One day I may go to Britain. That's my big dream. For this I must learn English. One would think that working in a Foreign Experts Hotel gives me the chance to practise spoken English, but it doesn't. I always hope that the foreigners speak to me, but they just ignore me, apart from requests for hot water and toilet paper. To them, I'm just a chambermaid. I get more respect from the Chinese: to them, I'm a worker.[8]

Gradually, China moved from a six-day week to a five-and-a-half-day week. In March 1995, the State Council decreed that from 1 May 1995, the Chinese would be working only five days per week.[9]

The traditional lazy, rich, corrupt official appeared in the communist structure, taking the same place as he had before in the imperial system. To the Chinese, the ideal career move is to obtain a job where you don't have to work and where you can get many bribes. You do not work hard to get promotion in order to do more work. You try to get promoted to cadre or managerial positions in order to 'rest'. Some educational and government institutions employ hordes of parasites who do little or no work, use up funds and take bribes. I read in a 1996 newspaper about a government appeal to the wives of tax inspectors not to accept gifts of jewellery, and to report any purchases their husbands made which were beyond their official salary.[10]

It is customary to buy a good job for the daughter, the son, the niece or the nephew if you can afford it. Of course, the sale of a job does not take place openly; the government would not approve of it. But the *guanxi* system is powerful, and bosses or personnel managers can be bribed. This applies particularly to clerical jobs. Selection by ability is still rare. In April 1996, *China Daily* had a whole article on page three about the authorities in Dalian, a harbour city in the Liaoning Province, who decided to choose the next 15 recruits for cadre posts by ability test.[11]

Of course those who paid for their jobs are seldom the best staff as far as talent, skills, efficiency and enthusiasm are concerned. You don't pay good money for a position in order to do hard work.

Historically, clerical and administrative jobs have always been regarded as prestige jobs with little work. This has not changed under communist rule. The atmosphere in a Chinese office is rarely hectic. Secretaries and clerks begin the day by cleaning the floor. Then they sit around, drink hot water, chat to colleagues, work a little, drink more hot water and continue to chat.

Every department is equipped with a bed, so that staff can have a nap when they are 'exhausted'. This bed is often placed in the middle of the office, and *xiuxi* (have a break) is an oft-used phrase for the workers.

Until the mid-1980s, sleep formed an important part of office life. Kevin Sinclair and Iris Wong Po-yee write in *Culture Shock! China*:

> The sleep lasted at least two hours and could easily, in the sultry summer months when the deep, humid heat settled on the cities, extend generously past this. Rousing reluctantly from this badly needed siesta, the cadre would stretch, go to the toilet, have some more tea and ponder the possibilities of dinner.
>
> This sedate pace of life was shattered rudely in 1986 when that bustling octogenarian Deng Xiaoping declared the afternoon siesta outmoded in the era of faxes, satellites and China rushing towards modernization. There was much muttering among the paper shufflers of the vastly over-staffed bureaucracy. No sleep in the afternoon? Impossible!

Even today, a deep and impenetrable hush settles over many a government office from noon until mid-afternoon. First it's a hurried lunch in canteen or noodle stall. Then it's back to work for a sleep.

Things are not as bad as a few years ago when a post-prandial snooze was almost compulsory. But if you should arrive for a mid-afternoon appointment and find the cadre you are supposed to meet rubbing sleep out of his eyes, don't be surprised.[12]

A teacher's job is seldom demanding either. Although many colleges are in arrears with teachers' salaries, they employ more teachers than they need. This is especially the case in cities and large towns. A typical week for a teacher would involve five to eight hours teaching per week. Some work more, some less, but there are many teachers on the payrolls who have no teaching obligations whatsoever. Especially in state schools, it's not easy to sack a useless (but well-connected) teacher: you just free him from his or her obligations.

This is in stark contrast to the situation of peasants who work hard for long hours and to whom the image of the busy 'blue ants' still applies.

Another feature of office life is the thermos flask with hot water. Every employee has a porcelain, earthenware, steel or plastic mug with a lid to keep the water warm. The Chinese drink hot water the way Westerners drink coffee or tea. Workers take water in glass jars (which were used for preserved fruit) to their workplace.

According to a report in *China Daily*, foreign enterprises are often the worst offenders against the rights of workers, particularly women's workers. China has about 230,000 foreign-funded enterprises, employing 12 million workers, more than half of them women. Zhang Ruiying, a deputy to the Fourth Session of the National People's Congress, said that some foreign companies neglect Chinese laws and deliberately postpone giving their women employees proper labour contracts. They also force women to work beyond normal schedules, and arbitrarily deduct their legal incomes. She alleged that 23 per cent of foreign-funded enterprises don't give the required 90-day maternity leave, and 33 per cent don't reduce work hours for breastfeeding mothers.[13]

However, this allegation must be seen in perspective. *China Daily* is a newspaper devoted to showing everything coming from abroad in a negative light in order to emphasize just how lucky the Chinese are to live in China. The newspaper did not supply information about how many Chinese firms ignore workers' and maternity rights. A regular reader of *China Daily*, I conclude that the record for Chinese-owned companies is even worse. However, I have not been able to obtain any figures to support my interpretation.

Talking to clerical staff and manual workers in northeast China, I found that employers care less and less about workers' rights. Especially in privately-owned enterprises, staff are exposed to the dictatorial whims of the new entrepreneurs, and I take this up again in Chapter 5.

Workers

I met a 31-year-old cleaner in a school in Harbin, the surprisingly clean and sparkling capital of the Heilongjiang Province with many historic façades. She could afford the occasional breakfast in a small tavern near the railway station. She always takes her little daughter with her; both enjoy spicy stuffed omelettes.

The child wore a smart frilly dress and shiny little shoes, and the mother watched her proudly. She was happy to talk about her job and income. Her work is hard and involves long hours, but she earns 50 *yuan* per day (6,000 *yuan* per month). This sum seemed enormous, and I asked Bao Tianren (a wealthy publisher of English language textbooks) if I had heard correctly. He assured me that this was the case and confirmed her claim that a senior teacher at the same school earned only 1,200 *yuan* per month. The woman was proud of what she was earning: 'Working at a school is prestigious. I'm a worker, that's better than a teacher. I earn much more.'[14]

The salaries and the prestige of railway workers are even higher than those of school workers. Working for the railway means job security, career prospects, prestige and more money than elsewhere for the same work.

The railway sector encompasses far more than trains and stations. There are railway hospitals, railway middle schools and railway supermarkets: in many towns, they are the best hospitals, schools and supermarkets. They all belong to the 'railway' unit and are there for the benefit of railway staff. However, their services are also available to people outside the work unit and are usually profitable.

Women workers are on the whole accepted as equal to men. On building sites, women work side by side with men, doing the same job. I saw them swinging pickaxes to demolish old buildings in Tonghua (Jilin Province), wearing the traditional navy blue Mao suits but no safety helmets or protective toecaps. Tonghua, an industrial town with an estimated 200,000 inhabitants, has had more than a quarter of its existing buildings torn down and replaced over a two-year period (1992–1993), and the work goes on. There is no shortage of work for those in building and construction.

In the Baishan Printing Factory (Jilin Province) the proprietor proudly points to the high skills of the workers. The staff are men and women in approximately equal numbers, but the workers he picks as shining examples are all women. One woman, a typesetter, stands between three large boards containing the cases for the metal characters. It is her job to replace the used characters into the right cases – and there are 5,000 of them! In pre-communist China, anyone who could read more than 2,000 letters was revered as a scholar. The young printing worker spins around like in a graceful dance, her arms moving up and down and reaching out to the cases, not once pausing to think about which letter goes where.

Women from rural areas who wish to leave agriculture often seek work in the new factories in the growing textiles industry. These jobs require 'nimble fingers' rather than education or skills. Rural industries in which the percentage of women in the labour force is particularly high include packaging materials, silk weaving, the chemical industry and cotton textiles.

No free choice of careers

Students can get grants for higher education only if they commit themselves to studying whatever subject is required, and to work in this skills area for several years, going wherever the state sends them (see Chapter 2). The case is most severe in teacher training. China needs teachers, and for many young people the grant for teacher training is the only possible route to escape poverty and to gain a further education.

Teachers against their will

When I lived in Tonghua, my flat was on the campus of the Teachers' College. Daily contact with the students allowed me to conduct an informal survey among several hundred students. I estimate that out of the 1,200 or so students at the Teachers' College in Tonghua, only about 20 have a vocation for teaching, another 200 don't mind becoming teachers and the rest dream or plot about how to escape from teaching.

Song Yuqing from Huinan (Jilin), 22, comes from a peasant family. She appreciates the education as an alternative to agricultural labour:

> I don't mind becoming a teacher, because I like children and get on well with them. There are worse jobs. But if I had had the choice, I would have chosen business studies. That's where my real talent and interest is.[15]

Twenty-one year old Jiao Hongyan comes from Baishan (Jilin).

> I'm undecided what type of career would suit me. Sometimes I'd like to be lawyer, on other occasions I fantasize about being a tour guide, a translator, or a businesswoman. I don't really know what my vacation is. Being a teacher will remind me of my childhood – these are fragrant memories. Giving my knowledge to pupils will make me proud. But I don't want to be in the same job for my whole working life – it would drain me mentally. A new job brings variety and refreshment to the mind, like fresh air and cool air.[16]

However, the majority are scheming and planning an escape from the unwanted career. Typically, they study with energy and favour to acquire skills in the subject they are supposed to teach – politics, English, arts, mathematics – and they look for ways of utilizing these skills outside teaching.

Short-haired, jeans-clad Li, 23, would have liked to become a secretary. She is practical, sensible, well-organized and efficient, and enjoys administrative tasks.

> I want to be a bilingual secretary in a big company, preferably in the south. I certainly have no vocation to become a teacher. Indeed, when I imagine standing in front of a class of 60 middle school students, I start sweating.

But her parents are both teachers, living on a modest income in Liao Yuan. Both her elder sister and her younger brother suffer from brain damage and are not able to contribute to the family income. One day Li may have to support the whole family with her income. The two-year teacher training on a part grant is all they can afford.

> We still have to pay tuition fees, 200 *yuan* per year, plus money for worksheets, books, dormitory accommodation. But the rest is being paid for by the government. This is just about as much as my parents can afford. But there are some girls here who come from poorer families, and for them it's really difficult. On the other hand, some of our classmates come from rich families. They have not won scholarships or grants, but their parents are wealthy enough to pay the whole 1,700 *yuan* for tuition.[17]

Her friend Xiao from Mei He, a romantic, soft-spoken 21-year-old, adds:

> These families want their children to go to college and gain some knowledge, even if they don't have particular talents. If I had the choice, I would do something creative – become an editor, an artist, or a designer. But I won't complain. For me, it means an opportunity to have a different lifestyle to my parents who are peasants. I'm grateful that they restrict themselves to finance my education.
>
> All of us who graduate as teachers with the help of a state grant have to become teachers. We can't get another job. We will have to go wherever we are sent, we can't choose. This may mean going into very rural areas, where infrastructure, hygienic conditions and resources are basic, to say the least. This system works because there are not enough teachers in China. Maybe in the future this system will change. But at present, it is the same all over the country. The system is just to get students to go the villages. There are not many good teachers in the villages and too many teachers in the cities. Most of us want to work in big cities. But often the living and working conditions in the countryside are not as bad as people imagine. And at least everyone of us is guaranteed a job on graduation. After six years, we are free to change jobs. You can leave earlier, but

you must pay a lot of money – more than anyone can afford, except a wealthy minority.[18]

Xin Xuelian from Tonghua (Jilin), 19, refuses to accept teaching as a lifelong career:

> No, I don't want to become a teacher. It's such a hard, repetitive job, with a small scope of activities – really very dull. Teachers haven't enough chance to touch society. I'll try to acquire knowledge and money, and as soon as there is a chance I'll change jobs. My dream job is to be a tour guide. My father is a chemist in a medical examination institute and my mother has just retired. I don't want to be a teacher for the rest of my life.[19]

The first generation of policewomen

Work in the police force is one of the few careers that have become open to women only recently. A brigade of policewomen was formed and trained in Beijing in 1994 to police the Fourth World Conference on Women in 1995. In one year, they were taught public security, political theory, discipline, laws, policies and a foreign language.

Before 1994, there were only very few policewomen, but today China is encouraging women in the police force, apparently to adapt public security work to focus on social development.

The head of the brigade of patrol policewomen is Wu Shurong who worked as one of very few policewomen on the outskirts of Beijing for several years, and then went to study at the Beijing College of the People's Policemen. She says that a brigade of patrol policewomen should be an 'etiquette brigade, a service brigade, and a law-protecting brigade worthy of its name'.

Wang Lina, a police squad leader, graduated from university after majoring in public security. She says: 'In front of Chinese people, I represent the capital, and in front of foreigners, I represent China. It is exciting to be a policewoman. It was a mystery to me when I was a child.'[20]

Dream jobs and ambitions

Secretary, interpreter, translator, businesswoman and tour guides are the top dream jobs for Chinese women. A random survey among 20 female first-year students at the Beijing University of Post and Telecommunication reveals their ambitions. One wants to become a language teacher. Two want to be housewives ('Not having to go out to work would be the ultimate luxury', 'I want to be cherished and pampered by my husband'). One has no plans whatsoever. A fifth one is determined to go to America, one way or another.

Two students don't mind what job they do as long as they earn a lot of money. Their aim is to become rich. One of them would use her wealth to travel, the other says: 'I want to enable my parents to have a comfortable life. They are working hard to finance my studies here. I want them to be secure and comfortable when they are old, with no worries.'

The other 13 would like to be interpreters or translators; one of them says: 'But I don't think I could do it.' Why not? Is she concerned that she doesn't have the necessary language skills? 'Oh, the language is not the problem, that's not important. But I'm not tall. Interpreters and translators must be tall. That's why we women have little chance.'[21]

Lin Yanmei from Dongfeng, one of the students at Tonghua Teachers' College, cherishes her private dream:

> I've wanted to be a designer of clothes since I was very young. I enjoy designing beautiful clothes. Seeing people wear the dresses I designed would give me such a thrill. I'm sure that clothes' design is a sector with a good future. Both my mother and my father are workers, and teacher training is the only education I could get. I'm an optimist. I think one day I will be free to change my career. It will be very difficult, but if you try hard, you can do it.[22]

The glamour of being a secretary

In China teenage girls long to become secretaries just as girls in the West dream of becoming an actress or a pop star. The reality is less exciting: filing and local telephone calls take up most of a secretary's working day. Very few offices are equipped with computers; even typewriters are rare. Despite the official introduction of the *pinyin* system, most people still use the old Chinese symbols and no effective typewriter exists for those. Most letters are written by hand.

Criteria for candidate selection for a secretarial post are height and beauty rather than skills and experience. Exceptionally good-looking women may be able to find a secretarial job; if they are tall, they even have the prospect of becoming a bilingual secretary. The Chinese believe that height is essential for linguistic work. If a woman is neither tall nor beautiful, her only chance is to ask members of her family to bribe a personnel officer.

Wang Meiliang (pseudonym) is a bilingual secretary, but has only mastered a few English sentences. However, her boss regards a bilingual secretary as a status symbol, and Wang's uncle was prepared to pay more for the 'bilingual' title. Her average working day consists of making tea for visitors twice daily, filling her boss's thermos flask with hot water every morning, and half an hour's filing. Her main task is to make phone calls: it can take up to six hours to get a local connection.

Secretaries are expected to dress according to 'Western' fashion. Wang Meiliang for example wears black leggings, a brown-checked miniskirt, a frilly white blouse with pink sequins, a red-and-blue checked jacket and red-and-white checked high-heeled pumps. A woman who wears make-up under the age of 25 is still regarded as decadent, but secretaries are the exception: they must make up. Wang chooses the brightest colours from the supermarket range. She dreams of working for an international company in Beijing, maybe an American or German joint venture. 'This would be great. Everyone would envy me. But my uncle doesn't want to pay for it. Anyway, I've heard that secretaries in international companies must work really hard. I don't think I would like that.'[23]

The appeal of secretarial work to Chinese women is similar to that of acting for Western women: glamour, prestige, being envied by others, being considered attractive and the chance to meet interesting men.

Career women

Teaching and education is a field in which more than two-thirds of all employees are women – yet less than 5 per cent of head teachers and senior officials are women.

Wang Yuying is a successful career woman within the education system of the Heilongjiang Province. Her work has even taken her to London on a research project. But there is a lot of resentment among her colleagues and subordinates. After she had given what appeared a brilliant presentation, I overheard one man saying to another: 'Is her English really that much better than mine? I'm sure she can't be as good as she pretends to be.'

Wang Yuying works long hours. Her job often involves weekend conferences and evening meetings. Whenever possible, she takes her four-year-old son with her. When she comes home, she has to do the housework, cooking and washing. She admits: 'I'm often tired in the mornings at work. And colleagues have already commented on this. It worries me.'

What about her husband? Can't he take on half the housework? 'Of course he could not. He is a brain surgeon. His work is important. He works hard. I work hard too, and my work is equally important. But I would not think of making him do housework in the evenings.'[24]

Another sample career woman is Sun Lianfen. She is head teacher at the Petroleum Primary School in a village near Tonghua with 598 pupils, 37 teachers and five workers. Thirty-two of the 37 teachers are women – but everyone proudly points out how exceptionally successful Sun is.

More women than men are attracted to teaching, possibly because of the job security, or because it is a job which can be carried out anywhere, and newly graduated teachers are usually sent to work in or near their home villages.

It appears that whenever a man is seriously interested in teaching, his career progress to head teacher is guaranteed. For a woman, success involves hard work and is by no means certain, although in theory men and women have equal chances to become head teachers. Sun says:

> It is important that I have achieved this status. It is true, I have had to work much harder and be much better than a man. I still have to. But what counts is that it is possible. This way, I can set an example for other women to follow.[25]

At colleges, universities and middle schools it is even more difficult for women to achieve a managerial or senior position.

Geng Hong, a woman in her early thirties, lives in Changchun (Jilin Province). She is one of the many women who have managed to change their careers to earn more money.

> I used to work as a midwife at the Changchun Railway Hospital for 500 *yuan* per month. Now I'm a sales

representative for a company called Large Screen News Advertisements. I sell cinema advertising. I get commission and earn at least 1,000 *yuan* per month – often 2,000 or more. The only thing I miss is the prestige of belonging to a railway work unit. But earning good money is more important.[26]

Liang Zhiqiao is in charge of the accounts department at a publishing firm in Tonghua.

I feel I was cheated of my education. We only learnt political slogans, and were sent to do hard labour. There was no skills training. I learnt to read and write, that was all, and I was lucky in that. I envy the younger people who have a chance to get a college education. But I'm learning from experience, and I've been able to work my way up. You need a lot of energy to succeed in a career if you've missed out on your education. But then most of the women of my generation are in the same situation.

She uses an abacus with flat white beads for calculating. 'This one is faster than a calculator, especially for additions and subtractions.' For multiplying and dividing she occasionally uses a calculator.[27]

Jenny, a secretary at the Foreign Experts Hotel, part of the University of Post and Telecommunications work unit in Beijing, is dissatisfied with her job:

I have a university degree in English. But whenever I apply for a job as an interpreter or translator, the interviewers talk down to me. They leave no doubt that they are looking for a man. I just don't have the confidence anymore to continue job-hunting. I'm bored with my job here. It would not be so bad if I was really a bilingual secretary. But I don't use my language skills at all here, and they are becoming rusty.[28]

Pan Quinyue, 57, is the president of the Linyi Maternity and Child Care Station in the Yimeng Mountains, a particularly poor area. Pan Quinyue has devoted herself to the health of rural women and children for more than 30 years. A trained midwife, she worked several hears at a hospital before she was sent to the countryside. She introduced contraception in the 1960s and modern delivery methods in the 1970s. Pan performed tubal ligations, vasectomies, and inserted IUDs (intra-uterine devices). In the 1980s, the state issued additional laws protecting women's and children's health and Pan helped set up managerial systems for pregnant and lying-in women, and for children. She became deputy director in 1981, director in 1992 and finally president of the centre in 1995.

Pan Quinyue describes her work, which involves continuous medical studies and the training of her staff as well as working with rural women, as 'half-medical and half-social work'.[29]

The state emphasizes the training and promotion of female cadres (government officials). Special efforts at recruiting and training female cadres for leading posts are guaranteed by law,[30] and there are even special women cadres' training colleges (see Chapter 2). The number of women working in government offices increased dramatically from 366,000 in 1951 to 8.7 million in 1996,[31] but the leading cadre positions are still mostly occupied by men.

Nevertheless, more women are moving up the career ladder within authorities and the government. For example, Wu Yi, minister of foreign trade and economic co-operation, is a woman.

Deng Zaijiun is senior director at China Central Television Station. She is a determined, confident, highly efficient woman. Her previous career in the army taught her how to overcome obstacles. Despite her success in her chosen career, a magazine article in *China Pictorial* emphasized her feminine attributes: big eyes, calmness, modesty, motherliness, making and ironing her children's clothes. Her husband Zhou Erjun is quoted as saying: 'She is anxious to outdo others in her career, but she is also a good hand for house chores.' Deng herself says her two happiest moments were the public recognition of television programmes she directed, and her husband's and children's visits to her office.[32]

Gulixiati Abendukar is the only woman of the Uygur nationality who has achieved the rank of vice-mayor in China. She obtained a university degree, then worked as manager of a small shop, and was later promoted secretary of the party committee of the Bureau of Commerce of Kashi. Gulixiati is a natural leader who can motivate and stimulate staff. Since 1993, she has been vice-mayor in charge of finance, commercial trade, statistics collection, civil affairs and tourism work in Kashi, a city in the Xinjiang Province. But Gulixiati is an exception: among the Uygur ethnic group in the Xinjiang Province, it is still unusual for women to have a significant career, let alone to hold a position of power and responsibility. Gulixiati encourages women in Kashi to embark on careers or to become self-employed. She is proud that the managers of most of Kashi's most successful shops are women.[33]

Risky career changes

Those who change their careers almost always have to leave their work units, and with them their social security benefits, behind. If they cannot get permission to leave, some do it without permission. In some cases, they claim long-term illness while taking up a job with another work unit.

Zhang Meiling (pseudonym) left her job as a teacher with a state middle school when she was offered a job with a railway middle school which was more interesting and paid twice as well.

> I enjoyed my new job so much. But the head teacher of my old school applied pressure to get me back. I did not have his permission to start a new job. What I had done was a crime. He forced me to go back to my old job. But he was very good: he told everyone that I had been ill, so there were no recriminations for me, and my pension and social security remained intact.[34]

Nicholas Kristof, former *New York Times* correspondent in Beijing, interviewed one young woman who told him that she had needed money urgently to bribe doctors to give good treatment to her mother who suffered from cancer. Additionally:

> I got a doctor to write a letter saying that I was ill and needed a medical leave for three years ... I still get 70 per cent of my wages even though I'm not even in town. If I didn't have the doctor's letter, I would have to quit my work unit, and then I wouldn't get a penny. Anyway, my company was state owned, and so my bosses don't really care about my salary. They know I'm not really ill, but this is what everybody does now.[35]

Women of all levels of education – from peasants, who may not be able to write their name, to college graduates – float to the cities in search of jobs. But as most of the clerical jobs are allocated on a *guanxi* basis, a complex system of connections and bribery which dominates life in China, it is difficult for new arrivals to break into this closed network. Even jobs which are open to outside applicants will rarely be given to someone who applies without permission from the previous work unit.

In many cases, good jobs are often sold to the highest bidder. 'The people who get the best jobs are those who have the best-connected parents or whose relatives have a lot of money. I don't think candidate selection has much to do with exam results,' says Xiao.

Zhin Xuelian, 19, is in a luckier position.

> I'm doing a two-year course for English teachers, just to get a language qualification. But I will definitely not become a teacher. My father is a graduate engineer, and my mother is manager of a supermarket. I have one brother who is a soldier. My parents will pay the fine when I quit teaching. My father has many contacts in the rich cities in the south, and some of them owe him a favour. He will find me a job as an interpreter.[36]

Unemployment

Women enjoy special protection during pregnancy and menstruation, which is why employers often regard women as less flexible and more expensive than men in the same job. Consequently, unskilled women are often the first to become unemployed when a company cuts jobs.

It is difficult to estimate just how many women are affected, but *China Daily* reports that in Guangzhou (Canton), in 1995 alone, 15,000 female employees were dismissed. More than 60 per cent of them said that they found lack of marketable skills was the greatest obstacle to finding work again.

A recently launched programme in Guangzhou, which is one of China's richest cities and has about 5 million inhabitants, aims to train women in work-related skills which are currently in demand. These courses appear to be popular, with 170,000 female workers learning computing, accounting, cooking, electrical engineering, sewing, driving and other skills. Most women choose to learn at least two new skills. The programme is run by trade unions, branches of the state labour department, employment agencies, and work units (state-run enterprises).[37]

A similar project was launched in Beijing's Dongcheng District in March 1995, the only programme of its kind in the capital. The

Dongcheng Employment Service Centre for Women was established by the local labour bureau. On Mondays, women looking for work can get free consultations. During the first year, more than 4,000 women took the opportunity for free consultations and a further 2,700 received professional training. But unlike British employment agencies, for example, women who are placed successfully have to pay a fee, which is currently 20 *yuan*.

Most women who seek work through the Centre are between 30 and 40. One of the consultants, Liang Wenfang, is a woman in her thirties. She said that women who have been made redundant often feel deserted by society and can be aggressive, demanding to be found jobs instantly. Liang believes that most of these women lost their jobs not only because they were not trained but because they were ageing. She was talking about women who have passed their thirtieth year! It looks like the victims of ageism in China are younger than those in the Western world, at least as far as women are concerned.[38]

Prostitution and sexual exploitation

Many of the educated young women flocking to Beijing, Guangzhou and Shanghai to become secretaries or interpreters end up working in nightclubs or in prostitution.

Bosses are said to abuse their power by demanding sexual favours from their secretaries, in some circumstances 'secretary' has become the new title for what used to be a 'concubine', the dependent mistress. They rarely know in advance what their 'job' involves. Others are used as bait to stimulate and lure business partners.

Sheryl WuDunn, a Chinese American who spent the years 1988–1993 researching the position of women in China, describes a party given for political VIPs in her book *China Wakes*:

> A dozen beautiful female assistants and secretaries, dressed in black and glitter and balancing awkwardly on high heels, stood by a row of foldable steel chairs ... The young women had been summoned to serve as dancing partners for high-ranking male cadres.

She recounts how a cabinet minister mistakes her for a secretary and gropes her on the dance floor. 'Being groped by Minister Lin was not one of my most pleasant moments in China, but in some respects it was among my most insightful. I realized that most Chinese women at the party would have had to put up with Minister Lin's squeezing, and perhaps with other requests as well ... '.[39]

Some women, delighted at having secured the desirable post of secretary, discover too late what it involves. They will either leave – and be without money again and have lost face – or adjust to the situation.

A secretary who was faced with this situation recalls:

> So I went down south, and a friend helped me get a job at a joint venture factory in the city of Dongguan. Really rich place, Dongguan is! Right near Hong Kong ... I was the personal secretary to the manager. I got 900 *yuan* a month – that's more than six times what I was getting in my old job. I should have known it was too good to be true ... And then he began to hint that maybe I should sleep with him. A lot of girls do that, you know, especially in the south. The secretaries are always the prettiest girls in the factory and they all sleep with their bosses. But I wasn't ready for that, and so I told him I was quitting.[40]

Sheryl WuDunn told me it is different with nightclub work, a career which women choose in full awareness of what it does, or does not, involve.

> One of the popular careers, believe it or not, is prostitution, even for college graduates. Young women flock to the glitzy nightclubs in the south where they can earn many times their hometown salaries. They wear nice clothes, make-up and live stylish lives, or so goes the dream. I was surprised and disbelieving at first, but then I interviewed some of these women.

She adds that the prostitutes looked upon it as a 'good job' although many nightclub workers drew the line and insisted that they didn't 'go home with the men'.[41]

Domestic slavery

The Beijing Labour Market, a narrow road cluttered with litter, is rumoured to be the centre for female slave trade, but I was unable to find any evidence for this claim. I met several women who said that they knew something but did not wish to talk about it or that they had observed something but could not provide proof. A divorcee in her thirties said:

> I often go to the Labour Market in the mornings and hire myself out for temporary work. This is usually as a nanny, or washing and cleaning in a private household. I'm experienced, I can smell it if something's not right. For example, a man came and said he wanted a maid for his wife. But he had recruited a new maid only a week ago and another one the week before that. So I was suspicious and did not accept. But many women come to Beijing looking for a job have no experience and no relatives to turn to for advice. They can't read, they have no skills. They are glad if someone comes and hires them on the spot as a maid. I believe many employers take advantage of the women's naivety.[42]

But the Chinese police are efficient in this matter: in 1993, for example, the police caught a slave-trading gang that had abducted 1,800 women from the Beijing Labour Market and sold them to the Shanxi Province.[43]

Sheryl WuDunn says she met one young woman who had been sold into slavery as a child together with her mother, and another who was abducted by traders when looking for work in Beijing, but who managed to escape after two days.[44]

Women as entrepreneurs

From 1978, Deng Xiaoping gradually introduced principles of free market economy into the communist system. One of the most revolutionary programmes was based on the simple observation that Chinese farmers produced best results if they worked in small family groups rather than in large collectives. Peasants were given their own land to farm and could sell their produce in the open market. There were still some restrictions, for example in pricing, but within five years, the output from farms had doubled and the living standards of peasants increased. In urban areas, bonuses and piecework rates were introduced, factory output rose and factory workers' living standards also increased. The only people who could not raise their income were those on a fixed salary: teachers, government officials, soldiers and officers. Some of these resorted to bribes, others decided to start a small business. If peasants could sell their produce in the street, why should a teacher or bureaucrat not treble her salary by becoming a street hawker? Many of these small enterprises folded, but in the general atmosphere of economic growth, many succeeded. Self-employment is a dream for many Chinese women of any age.

Song Yuqing is ambitious:

> My parents are both peasants, working in the fields. I would like to start my own business, but I don't have any marketable skills and I lack the experience. Somehow I'll have to get business experience, but I don't know how I could possibly acquire that as a teacher. As soon as I have a chance to work in a business-related field, I'll take it. Any job! And then I'll gradually work my way up. When I have the skills and the funds to start my own business, I'll do it. I think I'd be good at it.

There are 14 million self-employed people in rural areas, engaging in commerce and service trades, and two-thirds of them are women.[45]

Mei Lutang (pseudonym) is a peasant who has entered into the spirit of the free market with enthusiasm. Every day, she loads her tricycle with agricultural produce, places her four-year-old daughter on top of it and cycles the five miles to Tonghua street market. The vibrant speckled band of the street market stretches like a lazy snake for three miles between the grey concrete blocks of the town centre. Despite the cold climate, peasant women like Mei Lutang bring a wealth of their surplus produce for sale on their tricycles which also serve as market stalls: onions, sweet potatoes, bundles of fresh coriander and cabbage, which form the staple diet in Jilin.

The warm smell of freshly baked pancakes lures shoppers to the pancake makers, who have invested their savings in a mini-carriage with glass windows and hotplates. They use brushes to spread the dough paper thin onto a huge hot plate, cover the pancakes with a layer of chopped chilli and chives, fold them and wrap them in pages torn out of a book. They are so hot that it's difficult to eat them without gasping, but delicious.

Customers bargain for oranges, apples, small bananas, pineapples, fermented-tasting pears, noodles, brown eggs and vegetables. In winter, they walk through knee-deep snow; in spring, through ankle-deep mud. In summer, they wrap thin gauzy scarves in bright colours around their heads, which makes them look as if they are carrying huge pumpkins on their shoulders. This is to keep the fine dust and sand out of their eyes and nostrils.

Other items on sale are live fish and skinned, dark red little birds on spits. Another vendor offers brown, arm-long snakes which try to escape from his red plastic bucket. Half the traders are women, most of them self-employed like Mai Lutang.

> We are now allowed to sell our goods at our own prices. Deciding the price is not difficult. Every morning, I look how much the official state stall charges, and I set my price just a little below that. If someone buys a lot or comes often to my stall, I'll give them a better price. It's easy. I just sell whatever my husband has harvested. At the moment it's green beans. I also watch how other traders do it and learn from their approach. It's less hard work than farm labour, and I can look after my daughter. I earn more than before. I will be able to pay for a good education for my daughter.

Mei Lutang plans to expand:

> I think of buying bananas from the south. They sell well in this market, but of course they don't grow here in the north. But I need to invest money. Sometimes I wonder: am I a peasant or am I a businesswoman? A bit of both, perhaps. But when I buy in fruit from the south, I'll know I'm a businesswoman.[46]

Cai Shuzhen, 46, from a village in the Jilin Province, made several attempts at becoming a self-employed businesswoman. In 1982, inspired by seeing other people making a fortune by starting small businesses, she borrowed 3,000 *yuan* – at that time ten times the average farmer's annual income – and decided to raise chickens. However, she knew little about the subject, lost most of her 8,000 chicken in chicken pests, and ended up 4,000 *yuan* in debt – an astronomical sum for a peasant.

Only three months later, Cai started raising rabbits for which she was aware there was an eager market. A virus killed most of the rabbits. She said:

> I cried and cried for my ill luck until no more tears came out. I thought of suicide ... I came to realize that I shouldn't

yield to failure. From the bottom of my heart I knew some day I would get over all these misfortunes ... I owe a great deal to my family, because during my ups and downs they were always there to support me ... At last I figured out that my biggest enemy was illiteracy, especially illiteracy of science and technical know-how. So I began to learn to read and write bit by bit during farm work and housework. Sometimes I stayed up late into the night studying.

A crash course in mushroom growing finally led to her first successful enterprise in 1987. In 1989, she turned to planting rice using new technology from Japan, and in 1994 she set up a service centre providing quality grain seeds to local farmers. She is now one of the provinces most successful businesswomen and she plans to expand.[47]

Self-employment is particularly difficult for women among those ethnic groups which are based on a strict patriarchal society. But there are some women who have shed the fetters. Rebiya, an Uygur Woman, is a striking example.

Tradition restricts married Uygur women from showing their face to men who are not family members. The veil covers the whole face, including the eyes. More and more women shed the veil, but the old ideas remain, which makes it difficult for women to conduct business.

Rebiya was born in a small remote town in the Xinjiang Province in northwest China. Her father, a poor barber, married her off when she was 15 to a man who, according to a fortune teller, would become an official. Unfortunately, the fortune teller got it wrong and the husband's glorious career did not happen. Rebiya gave birth to six children and lived in poverty. Desperate for money, she made children's shoes and clothes and sold them in the street. Women in those days had to wear the chador and stay at home. Rebiya's appearing in public earned her the name 'the bad woman.' Her husband found out and divorced her.

Without a home to go, Rebiya rented a six metre square room, put on her chador and went from door to door to collect dirty clothes. She just managed to survive on the money and put a little to the side. Then she took her savings, travelled to cities like Kashi, Urumqi and Shanghai. Rebiya possessed business instincts which helped her to spot opportunities. For example, she bought 10 kilograms of artificial pearls in the Fujian Province, made them

into necklaces, and sold them for good profit in the Xinjiang
Province: her business was started.

When Xinjiang began to do foreign trade, Rebiya established
Akeda Industry and Commercial Corporation Ltd, and made
herself president and general manager. Akeda is the largest private
enterprise in the Xinjiang Province, and Rebiya is believed to be
the richest woman of the province.[48]

Aiming for idleness

The government makes genuine efforts to encourage and assist
women into skilled and responsible positions. But while some
courageous women take up the opportunity and work their way
up in a men's world, many others are willing to forego the career
in favour of feminine accomplishments. These include
housekeeping, cookery, looking beautiful, and pursuing genteel
hobbies such as painting or music – in the home. I get the
impression that the pre-1949 ideal of the woman staying at home
is re-emerging. I believe that non-working wives are about to
replace fridges, washing machines, television sets, Japanese cars
and mobile phones as the number one status symbol. Strangely,
even young educated women increasingly aspire to this ideal of
wealthy, genteel idleness.

The ratio of women and men in managerial positions is likely
to improve slightly over the next decade but there is enormous
pressure from society for women (even successful career women)
to put husband and household duties first. Women feel they are
giving a noble sacrifice if they give up a career opportunity to serve
their family. These attitudes are not likely to change soon.

Jobs are allocated by the authorities, and the Chinese have little
opportunity to choose their careers. Bribes are more effective in
getting a desired job than talent or skills. Unwanted assignments
and bribery lead to a workforce which is, on the whole,
unmotivated. The communist system guarantees comprehensive
protection for workers, especially for women, but lack of funds
and the upcoming of independent enterprises decreases the level
of protection and workers' rights.

The unmotivated workforce is a serious obstacle to China's
economic development. The introduction of piecework rates and
profit-sharing schemes will change this. Officials, who cannot
benefit from such schemes, may resort increasingly to corruption.

Over the next decade, there will probably be more freedom for people to choose where and how they want to work, but at the same time unemployment will soar in many rural areas as industries will continue to concentrate around Guangdong and Shanghai, and workers' rights are likely to be limited or ignored.

With greater economic freedom and more role models, it is likely that more and more women are going to start their own businesses, mostly on a small scale with enterprises which require little capital, for example as street vendors or providing services such as tailoring and bicycle mending. Self-employment gives women of any age group and educational level a measure of economic independence.

4 Love, sex, relationships

The pattern for choosing a partner has changed dramatically over the last 50 years. More and more women select their own spouse, or at least have a say in their parents' choice for them. The age for marriage has risen. But one aspect of the woman-man relationship has changed little: sex before marriage and even loving relationships without a firm intention to get married are nearly taboo.

Single sex friendships

Two young men walk, hand in hand, across the campus of the Teachers' Training College in Tonghua (Jilin Province); two girls cuddle up to each other on a rug, deeply concentrating on their textbooks, interrupting their studies only to kiss each other occasionally. Gays? Lesbians? Far from it.

These students are just good friends who like showing their affection physically. Kissing, cuddling and holding hands in public is the norm among friends. But there were no heterosexual couples to be seen in this town or in most others. Only recently have married couples begun to show their affection for each other in public, and only in 'modern' areas such as Shanghai. Unmarried lovers still consider holding hands in public to be as daring as we would consider having sex in public.

Many students avoid the issue altogether by not having a loving relationship until they leave college and 'enter society'. Boys often stick with boys and girls with girls, and they develop very close and intimate relationships. Hugging, stroking and kissing between members of the same sex are a substitute for lovemaking.

When the conversation turns to boys, the female students giggle in embarrassment. Then Song Yuqing, a 22-year-old peasants' daughter from the Hunan Province, decides that I, a foreigner who comes from the immoral West, cannot be expected to know the Chinese code of conduct. She smiles tolerantly, showing beautiful lips and perfect teeth: 'Of course I have no boyfriend. I will look for one when I have finished my studies. It's not good to have a boyfriend before you are at least 25.'[1]

Pressure from government and families

Traditionally, the Chinese married in their early teens. The communist government respected and promoted love between partners as a the basis of marriage, but demanded that couples put their love for their country first. To reduce the number of children and to raise the status of women, the communist government offered benefits to couples who married later, such as a few extra days' annual leave to enjoy their honeymoon.

For young women, this means pressure from two sides. The government urges them to marry as late as possible, but families in rural areas try to marry off their daughters as early as possible. A girl who has not found a husband when she is 25 is considered to bring shame to her family.

On the other hand, many young people rebel against social pressure to marry, especially girls, who are keen to further their own careers and enjoy their independence for as long as possible. Many of the students at Tonghua Teachers' College feel that they are breaking ground with their liberated views.

Jin Zefeng, a slim 22-year-old male in a new Western-style suit, folds his hands behind his back as he talks:

> Each time I go home during the holidays my parents ask me if I've got a girlfriend. Yes, they wait for me to get married, the sooner the better. I know they mean well, and are waiting for a grandchild. I will be happy to oblige them. But I want to wait until I am established in a job and career.[2]

Jin Xuelian, a lively 19-year-old, claims:

> I don't want to get married until I'm 35! But I'll let you into my secret. I have had a boyfriend for years. My parents know nothing about him. Oh yes, I see him regularly. Twice a year! He studies in another town, but we meet during each summer and winter vacation.[3]

Lin Yanmei, 19, has a boyfriend, too. She speaks in a low voice.

> I meet him everyday when we have dinner together in the
> refectory. I think I will marry him someday; we love each
> other very much. Our parents expect that I will marry him.
> Luckily my parents don't hurry me; I'm their only unmarried
> daughter, and they want to keep me with them for as long
> as possible.[4]

My friend Chen (pseudonym), 23, told me in May 1994:

> I won't get married until I can no longer avoid it. Marriage
> would mean giving up my ambitious long-term career
> plans. I want to be a secretary in a city, which is incredibly
> ambitious for a country girl. But I have the willpower, and
> if anyone can do it, I can, although it may take ten years
> or more to achieve my aim.
>   The only thing which can possibly stop me is pressure
> from my parents to get married. They say I bring them shame
> if I'm not married at 25. I wonder how long I can hold out
> against this pressure ...[5]

Two years later, in April 96, I received a letter from the now 25-
year-old Chen who had become a teacher and dreaded every
working day. 'On 5 May, I'll marry. So these days I am busy
preparing for my marriage ceremony.' She continued describing
the wedding ritual and her family's delight in detail. She did not
mention her husband-to-be or her feelings at all.

I sent her my best wishes for her marriage, and asked about her
husband. She simply replied 'He's a worker. My parents introduced
us. They like him.'[6]

Talking love

In the countryside as well as in urban areas, courtship is a two-
way communication and girls as well as boys can take the initiative.

Ding Xianqian (pseudonym), a 42-year-old railway engineer,
explains how he met his wife:

> I was studying at college and was introduced to a fellow-
> student's sister. She seemed a nice girl, but I wasn't
> particularly interested. But after that party, she contacted
> me several times, always with an excuse: could she borrow

some maps? Could I explain something technical she needed for her studies? Usually it had something to do with studying, never any personal reason. It was obvious that she was personally interested in me, although she always used an excuse. I never made a move myself, but I enjoyed her efforts. I was amused, and flattered. I found I liked her more and more, and soon grew really fond of her. I'm really glad she was so persistent.[7]

Among the Bouyei people in Guizhou, young people mix freely at the markets and fairs and have plenty of opportunity for flirtation. Gina Corrigan writes in her book *The Odyssey Illustrated Guide to Guizhou:*

... the unmarried often sing to each other, signalling the beginning of a courtship. In the low work season, the festivals and family get-togethers provide an opportunity for the young to continue their courtship. Each village will have its own set of melodic tunes and the girls invent appropriate words to sing to each guest as they offer him a drink. He must then reply in song before he can accept. Replies should rhyme, be clever and amusing to entertain the gathering of family and friends. Both boys and girls express their feelings strongly and openly. Singers must be quick-witted with their replies – the songs are a test of each other's intelligence. Although good looks are appreciated, the value placed on antiphonal singing in the Bouyei culture is such that a village girl would find it difficult to get a husband if she could not sing. Courting by song often continues while working in the fields. Even the urbanized Bouyei often sing to each other in the parks of Guaiyang on a Sunday ... Another way for a girl to show attraction for a particular boy during certain festivals is to throw him a ball of silk strips that she has made herself. If he finds the girl attractive, he will seek her out and courtship will continue with singing playing a major role.[8]

Choosing a partner

There are four patterns of selecting a spouse:

A) In urban areas, the woman and the man meet at work, during their education, or social activities, or through dates set up by friends and colleagues. They get to know each other fairly well because of their common interests. They fall in love and marry on the basis of mutual affection. This pattern is similar to the one in most of the Western world and is increasing in China's urban areas.

B) In both urban and rural areas, a matchmaker introduces the partners to each other. The two gradually develop mutual understanding and affection before they decide to get married.

C) The parents of both partners arrange a meeting. If the young people consent, a marriage is arranged. This pattern is popular in the countryside.

D) The parents arrange the marriage without seeking the consent of the couple. This pattern still accounts for many marriages in the countryside.

An undated random survey, cited in *Mother Wife Daughter*, says that 74 per cent of all marriages in the 1990s are decided either by the couples themselves or in consultation with their parents (patterns A and B). This means that 26 per cent of all marriages are still arranged by the parents. The same survey claims that 80 per cent of women are married to men of their choice (patterns A, B and C). This leaves 20 per cent of young women getting married to men they don't know or don't like. These figures also indicate that 6 per cent of all marriages occur under pattern C, where the parents choose the husband but the daughter is content with their choice.[9]

What makes a woman a desirable partner in marriage? Criteria differ. In the northeast, among the educated students whom I questioned, (mostly of Han and Manchu peoples), girls are chosen for their connections, their gentle manners, their looks (white skin, Western eyes, big breasts), the location of their home village, their parents' wealth, and their 'gentle and caring' behaviour. Wu Naitao in *Mother Wife Daughter* reckons that 'good-looking' and 'good at housework' are still the men's main criteria.[10]

Among the Bouyei ethnic minority in the Guizhou Province, a girl is chosen for her beauty, educational achievement, weaving and embroidery skills, farming skills and singing skills. A girl who can't sing will have difficulty finding a husband.[11]

The young women I talked to were likely to consider the following aspects in a potential husband (in order of importance): career prospects, family background (especially reputation and age of parents), education, wealth (his or his parents'), looks (especially height). Wu Naitao says women want their spouses to be well-educated, enterprising and have a family with sound economic conditions.[12]

In 1985 a matchmaking institute in Shanghai questioned 1,132 unmarried women and 891 men. They found that 78 per cent of the women wanted their man to exceed their own education, professional status and income; 15.5 per cent wanted the man's conditions to equal their own and only 4.7 per cent were willing to take a man whose conditions were inferior. Just over three per cent of the men preferred a superior woman, 32.3 per cent preferred a partner of similar status and 64.4 per cent wanted a woman of lesser status. These preferences were confirmed by reports from matchmaking institutes in other major cities.[13]

Young people are still expected to marry their first boyfriend or girlfriend, so a young woman may not dare as much as flirt with a boy across the classroom until she has checked out his suitability as a husband. If she is interested in someone, she'll enlist her friends' and family's discreet help in investigating his background: does he come from a good family? How old and healthy are his parents? (The daughter-in-law is still expected to serve and care for her husband's parents, which can be an enormous job if it requires nursing an invalid.) What are his career prospects? Does he live far away?

After their studies, each will have to return to their home town, to the jobs assigned to them by the government. It is still difficult to move towns to join a loved one, but some students spend their whole last year at college pulling every string of *guanxi* (connections) to ensure that they can both get jobs in the same town.

One student's husband left shortly after their wedding at the spring festival to study in another province for two years. They'll see each other only in the holidays; long separations are considered normal for married couples. Couples who belong to work units in different parts of China are granted some extra annual leave so that they can visit each other once a year.

Lin does not know yet where she and her boyfriend will be posted and they may face such a situation. 'But if it happens, we will be strong. Love is the most important thing between a male and a female.'[14]

Matchmaking and arranged marriages

Matchmaking has always played a great role in China. Before the Communist Revolution, when most marriages were arranged by the parents, there was the professional matchmaker. The matchmaker was usually an old woman who was perceptive, practical and cunning. Parents used to engage her services to find a suitable husband or wife for their child. In Chinese folk dances and plays, there is still a 'matchmaker' dancing her role, identified by a basket, an apron, and an opium pipe.

During the Communist Revolution and the Cultural Revolution, it was often the communist party that introduced suitable marriage partners. While the communists fought against arranged marriages and promoted love matches, they also encouraged 'suitable' matches amongst party members.

Nowadays, the village matchmakers are not professionals; they are more likely to be popular, elderly women with a keen interest in human nature, who engage in matchmaking as a hobby. Young people in urban areas ask their families and friends, employers, teachers or colleagues for help in finding someone suitable.

Meng Xiaoxian (pseudonym), a middle school teacher, had her brother acting as her matchmaker.

> I was 24 and studying at college. My parents kept urging me to find a boyfriend and marry him. I said I would like to find someone, but didn't know how to go about it. Most of the fellow students were women, and the few men on our course were already spoken for or came from other provinces. My brother offered to help. He took me to a party at his college, and introduced me to a fellow student, saying we had much in common. Ding and I understood at once what my brother meant. Dutifully, we discussed music and cinema. There was no instant attraction between Ding and me, but if my brother thought Ding would make a good husband, he was worth investigating. He lived nearby and his parents were in good health. Ding did not encourage or discourage my interest, but I persisted. I asked his help with English grammar and offered to lend him some English novels. Helping one another with studies is a very good excuse. It's respectable, if you know what I mean.

> We are not in love with each other, but maybe we will
> be by the time we have finished our studies and are ready
> to get married. I value my brother's judgement.[15]

The parents of one of my friends asked tentatively if I could introduce their daughter to 'wealthy single Chinese men of good character'. They assumed that as a foreigner I would have close contacts with many wealthy Chinese.

Dating agencies which operate through magazines and television programmes are extremely popular, especially with people in towns and cities. In Beijing, there is even an agency which arranges marriages between people with disabilities.[16]

In rural areas, there are still pre-arranged marriages. Among some ethnic groups, marriage among close relatives is encouraged. For the Miao people in the Guizhou Province, the preferred spouse for a daughter is the father's sister's son; for the Yi in Guizhou, it is the mother's brother's son. Occasionally, a girl will be promised in marriage at birth if two families wish to strengthen ties, but in general the girls have certain amount of individual choice.

Until 1949, the Yi people had a strict system of family-arranged marriages to keep up their rigid class structure. This still exists to a large extent in rural areas, where arranged marriages are the norm. But in the towns of the region, more and more young women choose their own husbands.[17]

It is not only the uneducated peasant women who get married to a husband of their parents' choice. Two of the college students I met during my stay in China made the mistake of falling in love with men whom their parents thought unsuitable, for reasons such as family background and origin. Both were taken from college before graduating and quickly married off to boys from their village. One of the young women who was married against her will was a divorcee, which shows the power parents and society have not only over inexperienced young girls but over grown-up and fairly educated women. I did not hear from either of them in person after their marriages, although I tried to keep in touch. I believe that the husbands or parents intercepted the correspondence for fear that contact with foreign ideas could inspire rebellion. Mutual Chinese friends had heard about the fate of one of the brides but their information was second-hand and may have been based on wishful thinking. 'At first she was very sad, but she understood that it was inevitable. She consented to the marriage because the man her parents had chosen was a good man. She has known him from childhood and she is fond of him. In time they will grow to love each other.'

A survey on changes concerning marriage conducted in some of the districts in Beijing, Shanghai, Tianjin and Chendu showed that the percentage of people who married their acquaintances was only 19.34 per cent in 1950–1953. The figure grew to 32.98 per cent in 1977–1982. Those who were matched by their families but consented to the marriage accounted for 26.81 per cent, and those matched by their friends for 31.21 per cent in 1950–1953. These figures decreased to 15.79 per cent and 50.18 per cent in 1977–1982. However, the regions covered in this survey were the richest and most modernized areas of China, and cannot be considered representative of all China.

Premarital sex and enforced celibacy

By delaying marriage for as long as they can endure the pressure from parents or society, or until they are established in a career, the young people can avoid emotional pain. But what about their natural instincts for intimacy and sex?

Lin draws in her breath at the question and tries not to look shocked. 'Oh no, you can't have sex if you are not married. It's immoral!'

It seems it is not morals which prevent young people from sex, but fear. Xin says: 'Personally, I think it is all right for lovers to have sex before marriage. But in China, if you're caught, you'll be sent to prison. Premarital sex is against the law.'

Young men would not risk it either. Jin says: 'I know it's okay in Western countries for people to sleep together. But in China we have several laws which don't permit couples to have sex before they are married.'

But their knowledge of what exactly the laws do or don't permit is scanty. Jiao Hongyan, a serious, intelligent 21-year-old whose parents work in an iron mine, is more aware than the others:

> There is no danger if you are officially engaged, and have registered your intention to get married. It's only casual sex which is against the law and it doesn't matter whether people are of age or not. Engaged people are accepted as a couple by the law, so they can have sex if they like.[18]

I have not been able to find a Chinese law which makes premarital sex an offence; however, the perceived illegality seems to be enough to prevent sex.

Before the Liberation, premarital sex was an accepted feature for women and men in some minority areas. For example, the Jinuo in the Yunnan Province thought it normal that 16–17 year olds had sexual relationships. The man went quietly to his girlfriend's home late at night and stayed there until dawn. The parents did not interfere because they had done the same when they were young. It appears that some villages even had special houses where unmarried couples could spend the night; it was no stigma for a child to born to unmarried parents. The couple might not make their relationship known publicly until they had been together for some months, by which time they visited each other's families to help with agricultural tasks and housework. Once they had a child, the man would help his girlfriend's family more than before. There was no commitment on either side and each young person could have more than one relationship going. But once they were formally married they were expected to remain faithful.[19]

In the Miao (Guizhou Province) society, there is still considerable sexual freedom. Even after marriage, a woman may have sex with another man until she is pregnant. This is why sometimes the first child does not inherit the family land.[20] More about this in Chapter 5.

Nevertheless, in most areas, sexual freedom for women has always been unthinkable. Dongbei (the northeast of China) is extremely conservative and cohabitation is unheard of there. If couples have sex, it is almost always in secret and out of doors, for example in a forest. Having sex at home is impossible from the practical point of view: the work units allocate rooms and flats only to married couples, and even then you may have to live with your parents or in-laws for several years. Because of the strict and crowded conditions in college dormitories and private homes, secluded corners in parks and woodlands are the only possible venues for unmarried couples to make love. Late in the evening, couples seek out the small forest near the college, and on warm dark evenings there are often a number of couples petting, but they pretend not to notice each other.

In big cities in the more developed areas of China, such as Shanghai or Beijing, cohabiting couples can be found, and sex before marriage is more or less accepted. Sheryl WuDunn says:

Yes, there is sex before marriage. Once, when I was at Beijing University, I was walking by a grassy lawn and saw a large clump of what looked like a sculpture. Upon closer examination, I saw that it was a blanket thrown over two somethings, and then those somethings began to move. It was a couple of university students writhing together in ecstasy.[21]

Jiao explains the student's viewpoint:

China is a traditional country and people have still conservative attitudes. Even if a girl is engaged to get married, she takes an incredible risk if she has sex. The boy may reject her after he's had sex with her. If her shame becomes known, her reputation is ruined, everyone will look down on her. Once she's had sex with one man, no other will want to marry her, except perhaps a man who is too poor to find a wife with an unsullied reputation, or someone who hasn't got a job and needs a wife's income to support his parents.[22]

Unmarried pregnancy: suicide expected

The prospects are even bleaker if a woman gets pregnant. Jin is decisive in his male point of view: 'A girl who gets pregnant is a bad woman.'

His friend Paddy, a serious and ambitious 20-year-old, is at least willing to concede that it may not be the girl's fault: 'I would feel pity for her if she got pregnant after being raped.'

The girls, who had been hesitant to talk about sex, are eager to comment on unwanted pregnancy, which is such a stigma that society often expects the woman to commit suicide. Xin says: 'If an unmarried girl gets pregnant, her life is virtually ruined. The way single mothers are treated by society very often leads them to commit suicide.'

Jiao thinks carefully, then she says if a close friend got herself pregnant, she would stand by her: 'In many ways her life would be ruined, but I would encourage her not to throw her life away. She would probably have the whole society against her, if she continued to live, but I would do my best to give her courage to go her own way.' But Song thinks that unmarried motherhood should be avoided at all cost: 'If she cannot marry the baby's father, she must get rid of it.'[23]

Contraception: easy if you know how

The authorities encourage abortions of single women's pregnancies and even in the case of married parents when there is the slightest suspicion that the unborn child may have a physical disability. But to obtain an abortion, or any other medical help, a woman has to apply through her college or employer, which might effectively ruin her career prospects. So many girls delay this essential step until it is too late. It is possible to arrange for a private and discreet abortion in a hospital in another town, but few girls know how to go about it. The assumption that premarital sex does not exist in China means that the pill and the IUD (Intra Uterine Device) are available only to married women. Yet condoms are so easily available that it is astonishing that unwanted pregnancies – considering the stigma and problems attached – occur at all. Condoms are sold openly in the department stores in bigger cities.

The problem is that married women are usually forced to have a coil inserted until they get permission to get pregnant (see the section on family planning in Chapter 5), which means that buying a condom is to declare the intention to have extramarital or premarital sex, so the purchase can be extremely embarrassing for a girl.

Lack of sex education

The major hurdle is the lack of knowledge, especially in rural areas. Parents still avoid talking about sex other than in vague terms; there is no sex education in most schools and colleges, and teenage and women's magazines are not as widespread or as frank as in the West. When a couple gets engaged, they are usually invited to a marriage preparation seminar, which includes basic sexual information. The system differs from region to region. Sometimes this basic sex education is given only after the wedding, so for the teenage girl who gets pregnant from a casual encounter, this information comes too late.

Lesbian relationships

When I asked the college students in Tonghua and other young female Chinese friends if they had lesbian relationships, the girls were confused. They had never even heard of such a thing. Surely it is normal to kiss and stroke your best friend? Lin explained: 'Of course women touch each other a lot. It shows friendship. And also, we grow up with many people in a room, and we stay close together in terms of feelings as well as of space'.[24]

The situation seems to be similar to that in Victorian Britain, when homosexuality between men was unlawful, but homosexual relationships between women were not even considered a possibility.

In many ways, China is the ideal country for homosexual couples of either sex. They can caress each other in public without attracting attention, live together openly – something heterosexual couples usually can't without marriage – as long as they don't declare their homosexuality. One can only guess that what goes on in the dormitories, where up to twelve students share a room in strict segregation of the sexes, is not unlike the happenings at the average British boys' boarding school, possibly even more so because of the lack of knowledge.

Another outlet for sexual urges is masturbation, and here they are innocent too: I have repeatedly seen young men masturbating absent-mindedly beside a public footpath, neither embarrassed nor turned on by being seen.

Rape and violence

China has one of the lowest reported crime rates in the world – but the emphasis is on the word 'reported'. Violence against women is frequent, although it rarely gets reported. A woman who has been raped is likely to keep it secret because she fears for her reputation. Her main concern will be to terminate any resulting pregnancy which would ruin her life.

Society is more likely to stand up for women who have visual injuries to show for their ordeal. In 1994, during my stay in Tonghua (Jilin Province), a couple of rapists terrorized the town. Three girls were knifed and raped in two separate incidents on the campus of the Teachers' College, one of them in broad daylight on the sports ground. They were hospitalized and their condition was critical. It turned out that the same pair of men had attacked and raped over 20 women over a period of a few weeks. In this case the police were quite efficient: the rapists were arrested and convicted within a short time. But I heard about several other crimes which took place over a period of six months on the college campus alone: a corpse was found one early morning on a dormitory doorstep; a leg (minus a body) was discovered in the wood but not identified; a brick was thrown into a window which narrowly missed the victim's head.

One student told me:

> Women are particularly vulnerable, because they are small. There are more crimes against women than against men. Women who are tall are not as afraid as women who are short. There is the perceived idea that tall women are inevitably strong and can defend themselves. I am afraid because I am small. A rapist may think I'm the ideal victim. I don't think a rapist would attack Western women, not just because the punishment would be more severe, but because Western women are so much taller. There are many crimes happening all the time. But we are not told about them. The authorities like to keep them secret. It is only when many women have been attacked by the same criminal that we are informed. They now sell personal alarms at the Railway Department Store. These would be useful, but they are so expensive that only rich women can afford them. I wish I had enough money to buy one. I would feel safer.[25]

However, Chinese law is remarkably progressive in protecting women from marital violence. Chinese marriage law makes it a criminal offence for a husband to beat or torture his wife. Since the 1980s courts have convicted husbands for marital rape, something the courts in many Western countries are still hesitant or unwilling to consider.[26]

Prostitution and concubinage in modern guise

In 1949 a widespread campaign to eradicate prostitution and sexually transmitted diseases was launched. Women who had been sold into prostitution or forced by circumstances to sell sex were treated for VD and trained for other careers. If necessary, they were sent to re-education camps. Pimps were executed or imprisoned. A small minority of women who regarded sex work as their career fled communist China and continued their trade in Hong Kong.

The campaign was remarkably successful, particularly as the huge majority of sex workers were not prostitutes by choice and welcomed the chance for a new life. Dr Ma Haide led the campaign which eliminated prostitution even in places like Shanghai where one house out of twelve was reputed to be a brothel. Under his leadership, VD was virtually wiped out and for about 30 years, prostitution and VD were near to non-existent in China.

This has changed. Since the early 1980s, both have been increasing rapidly. Tourism and market economy have led to freelance prostitution. Even official sources and newspapers no longer deny that prostitution has made a comeback in cities like Shanghai, Beijing and Guangzhou. They blame Western tourists for this; however, no market can exist without suppliers – demand alone doesn't work.

The suppliers are mostly women in their twenties who chose this career with their eyes open. Their calculation is simple: in one night with a Western tourist, they can earn twice as much as in two months as a factory worker or a teacher. They want to get rich – quickly. Their ultimate goals are an easy, glamorous life now and enough savings to achieve financial security in old age.

Prostitutes can be seen parading up and down the streets in front of the big hotels where foreign tourists stay. They tend to wear miniskirts, high heels and make-up. In Shanghai and Guangzhou, there are also bars which provide services beyond drinks. Hotel rooms have warning notices pointing out that it is forbidden for foreign guests to take prostitutes into the room. Some hotels are so strict that staff will immediately alert state security; others may turn a blind eye.

The main risk for the freelance prostitute is VD. When Mao declared venereal diseases eradicated in China, VD departments in hospitals were closed, and medical students were no longer taught how to diagnose and treat sexually transmitted diseases.

Ironically, it was the late Dr Ma Haide who again took the initiative: he had to re-introduce treatment for VD.[27] However, the knowledge of sexually transmitted diseases is still limited among doctors as well as among the public. AIDS is known to exist, but most people assume it's something which afflicts only decadent Westerners and can't happen to the Chinese. Prostitutes are often unaware of the danger of VD and know little about prevention, diagnosis and treatment.

The prostitutes who ply their trade in the streets, the hotels and the bars are almost always self-employed; the coercion and slavery of pre-revolution days does not exist for them. The situation is different for women who, because of circumstances or naivete, enter a form of modern concubinage. Today's concubines are often 'secretaries' or 'domestic workers', forced to provide sex for their employer. The main customers here are almost always wealthy Chinese who abuse their power, and the suppliers are Chinese women who were betrayed by false promises and held by blackmail. Enforced concubinage seems to be on the increase, but it is difficult to estimate the number of cases, or indeed to act against it, as it is almost always disguised as an employer/employee relationship.

Modern courting and relationships

I am sure that forced marriages will become rarer, because women are becoming more educated in the countryside and consequently more aware of their legal rights. Weddings where bride and groom actively dislike each other will become the exception. However, marriages arranged by parents will still happen for a long time to come. Girls will continue to follow their parents' advice and society's pressure in the choice of their marriage partner, even if it means marrying someone they've met only once, as long as they have no strong objection to him as a person.

I believe that love and personal affection will play an increasingly important role in the choice of the spouse, although family ties and financial aspects will continue to be considered. Matchmakers will always play an important part in bringing people together, but in future it will be the young people rather than their parents who consult the matchmaker and make a choice. As the village crone disappears dating agencies will soar.

With the influence of the Western media, young urban Chinese will become less inhibited about premarital sex, but in rural communities the strict moral codes of many ethnic groups will remain in force for a long time.

5 Serving the mother-in-law: weddings, marriage and divorce

Wives' legal status

The family rule in pre-communist China was that the husband's word was the law. He was the boss in the family and the wife remained subservient, deprived of basic human rights, family property and inheritance. She did not even have the right to use her own family name. The law stipulated that the wife's property, name and residence were managed by her husband. The man was permitted to take concubines, but the wife had to remain a wife all her life.[1] Over 95 per cent of marriages were arbitrarily arranged.[2]

The communists raised the status of women radically. In 1950, the first year of its government, the communist regime passed a new Marriage Law that improved the status of wives significantly: it abolished marriages arranged against the bride's will as well as concubinage, gave women legal protection and wives rights equal to those of the husbands. It made it possible for men as well as for women to obtain a divorce, and gave unmarried, divorced and widowed women the right to hold land in their own names. Although the proclaimed equality was not always fully enforced, most women found that their position had improved to an extent they could not have dreamt about.

Couples encouraged to delay marriage

The second Marriage Law of the People's Republic of China, formulated in 1980, fixed the minimum age for marriage to 20 for women and 22 for men. During the Cultural Revolution, the minimum age had temporarily been even higher, for women 25 and for men 27.[3]

The government encourages couples to delay marriage until several years after the legal minimum and its campaigns seem to be successful. I talked to Chinese women and men of different age groups, educational levels, geographical and cultural background about what they thought was the best age for a woman and for a man to get married, and their answers were between 22 and 25 for women, and between 24 and 26 for men. Female college students usually suggested 25 as the ideal marriage age for a woman, whereas their parents' choice was 23 .

A woman's average age at her first marriage has increased from 18.46 in the 1940s to 22.67 in 1993,[4] despite a drop from being 22.80 in 1982 to 21.01 in 1987. Anna de Cleene, Beijing-based Far East Projects Manager of the University of Central Lancashire, points out that such fluctuations don't necessarily mean that women marry earlier or later. The statistics may simply reflect an improvement in statistic gathering techniques and accuracy, and greater accessibility to remoter regions and places.[5]

But the minimum age cannot always be enforced, especially in rural areas, where pressure from the family is stronger than the fear of the law. Two per cent of urban women and 5.5 per cent of rural women marry between the ages of 15 and 19.[6]

Wedding ceremonies: from spartan to lavish

Remembering her wedding, 68-year-old Guo Yun recalls:

> I was engaged at the age of seven and got married at 15, at the price of 200 silver dollars offered by my husband's family. On the wedding day I was helped into a sedan chair with my head covered with a scarf, and my husband rode a donkey to fetch me to his family. Just before entering his village, he asked me to ride the donkey and himself sat in the sedan chair so as to show his authority. I had no idea of what my husband looked like, even after the traditional wedding ceremony was over. A few days passed and I still couldn't tell my husband from his four brothers because they all spoke alike.[7]

Traditional wedding celebrations were lavish and costly, and the puritan communist regime banned them. Weddings became little more than an exchange of documents and signatures. Jung Chang describes her mother's wedding in *Wild Swans*: waiting for permission to get married, then taking her bedroll to her husband's accommodation. The mother of the bride was appalled that her daughter was not having a magnificent traditional wedding and felt that for a woman to walk to her bridegroom's house instead of being carried in a sedan chair meant she was worthless and that her husband did not really want her.[8]

Until the 1980s, the politically correct ideal remained to get married with just a set of new bedding, a thermos flask, and maybe a table and two chairs – and certainly without major celebrations and debts.

If both partners are marriageable according to the marriage law, all they need is their residence permits, identity cards and permission from their work units. The marriage registration centre, sub-district office or local town government makes out the marriage certificate and the couple are married. This sounds simple, although complications can arise for migrant workers who don't hold residence permits for the cities where they are working or if the work unit refuses permission.

Even if all the papers are in order, things are rarely so easy nowadays. Since the early 1980s, lavish nuptial feasts have made a comeback. More and more couples decide to splash out on their great day, mostly with the aim of impressing neighbours, and the main problem is how to finance a feast which may be beyond their means.

Teresa Poole, writing for the *Independent*, estimates that a wedding in Beijing costs '... about twice the average annual urban income, if you believe the official statistics.'[9]

Some brides wear the traditional *cheongsam*, a tight-fitting long dress. But 'Western-style' wedding gowns are more popular: frilly, sequinned dresses in glossy synthetic fabric. They may be white, but to many Chinese, white is not eye-catching enough. Women often prefer shocking-pink or scarlet-red (bright red being China's luckiest and most joyful colour), and the gowns may be rented. The groom usually wears a Western-style suit, often with a red flower.

As a compromise between the spartan communist style weddings and the lavish celebrations inspired by Western and by traditional weddings, many couples have a 'short' party. The aim is to display as much wealth within one hour as possible. After that, it is back to everyday life.

This hour may be spent at a scenic spot, a place on a hill which offers good views and is considered auspicious. The whole wedding party is carted there in hired cars, a few fireworks and crackers are lighted, and everyone departs again. Alternatively, the parents of the bride or groom book a lavish banquet in an expensive restaurant. Everyone eats as much as one can eat within an hour, gets drunk and goes home again.

A third possibility is to forego the banquet and enjoy a honeymoon trip instead. For many young Chinese, the honeymoon is their first holiday trip and they may not have the resources to have another one in the near future, so this is a special experience. In a survey among young couples in Beijing, half of them planned to have a honeymoon trip instead of a family banquet.[10]

In the cities, a whole industry of wedding organisation services have sprung up, similar to the ones in Western countries: photographers, shopping, dressmaking, banquet planning and so on.

The Purple House in Beijing, a popular wedding service company which opened in 1934 and closed 19 years later because lavish weddings were not considered appropriate in a socialist state, reopened in the early 1990s. Within four years of opening, 1,500 couples took their vows in this venue which also sells wedding outfits, rings, flowers, decorations and presents.[11]

In recent years, photo rooms have emerged in large and medium-sized cities. They provide styling, make-up and photography, guaranteed to make the clients look beautiful – at a price. Most patrons are newly-weds, some of whom say that they are willing to save up to preserve their youth, beauty and happiness at least on paper.[12]

In rural provinces, weddings are considered great, happy events, and they are almost always celebrated on a large scale, sometimes turning into a village festival.

Rural weddings among ethnic minorities can be more colourful. Their traditions were hardly interrupted or changed by the communist regime. In some areas, men marry into the women's families, in others, women into the men's. Among the Yi, the groom must pretend to kidnap his bride, to prove that she is wanted by both her old and her new family. Among the Hani, people hold up olive branches to offer their best wishes and to welcome the bride. Mongolian brides perform traditional dances after their wedding ceremony: a chopstick dance, a belt dance and a bowl dance. Among the Tibetan and Tajik people, everyone sings and dances all night long. A De'ang bride helps the groom put on a new turban which symbolizes white hair and therefore lifelong devotion. Tuja wedding etiquette demands a lot of crying: the bride, her mother, her sisters, her friends and her brothers' wives start a few days before the wedding with crying and sad songs to demonstrate how much they love each other and will miss each other's company. One particular part of the 'crying etiquette' which rarely happens today is the 'cursing of the matchmaker'. The bride used to mock and scold the matchmaker blaming her for the marriage in a song which was eagerly awaited by the audience.[13]

Gina Corrigan describes the typical Miao ceremony:

> It is common for the bride to be collected by unmarried male friends of the groom. She is dressed in a beautiful embroidered costume with all the silver she possesses, and is taken to the groom's house. Her silver represents her wealth and remains with her all her life. Her family will also give her a small present, such as chickens, so she retains some independence and is able to buy items like embroidery silks for herself from selling chicks or eggs. The wedding will be accompanied by much feasting and drinking and in some areas a bamboo cane is broken to symbolize the union. The girl remains with her new husband for several nights, but in some regions will return to her family on the day of the wedding. She will spend time with her husband during festival occasions and traditionally does not return to his house until becoming pregnant. As there is considerable sexual freedom in Miao society, she may have had sex with another man in the meantime, which is why in some cases the first child does not inherit the family land. Today, the bride usually returns to her husband's house after two weeks, bearing more gifts and again dressed in her finest clothes.[14]

Among the Dai in the Yunnan Province, the groom must knock on the bride's family's house, where the women guard the entrance. He will be cross-questioned and must promise to work hard to increase his bride's family's wealth, and to respect, and care for, his parents-in-law. Only then will the women reveal that the girl is not at home: she is hiding at the home of a girlfriend. Only when the bridegroom has promised to take care of her and her family and offered 'bribes' to people help him find his bride, everyone will skip down the path to fetch the bride.[15]

Bride prices emerge again

Traditionally, men (or their families) bought the bride from her parents in order to compensate for the loss of the girls' labour, or to pay for the girl's upbringing and education. The communists abolished bride prices, but the custom continues among ethnic minorities in some rural areas.

Among the Miao in south China (Guizhou Province), arranged marriages and bride prices are on the increase. As the market economy becomes freer, wealth becomes more significant. The only difference is that the man's family no longer pays the bride price in silver: bicycles, television sets and cash are more useful. If the man cannot afford the price, he can choose to 'earn' his bride by working for her family. The bride's family will give her bedding, furniture, chickens and silver jewellery for her dowry.[16]

In urban areas, dowries are playing an increasing role again. Household goods manufacturers target brides' and parents' pride to motivate them to buy expensive items. It is no longer the parents who try to extract as much value from each other in buying and selling a woman. Today, it is the girls who make the demands – and it is the bride's (not the groom's) parents who have to pay the price.

Chang Keting (pseudonym), a 24-year-old factory worker from the Liaoning Province, admits frankly to blackmailing her parents – both factory workers.

> I told my parents that I want a washing machine, a television and a refrigerator. I told them that I will lose face if I don't have them. My parents don't have these things themselves. They cannot afford them. But they must give them to me. Otherwise they lose face, too. I have two sisters. They will also get married next year. They will ask for a fridge, TV and washing machine as well. I know that my parents do not have the money. They will have to take a loan. They will have to pay back instalments until they die. They will still have enough money to eat food every day. But I want to have a better life. Getting married is the one opportunity in a girl's life when she can better her status and acquire some wealth. I am not going to miss this opportunity. Perhaps I am sorry that my parents cannot afford a television for themselves as well as giving one to each of their

daughters. But it is their own fault. They should have had only one child, then they would not have this problem.[17]

It is possible that the attitude of girls like Chang – who is by no means a rare exception – will add to the unwillingness of parents to have girl children.

According to the young women I interviewed in northeastern urban areas, washing machines, refrigerators, jewellery, and television sets are the most popular dowry items. Size is important when it comes to that prestigious television set, according to *China Daily*. In an article in March 1996, the newspaper reported that the sale of TVs has increased sharply and the best sellers were the ones with 54 cm screens. The major target consumers for these are apparently the 8 million couples marrying in China each year.[18]

Wedding guests usually present the bride with money or gifts. The desire to demonstrate one's wealth by giving valuable presents to the bridal couple has led to some excess in Shanghai, Beijing, Nanjing and Guangzhou, where gift recovery stores form a new type of business. In these shops, the recipients of gifts can put unwanted items up for sale. The main suppliers are newly-weds, and the gifts range from 5-*yuan* key rings to stereo systems and air-conditioners worth thousands of *yuan*. Yang Lin, visitor at the Xin Ya Gift Recovery Store in Beijing, is typical: 'When I got married several months ago, I received four tea sets, three coffee sets and all kinds of other gifts. I considered sending them to other friends, but selling them is, of course, a better way.'[19]

Bring a little brother

A typical Chinese name consists of two or three words. The first is the family name – the equivalent of a surname in the English language. The five most common surnames are Chang (or Chan in Cantonese), Wang, Li, Chao and Liu. It is estimated that one in twelve Chinese people has the name Chang or Chan, which means 'Archer'.[20] Other common surnames include Liang, Wong, Lin, Ding, Deng, Hao, Guo and Shu.

The second and often a third syllable form the individual name. For children, a double syllable is often used as a term of endearment, for example, Ying-Ying.

The individual names are usually recognizable as typically 'male' or 'female'. For example, *ting* (graceful) would be found only in a female name. People rarely call one another by their individual names, except within the family.

Until the turn of the century, women were often given no individual name at all. They were just called Eldest Daughter, Second Daughter and so on. After their marriage, they put their husband's name in front of their father's name. They could not have their own name even when their children were born.[21]

Deng Xiaoping's mother had no given name.

Sheryl WuDunn reports a conversation with a friend: 'We asked what his father had called her (his mother), and he thought for a long moment. Then his face lit up with the memory. "Eh!" he beamed. "He would just call out "Eh!".'[22]

Today, it would be unthinkable for a girl or woman not to have her own name. But in rural areas, the name chosen for a girl can still damage her self-esteem. Many first-born daughters are called Alidi, Zhaodi or Yindi – all of which mean 'Bring a Little Brother'.[23]

Women retain their own family name after marriage, they don't take their husband's name. I've also noticed that most Chinese women object to the title Mrs. If they are addressed in English, they prefer being called Miss, irrespective of their marital status, although recently the title Ms has become popular. So if Chang Keting marries Liang Xinya, she remains Chang Keting. She'll be addressed by her colleagues as Chang and would expect foreigners to call her Miss Chang.

Their daughter Liyunn will normally carry her father's name. She will be Liang Liyunn, or Miss Liang.

However, there are exceptions. Parents can decide for the child to carry the mother's name. This is usually done if the father has brothers but the mother is an only child. In cities, some feminist girls choose to take their mother's names.[24]

Husbands and fathers

In a family survey in 1991 one third of all couples described their relationship as 'very harmonious', and 50.3 per cent as 'harmonious'. Nearly half the respondents in a 1994 survey of the Beijing Marriage and Family Studies Centre said they and their spouse were deeply in love.[25]

Most Chinese men are proud to be good husbands. During 1990–92, the national government initiated 'Modern Good Husbands' public campaigns, to be carried out by local governments. These encouraged men to support their wives's careers, to prepare meals and to share responsibility for the family's finances with their wives. This initiative was met with the greatest enthusiasm in the three biggest cities: Beijing, Shanghai and Guangzhou, but rural areas showed less interest.[26]

In Beijing, when couples argue, it seems to be usually about their children's problems and rarely about emotional problems connected with their relationship. The most popular way of expressing discontent is not to talk to the spouse for several days. The husband is said to be four times as likely as the wife to give in and speak the first word of reconciliation.[27]

The one-child policy has made children a precious possession and childcare a prestigious duty. Men are proud to wash, dress, feed and play with their child. They are also eager to demonstrate that they care for their wife, and the ultimate status symbol is – as in Victorian England – the ability to support and pamper an idle wife.

Bao Tianren, a 44-year-old publisher in the Jilin Province, is typical. He came from a poor peasant family with eight children, acquired some education and worked his way up as an English teacher before starting his own business. By local standards, he is an incredibly rich man. He has all the status symbols the people in his area dream of. His most prized possession is a foreign car with white lace curtains, gold-coloured velvet upholstery and pink satin cushions. He is also proud of a large-screen television and a mobile phone. Recently he has added to this by making his wife a homemaker. He told me:

> My wife, Liu Yünxiang, was a printing factory worker. She was the one who knew all about the business I was going to start. She gave me all the knowledge of printing affairs; I knew nothing. Now that I'm successful I don't want her to work in my company any more. I want her to stay at home. My wife's duty is to look after our twelve-year-old daughter, Bao Yü. More importantly, it is her duty to look after me and to wait at home for me until I come home in the evening, or after a few days on a business trip. Whenever I go on a business trip I buy her clothes. She has many clothes now, more than any other woman in the neighbourhood.

Recently she told me that she does not want yet another skirt, so I'll buy her a sweater instead. Of course she is happy. She does what I think is right for her. She believes in me unconditionally.'[28]

I had no opportunity to talk to Liu without her husband present, so I was not able to hear her own point of view. However, she appeared content and always greeted her husband affectionately.

Younger women take more decisions

The man is still the main decision-maker in the typical Chinese family, but more and more wives participate in the decision-making. The higher the wife's income and education, the more she has to say. In towns and cities, decisions are mostly made jointly between both partners, but in the countryside, the man usually has the final word although the woman contributes to the decision-making process.

A feature in the magazine *Women of China* looks at the decision-making in rural households, which I will try and summarize.

The traditional situation, in which the husband made all decisions without consulting his wife, has gradually declined to a state in which both partners participate in the decision-making. The key decision areas in rural Chinese households include type of production, building accommodation, the purchase of farming equipment, how to allocate money, and who does which and how much work. In 46.88 per cent of rural families, wife and husband make joint decisions in those matters (which does not mean that their opinions carry equal weight!), in 27.95 per cent the husband has exclusive control, and in only 8.68 per cent it is the wife who is in control of all decisions.

Younger wives play a more important role in decision-making than older wives. This is a reversal of the traditional set-up, when old women had little, and young women, no influence at all. It seems that women aged 30–39 have the greatest power. This may be due to education, skills training, capability, self-worth and sense of equality. In families with illiterate women, only 41.6 per cent of wives are involved in the decision-making, but nearly 70 per cent of college educated wives are.

The wife's income is significant. The more she earns, the more her husband respects her opinion and trusts her judgement in household matters.

Xu Shan and her husband live in a fruit-growing village in the Hebei Province. She earns around 4,500 *yuan* per year, and her husband twice as much. They discuss all important matters, but if their opinions differ, her husband has the final word.

Wang Yongmei, who lives in a town in the Hebei Province and is involved in greenhouse vegetable production, earns about 6,500 *yuan* a year, while her husband, a labourer who works building railways, earns about 2,500; Wang has more decision-making power than her husband.

Shi Xiuzhi is a a family planning worker in a village in the Hebei Province, earning about 2,000 *yuan* a year, and her husband, a carpenter, who is away from home most of the time, earns 5,000 *yuan* a year. Shi takes all the everyday decisions in her husband's absence, but leaves important, non-urgent matters for him to decide.[29]

The amounts mentioned in these examples refer to 1995/1996 incomes in the Hebei Province and should not be compared directly with salaries in other provinces or other years.

Matriarchal societies

Before the Liberation, most ethnic groups had strict patriarchal societies, but some had a matriarchal structure. The communist system of equality almost destroyed both systems, but in some places matriarchies have survived.

For example, the Jinuo people had a communal society with farming communes and a traditional matriarchal system, but by the 1940s the influence from the more modern Han people had already introduced patriarchal ideas.[30]

The Naxi and the Pumi (also in the Yunnan Province) still have large families centred around an older woman who is the family head. The most honoured place is by the right side of the fireplace and is occupied by the eldest female of the family. Her sisters, nieces and other women sit beside her in order of seniority. Men sit on the left, also in order of seniority. The head of the family decides how the money gets spent, who should have a new skirt and so on. If she feels too old to fulfil the role, she passes the responsibility on to her daughter.

Many women of the Naxi and Pumi groups still practise their traditional *Azhu* system of marriage, where woman and man regard each other as equal partners for as long as they choose to continue their relationship. Both live with their own families. The husband lives and works with his mother's family, but spends the night at his wife's house. The children belong to their mother. The husband provides economic support while the relationship lasts. The partners do not share long-term commitments or economic responsibilities. Children might never know their father, but there was no such thing as 'illegitimate children' before the communists introduced the term.

Zhong Xiu tells of a woman who had a 'modern' marriage and moved into her husband's home, but left her three sons behind with her mother because her mother and sisters were missing her so much.

The Naxi and Pumi system of matriarchy and *Azhu* appears to have provided a well-ordered, well-functioning society. But the Chinese regard it as old-fashioned, outdated, and even more backward than patriarchy. To them the natural way for a society to become modern is to shed matriarchy in favour of patriarchy, and finally patriarchy for communism. Zhong Xiu in *Yunnan Travelogue* concludes her observations of the still existing matriarchal family system with the promise that 'there will be an evolution into a higher stage of social development'.[31]

Division of household chores

Fifty years ago, it would not even have occurred to most men to get involved in household chores. Today, most husbands are willing to support their wives' jobs and share the housework, although the workload is rarely divided equally.

The Sociology Institute of the Chinese Academy of Social Sciences researched 420 households in 1980. Their results showed that one quarter of husbands made the breakfast, over one quarter made supper and more than one quarter emptied the rubbish bin. These results were greeted as a 'warm picture of home life',[32] but this still leaves about three-quarters of breakfasts and suppers prepared and rubbish bins emptied by women. With other chores, the picture looks even bleaker: only 5.9 per cent of all husbands regarded cleaning floors and making beds their duty.[33]

Nevertheless, the progress is remarkable when you compare the situation with pre-communist China and it is likely that the situation has improved since the survey was made.

I visited many families in northeast China, and in all of them, except one, the husbands naturally took on between a quarter and half of the housework. I noticed that the men's household duties were always the more pleasant or prestigious ones. Men did the cooking and took responsibility for looking after the child. Women were left with the washing and cleaning jobs.

Liu Funü is a department store manager, her husband Zhin Zhangxiu a graduate engineer. They have two children: a daughter who studies at college, and a son who is a soldier.

> My husband does a lot of housework. Perhaps I do a little more, but I'm in charge. I manage the household, he follows my instructions. He does a lot of cooking, because he's good at it.

China's career women are still expected to carry the burden. Xu Xuehua, the youngest deputy director of the Economic and Trade Department of the Hebei Provincial Government is in charge of the province's import and export. In the book *Mother Wife Daughter* she is praised as a perfect example of a dutiful worker, wife and mother.

> My husband is also in the foreign trade business. We share a common sense of responsibility and dedication. But at home we differ greatly in the sense of one's responsibilities. I have to manage all the household affairs. Sometimes my husband would help in some simple housework, but I never ask more of him because I'm the woman of the house. I think this way and so does my husband.

The director and the other deputies of Xu's department are men, all looked after and pampered by their wives. None of them are required to do housework.

> Each time they travel, their wife will do the packing, and when they get back home, the bath water is run for them and a square meal ready. I, too, have to travel. But each time before I leave, I tidy up the rooms, go shopping and cram the fridge with food. When I come back, the house is just like it has been being broken into. I have to clean it up immediately and then cook a good meal for the whole

Grandmother in a village in the Jilin province. She looks after her only grandchild while the rest of the family are out at work.
Photo: Christine Hall

In the richer provinces, almost every village has a small clinic, although medical standards can be low.
Photo: Christine Hall

Many people still live in squalor. Huts like this, built from rubbish and leftover material from modern building sites, still house three generations in a single room, without water, electricity, or sanitation.
Photo: Christine Hall

Middle Class urban accommodation: a family has a one- or two-roomed flat.
Photo: Christine Hall

Urban housing for the new rich.
Photo: Christine Hall

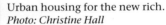

The Petroleum Primary School in the Jilin Province. Girls and boys are taught together, and discipline in the classroom is strict. Parents like to dress their children in 'western' clothes, although some schools have school uniforms. These children wear the red scarf which shows they are 'young pioneers', which is the approximate equivalent of being a cub, guide or scout. *Photo: Christine Hall*

A girls' dormitory room at Tonghua Teachers' College. Six to twelve students share a room. They create privacy and individual atmosphere by putting curtains in front of their beds and putting up posters and paintings on the wall. *Photo: Sarah Lowis*

Early morning exercises are
compulsory at most colleges and
universities.
Photo: Christine Hall

Students at Tonghua Teachers'
College. Very few of them have
any vocation to become teachers.
Photo: Christine Hall

Students of the politics department of Tonghua Teachers' College perform the traditional Manchurian dance with two large silk fans. Folk dances are part of the curriculum of most schools, but the young people prefer 'modern' dances such as the tango and foxtrot.
Photo: Christine Hall

Students' leisure time is controlled. They are supposed to study all the time. Just lazing in the early summer sun would not be acceptable, but sitting in the sun with a textbook is. Chinese women like to cuddle up to women friends. Physical contact between members of the same sex is the norm.
Photo: Christine Hall

Construction worker in Tonghua, Jilin Province,
working alongside men in demolishing old
buildings. They wear no protective helmet or boots.
Photo: Christine Hall

A typical enterprising woman in Tonghua, Jilin
Province. Like many new self-employed women,
she sees her chance in providing services for which
she does not need much equipment. She offers
bicycle and shoe repairs.
Photo: Christine Hall

More and more women dress in sequinned gowns, even for everyday errands to the street market.
Photo: Christine Hall

Chinese girls admiring western fashion in the department store.
Photo: Christine Hall

The wedding is – apart from the birth of a child – the most important event in a woman's life. Wedding dresses are costly creations, usually modelled on western fashion, but often in pink or red rather than white.
Photo: Sarah Lowis

At the Taoist White Cloud temple in Beijing. Most of those eagerly touching the animal horoscope images declare that they are atheists and free of superstitions.
Photo: Christine Hall

Graves in the haunted hills of Tonghua. People still prefer burials to cremations, although grave sites use up valuable agricultural land. Most graves are marked by mounds of earth or by gravestones, but here is a rare – and courageous – grave with a Christian cross.
Photo: Christine Hall

family, feeling a bit guilty to have left the rest of the family to look after themselves. So this is the difference between me and my male colleagues.[34]

Inheritance and property rights

In the pre-communist society, all property was owned and inherited exclusively by men. Widows who remarried were not allowed to take any family property with them. Daughters could not inherit their parents' property unless they remained unmarried until their parents' death.

Today in the average family, husband and wife own family property jointly and enjoy equal rights of control and use of their possessions. The law guarantees equal rights of inheritance among children, whatever their gender.

Serving the mother-in-law

In the traditional family hierarchy, a young woman reported directly to her mother-in-law. She was as much her mother-in-law's servant as her husband's chattel. She could only look forward to the day when she had a grown-up son who would marry and provide her with a servant daughter-in-law. Strangely, while the inequality between husband and wife has been nearly abolished, the mother-in-law/daughter-in-law relationship has changed little.

Few urban young women today would obey their husband in every matter – but they follow their mother-in-law's command. The problem can seldom be avoided because most young couples live with the man's family during the first years of their marriage.

Today, serving a mother-in-law may require that a woman has to spend all her spare time nursing her elderly parents-in-law, and if necessary has to give up her career to look after them permanently. Looking after and nursing the mother-in-law is a duty which has priority over caring for one's own parents.

Many of the college students I met in China said as a matter of course they would not marry a man who demanded that they give up their career to serve his interests. But they accepted that their mother-in-law had the power to demand such a sacrifice. It did not occur to them that they could resist. Their thoughts about how to prevent the situation were evasive, and their attitudes seemed little different from nineteenth century ideals:

> I'll try to marry a man who has several brothers, so that the duties can be shared among several sisters-in-law.

> Before you agree to marry a man, you must find out about the character of his mother, and also about her health. It is wise to choose a man with a gentle, young and healthy mother, then maybe you will never have to nurse her.

> You must be nice to your mother-in-law and do everything to make her like you, then she will be kind to you.[35]

Mrs Zhang, a worker, was in this situation: her husband is a research scientist and his parents objected to the marriage on the grounds that her educational level and social status was far below his. Instead of setting up her own household with her husband, she decided to move in with the in-laws and serve them until they approved of her.

> As soon as I came back from work, I would attend to the housework, cooking according to the taste of my parents-in-law and taking good care of every aspect of their life. My mother-in-law said nothing but her attitude to me was getting better and better. Before long I became real close to my husband's family ... I am simply fulfilling the duty and obligation of a woman ...[36]

There are possibly more wedding rituals referring to the bride/mother-in-law relationship than to the bride/groom relationship. These vary between ethnic groups: a widespread custom is for the bride to kowtow (kneel and prostate herself) in front of her in-laws. This custom was common all over China, and although it has nearly disappeared in urban areas, it is still carried out among some ethnic groups.

One exception is the She ethnic group in the Fujian, Zhejiang, Guangdong, Jiangxi and Anhui Provinces. She women don't worship their parents-in-law on their knees at their wedding ceremony. The bride greets her in-laws standing; it is the groom who has to kneel for his in-laws. This custom is explained by the wedding ceremony of a legendary princess on which today's wedding rituals are modelled. The princess married a commoner – unthinkable that she would kneel in front of common people.[37] Instead, the She bride lifts her veil to her mother-in-law (not to her groom) when greeting her for the first time. This bridal veil is not made from fabric, but from strings of silver beads and silver ornaments. The strings reach from the bride's forehead to her shoulder or chest level.

Divorces end loveless marriages

Historically, only the man could divorce his spouse, and he could do so for almost any reason. Local and national laws promoted the following acceptable reasons for divorce: inability to bear a male child, wanton conduct, being disrespectful to parents-in-law, being talkative, theft, jealousy, incurable illness. The wife had no opportunity to escape an unhappy marriage.

The first Marriage Law of 1950 stated that a divorce should be granted if both partners wished it. Between 1950 and 1953, 1.2 million couples took advantage of this law. They were mostly people trapped in unhappy marriages arranged by their families. These divorces were on the whole amicable.

From 1958 onwards, the courts became cautious about granting divorces. Couples had to prove that they had a justifiable reason for divorce, such as serious confrontations between husband and wife. This was the end of the amicable divorce for a long period: in an endeavour to preserve marriage, many appeals were rejected because of 'inadequate reasons'. The cases could drag on for a long time – sometimes as long as 20 years.

In the 1980s, people placed more value on harmonious family life and mutual affection between husband and wife. The revised Marriage Law of 1980 stipulated that a divorce could be granted even if only one spouse wished it 'in cases of complete alienation of mutual affection, and when mediation has failed'. Divorce by mutual agreement is made easy. If both want the divorce and if there is no dispute over children or property, the couple can get divorced easily at the marriage registration office of the local government. Either partner can initiate a divorce. The family property is divided equally between both partners and they can agree on the division by mutual consent. Failing this, the courts will allocate possessions on the principle of equality.

Nevertheless, preserving a marriage is still the ideal. The divorce departments of marriage registration offices display warning posters. The marriage registration office of Beijing's Xicheng District which handles divorces by agreement, for example, greets prospective divorcees with a sign 'Think carefully' over the doorstep. On the walls inside are slogans such as 'Take marriage seriously' and 'Faithfully abide by agreement of guardianship of children. Bringing happiness to your children is your obligation'.[38]

Since 1950, most complainants in divorce cases have been women. Today, about 70 per cent of all divorce cases are instigated by women. The reasons have changed: in the 1950s and 1960s, the main reasons were undesired arranged marriages and maltreatment from husband or in-laws. A random survey in 1984 picked 100 out of 589 divorce cases handled by the People's Court of the Hexi District in Tianjin. Forty-one out of the 100 were due to the husbands beating their wives violently, regarding this as their right. The main triggers for such violence were the wife being unable to produce a male baby, the husband suspecting her of having an affair, the wife being unable to get on with her parents-in-law or refusing to be absolutely obedient.[39]

To view this survey in the right perspective, four factors must be taken into account.

1. The survey was conducted more than ten years ago.
2. It covers only divorced marriages.
3. The random examples were taken only from court divorces, and did not include amicable divorces by agreement which, in the mentioned district, account for about 95 per cent of the whole divorce figure.
4. Tianjin is one of China's wealthiest and most modern areas, a metropolis with a highly developed economy and culture, and a population which includes different social groups including workers, cadres and intellectuals.

Even allowing for the fact that this small survey cannot be representative of the whole of China, it throws a frightening light on the still prevalent mentality of the husband's (and in-laws') authority in urban areas.

Another survey, carried out by the Xi'an Municipal Women's Federation, reported that a people's court located in a poor and remote mountainous area had handled 13 divorce cases in 1986. In all of these, the engagements had been arranged by the parents when the couple were still children.[40]

The divorce rate is rising every year in China, but it remains relatively low. There were 9.247 million marriages and 0.581 million divorces in 1987. The divorce rate in the early 1990s is estimated at 0.154 per cent.[41]

China Daily reports that in 1995, 1,055,000 couples divorced, 74,000 more than in 1994. Divorced people in 1995 accounted for 0.175 per cent of the nation's population.[42]

Today, lack of affection and love has become an important reason. Li, a 36-year-old manual worker, left her engineer husband and a family which seemed ideal but lacked love. She could no longer stand such a make-do type of loveless life. With all her courage, she requested a divorce. She recalled: 'When I went to the court, I was prepared to die should the divorce be refused.'[43]

Zhang, a registrar, lists six features as a current pattern of divorces.

1. The view on divorce has changed. In the early 1980s, a lot of people still regarded divorce as an ignominious act. Now ... they simply apply for divorce when there is no longer mutual affection.
2. Divorces include people of all age groups, mostly in the 30–40 age group. There are also some in the 60–70 age group.
3. The reasons for divorce are more complex. In the past, quarrels between husband and wife over housework, or because of difficult relations between wife and mother-in-law were often the causes of divorce. Today, many divorces are due to conflicting convictions or ambitions.
4. In the past, children were placed more often than not under the guardianship of the mother at the time of divorce. Now the picture is half and half.
5. In the past, the two parties at divorce were often engaged in endless quarrelling over division of family property. In recent years, with improved living standards, people are less concerned with it. Family property is often shared between the two parties, and in some cases offered entirely to the other party. Disputes and fights are rare.
6. There are more divorces by mutual agreement than by court ruling ...[44]

Remarriage: sunset love

Widows and divorced women have the right to remarry. This has not always been the case. In the feudal system of marriage, divorcees were often social outcasts who could not find a new partner and widows were prevented from remarriage.

The 1950s Marriage Law helped these women by stating: 'Interference in widows' freedom to remarry is prohibited.' But public opinion changed slowly, especially among ethnic minorities. Traditionally, women of the Hui and Yi could only get remarried to brothers of her husband; if their husband had no brothers, they had to remain widows for the rest of their life.[45]

Gradually, the remarriage of young widows was viewed as reasonable, and from the 1980s it was accepted that older widows could have another marriage. Second marriages among older people are often referred to as 'sunset love'. But in rural areas, remarriages among older people are still an exception, and even in cities they are met with scepticism.

Jiang, who lived in a town, had been a widow for 20 years. She braved all hardships and brought up eight children. By the time she was 64, her children had all found jobs and were married, and she began to think about remarriage. She had the support of her friends and she found a man she really loved. Her wedding ceremony was held in a bridal chamber decorated by all her children. In recalling her experience, she said:

> Remarriage is sometimes regarded as a difficult test for old people. But in my view the real test is whether the old people can emancipate their own mind which can be a true prison. If progress is to be made, one must break the self-imprisonment of the mind.[46]

According to a 1990 survey of 841 divorcees in Guangzhou, more than three-fifths had remarried within three years. The survey also showed that most remarried people were satisfied. However, Guangzhou is one of China's wealthiest and most progressive areas, and the situation will be different elsewhere.

In some areas, widows, particularly the elderly, will meet greater obstacles. Children may protest, thinking it a disgrace for their mother to remarry. Some women regard remarriage as an invitation to sneers. Few widows remarry in the countryside, particularly if they are past childbearing age.

Wang Jianning, a marriage registrar, says:

> There used to be a well-established view in China that for a man in his first marriage his wife must be a virgin, which means that divorcees or widows are no good. The issue at the core was chastity and such women were left at the mercy of men. In those days it would make headline news if a

divorcee or widow was married to a man in his first marriage. Now things are different. Quite a few such couples registered at my office ... I learned from them that in most cases it was those once married women who took the initiative in courting.[47]

About 830,000 divorced people got married in 1995, a rise of 40,000 over the previous year. But the remarriage rate is low when compared with the increasing number of divorced people: it seems that less than two-fifths of divorced people remarry.[48]

An article in the magazine *Women of China* mentions the case of Gong, a widow who married a widowed military service man. The husband's grown-up son treated her with respect, but her own daughter was opposed to the marriage and treated her stepfather with sarcasm. Xiao Yuan, the writer of the article, believes that some young people are more restricted by feudal ideology than their parents.

She also tells the story of Chen, a make-up artist whose husband divorced her because he found her dull, boring and predictable. Even when she discovered that he had had an affair, she just warned him gently and forgave him, the typical behaviour of a traditional, 'virtuous' woman. When they divorced, all she asked for was the guardianship of their daughter. Chen dated and later married a divorced bank clerk whose ex-wife had been too vain and pleasure-loving for his taste. Apparently the marriage between the make-up artist and the bank clerk was a happy one. When she was asked to set up a beauty salon in her spare time, she asked her husband's permission: he supported her plans. The grateful Chen reciprocated by going home to cook him a full dinner after a full day's work before going off to her second shop as salon manager. Apparently this virtuous behaviour combined with her success made her attractive again to her ex-husband, who repeatedly proposed that she should divorce her current husband and remarry him, which she refused.[49]

Women who choose to remain single

China had 7.86 million single people between the ages of 30 and 40 in 1990. More than 90 per cent of them were men, and bachelors made up 6.1 per cent of all men in that age group. Most of the single men live in rural areas and have little or no education.

In contrast, the single women are on average well educated and live in urban areas. They accounted for nearly 0.4 per cent of this age group. Experts say that some single people choose not to marry, but most are unmarried due to economic, social and cultural problems.[50]

Single women seem to be far happier with their lot than men. I met several single women in Beijing, Harbin Tonghua and Changchun (cities in the northeast), who stated categorically that they did not wish to get married. One of them was an ambitious college student who feared that a husband would restrict her in her career; the others were career women who had skilled work and clerical jobs. They did not wish to share their lives with a man, they said, and because of their jobs they did not need one. They liked their independence. Two said they had come to live in the cities away from their families, who constantly urged them to get married. A 30-year-old divorcee told me that her colleagues were worse than her family, constantly trying to match her with customers, business contacts, friends and relatives, and asking her daily if she hadn't found a boyfriend yet.

Pressure from families is probably the reason why no women aged 35 and over appear in the 'never married' columns of the 1990 Population Census which gives the percentage of population above age 15 by marital status. Unmarried women only account for 0.3 per cent of the female population aged 30 and above, compared with 5 per cent for men of the same age range.[51] The only two single men above the age of 30 I met were both desperate to get married. Both were skilled workers and were so keen to get married that they seemed to propose to every single woman who was friendly to them. One of them used to hang around the local colleges, trying to chat up female students, but the girls knew about him and avoided him.

Lingering stigma

There is strong pressure on a woman from society, family and especially in-laws, to put her husband's, children's and in-laws' interests before her own, and I believe that this pressure will often increase rather than decrease in the future, because so many Chinese are reverting to traditional attitudes.

Despite government efforts to change attitudes, it is still a stigma for a woman to be unmarried in her late twenties (which often leads to loveless arranged marriages), or for an older divorcee or widow to remarry (which often results in older, uneducated and untrained women living in poverty).

These attitudes are ancient and deep-rooted. The communists have not been able to eradicate them, but better education and job prospects for women, and consequently greater economic independence for them, as well as influences from the West will contribute to a gradual change of attitudes in the cities. However, these changes are unlikely to affect the countryside to a large extent.

6 Family planning and motherhood

Population control

The Chinese population has grown from 542 million in 1949 to 1.185 billion in 1993. By the year 2000, the State Statistical Bureau reckons there will be 1.272 billion Chinese people, despite a strict birth control policy.

The country simply cannot feed this increasing population, and if the Chinese continued to have as many children as they used to, this would soon mean mass starvation. Every square foot of arable land, even along road verges and between grave mounds, is already being cultivated. As the food production cannot be increased, the number of people must be kept low.

Since the 1960s and 1970s, the Chinese authorities have been worried about the population growth. In the 1970s, a campaign was launched urging couples to have 'late, spaced and few' children. Limit yourself to two children, have your first one as late as possible, and leave at least a four-year gap between the first and the second, was the message. Couples accepting this recommendation were rewarded in various ways: job promotion, better housing, financial incentives.

The decade saw impressive drops in birth rates but it was not enough. The government-encouraged baby booms in previous years had already set the powerful population growth in motion and it was impossible to stop it. It was calculated that about 20 million young Chinese would enter the childbearing age every year between the 1980s and 1990s. If each couple had, on average, three children, the population would double again in less than 50 years.[1]

The one-child policy

In the late 1970s, the one-child campaign was introduced: couples were asked by government to have only one child. Since then, the one-child policy has been adjusted and changed several times and the details differ from region to region. The policy is not based on national legislation but on city and province regulations, and regional authorities have some flexibility in adapting it to local conditions. On average, the regulations stipulate the following (but bear in mind regional variations):

- Every couple is entitled to have one child.
- After the first child, the woman has an IUD fitted (although there may be a choice of contraceptives).
- If their first child is disabled, they may apply for permission to have another child.
- If they live in the countryside but do not belong to an ethnic minority, and if their first child is a girl, they may apply for permission to have a second child seven years after the birth of the first one.
- If husband and wife are both single children, they may apply for permission to have a second child.
- To have the right to apply for a second child does not mean the right to have a second child. The authorities have the right to grant or reject second-child applications.
- Couples who have more than the permitted number of children can be penalized, for example they may be refused promotion in their jobs or have to pay higher school fees.
- Couples who belong to ethnic minorities, live in the countryside and need children to work in the fields can have several children, but are encouraged to restrict their number.

Western criticism is based on the individual's viewpoint: the woman's right to bear children should transcend the needs of society. The Chinese have always regarded the rights of society as a whole as more important than those of the individual. The individual must make sacrifices for the good of the community, and it isn't as if the state is taking away a woman's control of her own fertility: the Chinese woman has never had full control of her own fertility. In the past, the husband and the parents-in-law had more say in childbearing decisions than the woman; today, the woman can decide whether she wants a child or not. The state provides her with information and contraception to help her make her decision, and protects her from unwanted pregnancy, which is a great advantage over the previous situation where women had to bear children all the time, whether they wanted to or not.

There have been cases where women were forced to have an abortion even at a late stage of pregnancy. This is as shocking to the families as it is to a Western observer. However, these forced abortions are not the norm: the government is extremely strict as far as contraception is concerned, but it is *not* government policy to force abortions as a means of family planning. Enforced abortions do occur if officials in a particular area are over-zealous.

A likely scenario is that the officials in a particular region are negligent or incompetent in their handling of family planning matters and their region shows many unauthorized births in one year. They get severely reprimanded for this, lose their bonuses and are warned that if it happens again, they will lose their promotion prospects. This warning comes several months into the following year. By now, many women have heard that officials are indifferent to unlicensed pregnancies and have decided to have a second or third child. The officials realize that they are about to exceed their birth quota again and that their bonuses and promotions are in danger unless they do something drastic. With a typical Chinese disregard for the worth of unborn life they force women to terminate all unlicensed pregnancies.

A Chinese friend described a scenario along those lines. Apparently her relatives in another province were involved in what became a family tragedy. One woman in the family was pregnant without licence, the other worked for the authorities and had to ensure the quotas. My friend was evasive when I asked for details and refused firmly to even mention the province where this had allegedly occurred. All I could get out of her was that it had happened 'a few years ago, but not many years ago'. As she felt obviously unhappy talking about it to a stranger – fearing repercussions? – I left it at that.

I cannot say for certain that her story was true, but the scenario she described seems a likely one.

Enforced contraception

The law protects women's right to have or not to have children, but this is subject to the restrictions of population control.

After marriage, or after the first child, women usually have an IUD (coil) inserted. This is a more effective, easier-to-control device than the pill. An annual check-up is available; the IUD will be removed only if the couple receives written permission to have another child. Advice on side effects of the IUD and other contraceptives depends on the knowledge and professionalism of the family planning and medical advisers. It must be remembered that their qualifications and experience vary greatly (I will deal with this in Chapter 7), and some of them may simply be unaware of, or disinterested in, the disadvantages of the IUD.

The main aim of the family planning advisers is to make sure that the couples use contraception. They may consider any side effects and risks as unimportant, because of the priority of society's interests over individuals' interests. Other forms of contraception are available but the IUD. serves the purpose of long-term contraception best. It works even if the couple are not motivated to practise birth control: once the coil is inserted, it takes control of the woman's fertility for several years. It is also suitable for illiterate women who cannot understand instructions for oral contraceptives.

After the second child, one of the partners – almost always the woman – gets sterilised. At present, just below 90 per cent of married women in China use some form of contraception.[2]

Abortion made easy

The value of the unborn child is low in China; the general attitude is there are too many children anyway. If a couple loses one child during pregnancy, they have to wait many years before having another one, especially if they are not allowed more than one. A Western medical expert in China who wishes not to be named, told me:

> If ultrasound screening or other tests show that a child is likely to be ill or handicapped, doctors will quickly advise an abortion, and the parents will almost always take the decision to abort. If they can have only one child, then they want a perfect child. Even minor deformities, which in the West would be accepted, or could be operated on, such as a club foot, are a reason for abortion. It is easy to obtain an abortion.[3]

The level of induced abortions has risen from around 5 million in 1970 to about 10 million in 1993. There were peaks in 1981–82 and 1991–92, in both periods the number of induced abortions was around 14 million each year.

Boys preferred

As well as the traditional perception of male superiority, there are some psychological and practical reasons for wishing to have a male child. The main concerns are:

- The family line is passed on through the oldest male child. If there is no child, the family 'dies out'. The daughter keeps her own name after marriage, but her children will have her husband's family's name. A woman who has no brothers can apply for her child to carry her family name rather than the husband's, but unless the husband has an older brother his family is likely to object.
- The wife has traditionally been part of her husband's family. A woman who marries usually goes to live with her husband's parents. Her own parents may feel bereft: they have literally lost their only child.
- The married woman's labour belongs to her new family. Marriage means the loss of a worker for the bride's family, whereas the groom's family has gained one: this is an important aspect for some peasant families.
- It is every man's moral responsibility to care for his own parents in old age, but the woman's responsibility is to look after her in-laws. As there are not enough nursing homes available and affordable and the state pension is not nearly enough to keep old people alive, it is essential to have a married son. He and his wife will provide the financial security and the nursing care required. Those who have only a daughter have no 'social security'.

However, during my time in China, I didn't meet a single young couple who said they would prefer a boy, although many older people said they were hoping for a grandson rather than a granddaughter. Small children are cherished, loved and pampered regardless of their gender.

Research by the Chinese Academy of Social Sciences showed that 78.4 per cent of people in Beijing believed that there was no difference between having a son and having a daughter, and 6.5 per cent even believed that having a girl was better. However, this still leaves 15.1 per cent who would prefer having a boy, even in a modern, progressive and wealthy place like Beijing. I believe that in reality the percentage of Beijing citizens preferring boys is much higher than the survey indicates: this was an official survey, and many Chinese will simply give the politically correct answer.

There is little doubt that a similar survey in some rural areas would have brought very different results, with more people expressing preference for a boy. For peasants, a male heir is still considered superior. Traditions, which are more than a thousand years old, cannot be eradicated within a few decades.

Disappearing girl children

This traditional view of inheritance has resulted in a long history of female infanticide which was regarded either as a minor sin or as a worthy sacrifice. Sheryl WuDunn in *China Wakes* points to a popular sixteenth-century text in which the offence of killing your child had the same impact as urinating facing north or stepping over a person lying on a floor mat.[4]

The communists virtually eradicated female infanticide after 1949; censuses show no shortfall of girls until the early 1980s. At this time there was a wave of female infanticide, perhaps because the central control of private lives loosened. It is impossible to estimate just how many baby girls were murdered, died from neglect or were never born.

Three patterns emerged in the early 1980s which continue today:

- Many more boys than girls are born
- Girl children are often born 'dead'
- Girls are less likely to survive illnesses during childhood.

The difference between boy births and girl births is increasing. In 1953, 105 boys were born to 100 girls, which can be considered normal; in 1982, it rose to 107 and in 1990 to 114.[5]

Sheryl WuDunn quotes a 1992 figure of 118.5 to 100.[6] The number of boys' births is higher than girls' worldwide and the natural average may be 105.5 per 100. Unreported births may represent another very small part of the discrepancy, but it is unlikely that many parents get away with hiding a child from the authorities. There remains about twelve unborn girl children for every 100 girl children born.

The horror of large scale infanticide raised a new awareness in China: if so many parents were willing to sacrifice their daughters in order to have a son, then equality did not really exist. The government's admission of the problem stimulated investigations into other forms of discrimination against women.

The Law on Protection of Rights and Interests of Women, adopted in 1992, states clearly: 'Drowning, abandoning or cruel infanticide in any manner of female babies shall be prohibited; discrimination against or maltreatment of women who gave birth to female babies [...] shall be prohibited ...'[7]

The wording of this article refers to the situation of women who decide to kill their girl child because they fear severe abuse and maltreatment from their in-laws.

So how do Chinese couples prevent the birth of a girl? The answer is simple: by ultrasound and abortion, or by plain murder.

It is estimated that 100,000 ultrasound scanners were in operation in China in 1990. Their official use is to help doctors check internal organs and to ensure that women are still wearing their IUDs. In practice, unscrupulous parents get their doctor to tell them whether the foetus is male or female and if they are told that they are expecting a daughter, they request an abortion. In her book, *China Wakes*, Sheryl WuDunn describes the effect of ultrasound scans in the Fujian Province.

> Even the most uneducated hillbillies had heard of it. And they loved it. As a violent rainstorm pounded the paddies of one village, a half-dozen peasants sat around a stone hut and spoke with glee about the new age of ultrasound.
>
> 'Everyone has boys now,' Y.H. Chen said in a tone of awe, as the others nodded agreement. 'Last year we had only one girl born in the village – everybody else had boys. You go to the doctor and pay him 200 or 300 *yuan*.
>
> He tells you if your wife is pregnant with a boy or a girl. Then if it's a girl, you get an abortion.'
>
> Chen's brother, Y.C. Chen, interrupted: 'One family here in the village has five girls. They were desperate for a son, so they kept on having another child in the hope that it would be a son. But now you don't need to do that. Now technology is changing things.'[8]

One of the problems is that ultrasound cannot show the gender of a foetus until a late stage of pregnancy, which results in late and possibly dangerous abortions. The practice of using ultrasound to determine gender and decide about an abortion has been banned in China since 1987, but the situation has steadily become worse. The sex ratio in five provinces has risen to 120 boys for every 100 girls.[9]

People who cannot afford the ultrasound or don't have access to it may come to an arrangement with the midwife who makes sure that the female child does not survive birth. Some helpful midwives keep a bucket of water at the bedside in case the baby is a girl.[10]

Sheryl WuDunn states in *China Wakes* that all over the world boys are more likely to die from infant illness than girls. For example in Japan, there are 133 dead infant boys for every 100 girls. In the US, the ratio is 131 to 100. But in China, only 112 boys die for every 100 girls. She asks:

> What is skewing the statistics in China? Why are boys doing relatively better in China than in other countries? Presumably, because people treat sons better than daughters. They give them more food. They pay more attention to them. They are quicker to summon medical help for sons. It is not that they intentionally expose their daughters to mortal danger but that they take marginally greater risks with girls than with boys.

She talked to Li Honggui, an official in China's State Family Planning Commission, who acknowledged the problem: 'If a boy gets sick, the parents may send him to the hospital at once. But if a girl gets sick, the parents may say to themselves, "Well, we'll see how she is tomorrow".'[11]

Orphans: pretending birth has never happened

Parents who are desperate to have a healthy boy child but cannot bear to kill their daughter, often abandon the child in the hope that someone will discover and rear her or they take her to an orphanage: they pretend the birth of the child had never happened.

Chances of a happy childhood or indeed survival appear to be slim in some orphanages. On 14 June 1995, Channel 4 broadcast the documentary *The Dying Rooms*, in which a team of reporters gained access to several orphanages, in some of which children suffered from severe neglect. The crew filmed children who had apparently been left to die of starvation in special 'dying rooms'. A leaflet for the series states:

The orphanages, which are run by the state, are underfunded and understaffed, and the level of care in some instances amounts to outright neglect and abandonment. Babies have been crammed six or eight to a bed with bottles of thick gruel simply propped up against their pillows. Children have been strapped down to makeshift bamboo potties all day, their legs splayed over plastic bowls full of excrement. Babies and toddlers who have fallen ill have been abandoned in empty rooms and left to die ...

It is not possible to judge if the visited orphanages are typical of other or all orphanages in China, and there are no reliable statistics on the death rate of children in orphanages. However, it seems likely that the problems of lack of staff, of unqualified and often disinterested staff, lack of space and lack of finance are severe throughout China.

An official fact sheet from the Chinese embassy in London states:

Although tremendous progress has been made in setting up social welfare institutes and improving the living conditions for the children in them, China, a huge developing country with 1.2 billion people, still faces a lot of difficulties, one of which is the proper allocation of resources. There is still a lot to be done to improve the conditions in some orphanages. But anyhow, the so-called 'dying rooms' do not and are not allowed to exist in China.[12]

Birth customs: pig trotters for the mother

Tradition among the Hezhe ethnic group in north China demanded that a woman about to give birth had to leave home and give birth in a makeshift shelter, whatever the season or the weather. Winters in north China can be severe and it was possible for women in labour to die from hypothermia. Added to poor living conditions, lack of medical care and the spread of infectious diseases, this custom contributed largely to the near extinction of the Hezhe tribe. The Hezhe population decreased from 5,016 in 1851 to 1,200 in 1930, and by 1949, only 300 Hezhes survived.

These customs have been abolished after the revolution. The Hezhe is one of the ethnic groups for whom the family planning system is reversed and they are encouraged to have children. By 1990, the Hezhe population reached 4,255.[13]

Other ethnic groups have traditions of better care for the woman in labour and childbirth, although they may ignore the child's existence for a while. In some communities, a baby must not be washed for three days.

For one month after giving birth, the woman is being spoilt by her husband. Widespread customs include serving her with as much food as she can possibly eat, especially pig trotters which are considered a delicacy. The custom of serving pig trotters to new mothers has made this food a rare and costly dish.

The mother remains secluded, is encouraged to stay in bed and to let her husband pamper her. Chinese friends told me that by the time a young mother re-enters society she is sometimes 'bigger than when she was pregnant' because of all the food and lack of exercise.

Many Chinese, especially in rural areas, believe that it is bad luck if a stranger's eye falls on a mother or her new baby during the first month. Visitors may be limited to family and neighbours only. Sometimes even family members have to wait for three days before they may greet the new arrival.

The official celebration of birth is often held one month after the birth. Many of these customs are based on the fear that if you acknowledge the child's existence too soon you may lose it and go back to a time when infant mortality was high.

A generation of spoilt brats

There is no doubt that today's children are being spoilt by their parents. The ideal of the one-child family is two parents and four grandparents concentrating their love – and money – on a single child. Some older teachers told me that they have already noticed the effects: insolence, lack of discipline and lack of patience. Whether this is entirely due to the children having no siblings or to other factors is difficult to say. To cope with a generation of spoilt brats, an institute at Hangzhou University has been set up to observe the physical and mental development of the only children. It appears that today's only children are healthier and livelier and have a higher IQ than their grandparents.[14]

One positive aspect of the one-child family is that a child's special talents are more likely to be noticed and encouraged, whether it's a boy or a girl. Eleven-year-old Wang Jing, a primary school pupil in Beijing, is a typical example. She is profiled in *China Pictorial:*

Wang Jing is a gentle and quiet girl, who is always smiling ... an excellent student, who is often praised by her teachers and her parents. Wang Jing's father is a driver, her mother is a worker ... Like many others who want their only child to become a 'dragon of the future', Wang Jing's parents arranged that at the age of seven, she study calligraphy under the guidance of Mr Han Shi, a famous calligrapher ... She has participated in five national children's calligraphy contests and won prizes on every occasion ...

Like many only children, Wang Jing seldom does housework ... She stays at her grandma's home until her mother picks her up at five o'clock in the evening. Her mother takes care of her daily needs while her father is in charge of her lessons and calligraphy. Sometimes, her father teaches her to read classical books and to play the *xiao*, a vertical bamboo flute.

Wang Jing spends her weekends practising calligraphy. Her room is so cluttered with calligraphy that her parents have little room to move.

'We were born at the wrong time,' Wang Jing's mother remarks. 'And we place all our hopes on our daughter. It is the same for almost all families today.'

Wang Jing ... is aware that her parents spend all their energies and money on her. 'I must be better than others because I know that life is not easy for Mum and Dad.'[15]

Ultimately, girls benefit from the one-child policy. If an urban couple's only child is a daughter, or if a rural couple has two girls, they will give these girls the best food, the best healthcare, the best education they can afford, and lavish all their affection on them. If the girls had brothers, the parents would concentrate on giving the boys as much as possible, whereas the girls would have to do with whatever resources are left over after the boys have been cared for.

Furthermore, as the girls grow up, the parents will put all their hopes and ambitions into their daughters. They will fight for their daughters' rights to equal education and career opportunities and will not accept any discrimination against girls. Even in rural areas, people will no longer regard a daughter as a temporary household servant whom one marries off for as much money as possible. They will try to keep their daughters with them if possible and to find husbands for them who will treat them more as partners than as a commodity. It is also possible that they will influence their daughters to marry men nearby, so that daughters, not just sons and daughters-in-law, can care for old and frail people.

Adopting a child

Adoption is encouraged. However, couples can adopt a child only instead of – not in addition to – their own child.

Yu Zhijuan (a pseudonym) is a 41-year-old housewife, married to a businessman in Tianjin (near Beijing).

> My husband has an illness which means he cannot have children. We both like children very much. We decided to adopt a child. We asked at an orphanage. We were surprised that this was easy. Everyone was friendly about our request. We had to fill in many forms but nobody ever tried to stop us from adopting a child. We did not mind if we had a boy or a girl. But we would not take a crippled child. The authorities showed us one girl and suggested we adopt her. She was very young and very healthy. We said yes. She is now ten years old and we love her very much. But nobody knows that she is adopted, not even our families. Please do not tell my mother-in-law. My husband has not had the courage to tell her. She would be angry if her only son was not able to produce a child. She would probably blame me.[16]

Outplacing children

Another phenomenon which seems to be a status symbol is that of outplacing children. Some wealthy people pay foster families to look after their children. Bao Tianren explains:

> We love our daughter. But we have the money to pay for people to look after her. First I selected a very good primary school in the countryside, then I found a family living near the school. It is better for my daughter to grow up in the countryside than in the town. I visit her often, sometimes at school and sometimes at the family's home. I always take her home on weekends, so she spends weekends with Liu and me.[17]

Another reason mentioned by parents for outplacing their children is to give them the chance to grow up with other children of the same age. Under the one-child policy, children like Bao Yü will never have brothers or sisters. Staying in the countryside, children like her will grow up in a family with at least one other child – possibly several – if the foster family is in a rural area or belongs to an ethnic minority.

Status of the mother

Motherhood raises the status of a woman, especially in the countryside. Being the centre of the family is still a woman's most important function, whatever other roles she has. She is supposed to be a model of perfection in both her career and her family life, to serve her employer, her husband, her parents-in-law, her children and the country.

The super-mum's skills are acknowledged and she gains great respect if she manages to juggle all her roles. If she feels that she cannot fulfil all the roles equally, her career is almost always the first aspect to be neglected.

Traditionally, a woman could wait for her sons to marry and her daughters-in-law to serve her and her family full time. Today's younger women are more likely to have a career which demands at least some of their energy and dedication. For the older generation of women who had served their time of obedience to parents-in-law and who were looking forward to receiving similar servitude in their old age, the changes in society came as a shock. They may have to look after their grandchildren, and some confident young women expect the non-working older women of the family to look after the working generation's interests.

Shortage of women as marriage partners

Restricting the number of new children is the only feasible method to prevent large scale starvation in China today. The Chinese accept this drastic measure partly because they have no other choice, but also because to the Chinese mind the interests of society are more important than the interests of the individual and her desire for more offspring. I cannot see the government deviating from this policy, and I believe that measures may become stricter as the problem increases. For example, it may be necessary to curb the reproduction of ethnic minorities. The situation will only relax when China becomes wealthy and confident enough to afford, and depend on, imported food.

The traditional preference for male offspring continues to exist, resulting in abortions and the killing of female babies. As age-old traditions die hard and new technology spreads quickly, I expect abortions of females to increase further, although laws and severe punishment will help reduce the killing of babies.

Ultimately, there will be a shortage of women as marriage partners. This is partly the result of female infanticide and partly because more and more women become educated and financially independent, and an increasing number of them will choose to remain unmarried. One possible result of this is that women will have a wider choice of marriage partners and that husbands will treat their wives better, if only out of fear that the women will leave them if they don't. On the negative side, the shortage of women as marriage partners will almost certainly lead to a sharp increase in the existing problem of abductions and of trading women into sex slavery. It seems likely that prostitution will also increase.

7 Living conditions

Rising living standards

At first it was the farmers who benefited from the economic reforms in the 1980s, because they could sell their produce at free market prices. Now it is the urban people whose wealth is increasing rapidly while the rural population sinks back into poverty. Virtually everybody's income is rising, but rapid inflation prevents increases in the living standards of many. The gap between 'rich' and 'poor' is growing dramatically, both in the cities and in the countryside. A survey of 100,000 households showed that from 1978 to 1995 the gap between the income of 'rich urban people' and 'poor urban people' increased from 1.6-fold to 3-fold, and the gap between the income of 'rich farmers' and 'poor farmers' expanded from 2.9-fold to 6.6-fold.[1] While more and more people can afford bicycles, refrigerators, washing machines and televisions, there are also more and more people struggling for survival.

Accommodation: desperate building boom

China is struggling to provide enough housing for its increasing population and the 1980s and 1990s have seen a building boom in rural China. The area of newly built houses in the countryside from 1979 to 1994 alone reached 10.68 billion square metres. According to official information, the average living space per person in the countryside has increased from 8.1 square metres before 1978 to 20.5 square metres in 1995, and for urban people from 3.6 square metres to 7.7 square metres.[2]

In some areas, half the population has been moved to better housing. A visitor to Tonghua remarked that over a period of just two years, more than a quarter of that industrial town had been torn down and rebuilt.

The government plans to build more than 1 billion square metres of urban housing and more than 3 billion square metres of rural housing between 1996 and 2001.[3] This building boom has resulted in shortages of building materials such as timber, cement and roofing tiles, and led to inflation. Another problem is that the new houses are often built on the best agricultural land and thus contribute to the shortage of food.[4]

The new houses are more spacious, modern and pleasant to live in than the traditional hovels. However, in the countryside they are still often without water or electricity supplies and even with all the building activities, overcrowding remains a serious problem and can pose a health hazard. The All-China Women's Federation sent 15 cadres to 30 villages in poor areas in the provinces of Guizhou, Yunnan and Gansu, and in the autonomous regions of Guangxi Zhuang and Ningxia to investigate living conditions. They found that over 80 per cent of the rural families lived in thatched cottages, and some didn't even have permanent housing. The investigations showed that drought and lack of water were a major problem. These difficult living conditions affect the health of local people, especially women and children. The report pointed out that many women developed gynaecological diseases and a variety of regional diseases which would not have spread in better hygienic conditions.[6]

The style of housing varies greatly from province to province. The modern buildings are often inspired by historical housing styles of the region and they cater for the specific needs of each region, such as protection from heat, cold, sand, dust, rain, wind, flooding or snow. There are hundreds of different house design, ranging from tunnel-shaped cave houses of the Loess Plateau to compound houses which are built around courtyards in Beijing, bamboo stilt houses in the Yunnan Province, huge round earthen fortresses in the Fujian Province and Han houses with gabled roofs which look so typically Chinese to the Western eye.[7]

Modern urban accommodation

In northeastern cities such as Tonghua, the difference between the accommodation of the rich and of the poor becomes noticeable. The wealthier people live in blocks of flats with water and electricity (although supplies of either are erratic), with usually two or three good-sized rooms, plus a kitchen and a bathroom, for each family.

The inside walls are painted in two colours: the lower third is usually either wood-panelled or painted brown and the favourite colour for the two upper thirds is a bright turquoise blue.

Curtains and pillowcases are mostly made from nylon or other thin synthetic material which feels sticky to the touch. Again, bright colours such as pink, orange and sky blue are popular, and most items are decorated with machine-embroidered flowers. For those who can afford them, the refrigerator and the television have pride of place, and are displayed in the centre of the living room, for everyone to see and admire.

The bathrooms may contain a Western-style flush toilet or a Chinese-style latrine, a wash basin, a bathtub and possibly a shower. The bathtub is not used for bathing, but for storing water, because there can be droughts in the northeast and water supplies may cease for several days or weeks. The shower works on the principle of an electric kettle attached to a wall. To have a shower, the Chinese fill this kettle with water, turn it on until it has reached the desired temperature and have a shower. Every bathroom floor has a hole through which the water is drained away. However, for most Chinese a warm shower is a great luxury and generally they use enamelled or painted washing bowls for their daily washing ritual. Large towns like Tonghua have public baths with showers which residents can use for a small fee.

In Tonghua the poor live in groups of shacks made from leftover timber, corrugated iron sheets and other waste materials. Three generations live in a single-room building which offers little protection against the severe cold of the winter.

Peasants in the countryside around Tonghua often live in long terraced brick houses with gabled roofs almost tiled flat. Some of these groups of terraces were built in the time of the Cultural Revolution for agricultural work units. As well as for accommodation, they may be used to store farm implements and produce.[8]

Life in one of China's richest cities, Guangzhou (formerly Canton), in the Guangdong Province, shows similar contrasts. Shops offer luxuries such as home computers, whirlpools, CD players and reproduction Greek statues. Teresa Poole writes in the *Independent On Sunday:*

> The fabric of the city, its homes and basic infrastructure, are mostly ramshackle and crumbling after decades of under-investment ... Living conditions are basic; poorly

dressed children play by dirty gutters. When new money floods into an old city like Canton, it is easier to put a colour television in every home than to ensure each family has running water.[9]

A Chinese acquaintance described his visit to Shanghai in 1993 as follows:

> Parts of Shanghai are beginning to look like parts of Delhi in India of which I've seen a video. It's what you would call slums. People from the countryside flock to Shanghai hoping for a better life. But they cannot find jobs and they don't have accommodation. They build huts from whatever rubbish they can find. These areas are not large but I think they are growing.[10]

Food diversity: cats, rats, dogs and snails

Western gourmets divide China into four gastronomic areas: Guangzhou (Canton), Shanghai, Sichuan and Beijing. However, this does not reflect real life. Firstly, the average Chinese family simply eat what is available and what they can afford, and the 'cuisine' of their area can be enjoyed on feast days and banquets only. Secondly, each of the 50 ethnic groups have their own cuisine and these differ widely.

In the south, rice is the staple food and forms the basis of every meal. The climate allows two or three rice harvests per year. There is an abundance of fresh fruit available: bananas, apples, oranges, pineapples, lychees, honeydew melons, giant hawthorns, dates as well as many vegetables.

In the northeast, the situation is more difficult. In the colder climate, fewer fruit and vegetables grow. Rice, where it is grown at all, can be harvested only once a year. However, wheat, apples, soybeans, and cabbage grow well. There are more than a dozen cabbage varieties, and until 20 years ago, many villagers survived the winters almost exclusively on cabbage. Bread is a comparatively recent introduction and is spreading slowly. On the other hand, steamed wheat buns are a traditional staple food. Noodles are equally popular, eaten in hot soups or cold. Soybeans form the protein-rich basis of many food ingredients and dishes, from soy foods to sweet or savoury *doufu* (tofu or beancurd).

In the northern province of Inner Mongolia, the food situation is still difficult. There is little variety to the daily bread and mutton, and even these two staple foods are not always available.

In the very cold Heilongjiang Province, people of the small Hezhen minority live almost exclusively on fish, which is eaten (often raw) three times a day, although they now trade fish for other foodstuffs and some of them have turned to agriculture.[11]

The Chinese do not like milk and dairy products, which they find difficult to digest and the smell of which they find repellent. Milk powder with added sugar has recently been introduced and accepted, but only as a baby food. Milk powder bags are adorned with pictures of little rosy-cheeked blonde boys. Yoghurt is sold in earthenware jars as a Western novelty at street stalls, but only in cities. Another dairy product has become by far more popular nationwide: ice cream.

Gradually the Chinese are becoming more aware of the value of eggs in nutrition, although they are still regarded mostly as a diet for ill or recuperating people. Eggs are also made into omelettes, filled with chillis and other spicy ingredients, and sold as takeaway food.

Meat is expensive. Few people can afford it regularly, but it is an important ingredient if there are visitors, or at a banquet. The Chinese eat pork, beef, mutton, chicken, rat, dog, cat, snake and other animals. Each region has its own favourites: in the Jilin Province, for example, raw dog stomach was reckoned to be the most desirable meat. Fish is eaten mostly along the coasts, but shrimps and other seafood are often dried and used as cooking ingredients.

China has recently introduced a 'Green Food' label for organically grown and ecologically sound foodstuffs. The China Green Food Development Centre was founded in 1992, and a year later the Centre joined the International Federation of Organic Agriculture Movement (IFOAM). The range of 847 items of 'Green Food' includes grain products, fruit and vegetables, liquor, eggs, seafood, oil and meat. Most Chinese have never heard of 'Green Food', are not interested in organically grown fruit and vegetables, and are unaware of environmental problems influencing food quality. Nevertheless, a China Green Food Fair was held in Tianjin in October 1995, with 332 products on display. During the four days of the fair, over 100,000 people attended, 186 tons of products were sold and 60,000 tons of products were ordered.[12]

'Fast food' sold at the roadside is popular with the Chinese. Eighty per cent of urban residents occasionally buy fast food, and 57 per cent say they frequently have fast food meals.[13] Chinese fast food includes noodles or omelettes, for example. The variety is enormous, but as the food is often prepared long in advance and not covered while it is displayed by the roadside, there are food hygiene problems. Becoming a fast food vendor is a popular way for women to become self-employed.

Shopping

Shopping is mostly the women's duty. Most Chinese purchase fresh fruit and vegetables, eggs, spices and other foodstuffs, household items and clothing in the street markets. More prestigious – and expensive! – is a shopping spree in a department store. All cities and many of the larger towns have at least one department store, which is often part of one of the dominant work units of the area. There may be, for example, a Forestry Department Store and a Railway Department Store, just as there is a Forestry Hospital and a Railway Hospital, a Forestry Restaurant and a Railway Restaurant. Department stores offer a range of 'Western' goods, such as Nescafé, Mars bars, canned coke and other Western soft drinks, computers, videos, CD players and brand name clothes, which are so expensive that they are out of reach for all except the richest people.

Smaller shops sell the more standard items: stationery, candles, matches, instant noodles, sweets, sweet carbonated sticky soft drinks made from bananas or other fruit, and wine, but seldom fresh fruit and vegetables. Specialist shops supply cooking oils and rice.

Climate, customs, attitudes, wages, prices, availability of goods and living standards differ from region to region, and it would be foolish to measure, for example, the income of a woman in Inner Mongolia against that of a man in Shanghai.

For example: 2 *kwai* (or *yuan*) bought 1 *yin* (approximately 1 pound) of apples in a street market in the Jilin Province in spring 1994. In the Guizhou Province, the same amount bought a five *yin* bag full of mixed fruit such as bananas, pineapples, apples, melons and apricots.

Healthcare

For a developing country, China shows a surprisingly high life expectancy. From 1949 to 1990, the average life expectancy rose from 35 years to 68.55 years – 66.84 years for men and 70.47 years for women.[14]

For several decades, free healthcare was an important right in the lives of ordinary workers. It was introduced shortly after the founding of the People's Republic in 1949. In the state-run economy, where work units were owned by the state, this worked well: an employee who fell ill reported this to her employer, who usually sent her to a doctor or hospital and paid for the cost of her treatment and medicines.

However, with the free market economy came independent enterprises and the new entrepreneurs often refused to pay for their staff's medical treatment. In 1994, when I was working with a Chinese publishing house in Tonghua, one of my colleagues became ill. Not only did the employer refuse to pay for her treatment; he also deducted money for her absence and even reduced her salary for the next few weeks. He claimed that this employee was 'at risk' and that there was no guarantee that she could work efficiently after recovery.

The woman in question was a senior employee in charge of a small department. I asked her why she accepted this arbitrary treatment so meekly. She explained that, by getting a job in a private enterprise, she had left the protection of a state-run work unit and was thus at the mercy of the entrepreneur. He could hire, fire or abuse staff at will. She feared that if she protested, the boss would reduce her salary further to show his power.

This employer came from a poor peasant family with eight children. He used to be a red guard in his youth. Over the last four years, he had build a flourishing publishing business and could afford status symbols such as a foreign car and chauffeur, a mobile telephone and a European woman on his staff. Despite his wealth – he was one of the richest people in Tonghua – he claimed to be a communist at heart.

While private entrepreneurs cannot or will not pay for their workers' healthcare, state-run enterprises face a similar dilemma. Underfunded and in debt, sometimes they cannot even pay the monthly wages and pensions, let alone medical costs which are rising rapidly. *China Daily* reports that the medical costs of state-owned enterprises are rising faster than the gross national product and the state revenues.

The Jiangxi and Jiangsu Provinces were the first to experiment with a healthcare reform in 1984, and by February 1996, 28 provinces and municipalities have introduced similar reforms. These are based on social pool funds: state-owned enterprises contribute 10 per cent of their employees' salary, and employees pay 1 per cent to a medical insurance fund. Only after their personal deposits are used up, can employees apply to the social pool funds for a refund for further medical expenses.[15]

Children still die of tetanus

I talked to a Chinese professor of medicine and a Western medical expert in China. Both were based in cities in the northeast and were keen to publicize health information, but did not wish to be named.[16]

The rural areas of China are probably the most primitive on earth, with shocking hygienic conditions. Due to lack of good health education and preventive medicine, such as immunisation, children still die of tetanus.

Rabies, polio and Japanese encephalitis occur frequently. Apparently the rabies problem got worse in the year of the dog (1994), when it became fashionable to keep a dog for good luck. Chinese friends told me that some people engaged in a lively trade, smuggling dogs from the Russian Republic into China. These were usually big dogs who arrived without health certificate or vaccination.

Cholera has been declared officially eradicated, but there are rumours about local outbreaks in recent years. The typhoid problem is similar to that in England in the last century. The appalling hygienic conditions in some rural areas – for example, a family living in the same room as their pigs – make typhoid a widespread disease in the countryside. As more and more peasants migrate to the cities seeking work, typhoid appears frequently in urban areas. The problem is increased because many of the migrating peasants find employment in eating places. In addition, all types of hepatitis are found in China, including hepatitis A, which is carried by infected food, and hepatitis B, which is spread by contaminated syringes and needles.

Like many developing countries, lack of funds means China does not have a comprehensive public health programme for mosquito eradication. Awareness of health risks is low in China, and people are seldom aware that a neglected pond or water standing in pots for a long time may attract disease. Malaria is a frequent illness in the south, but not in the cold north.

Tuberculosis (TB), probably the most prevalent fatal infectious disease among adults worldwide, constitutes a serious problem in China. One quarter of all TB patients who can spread the disease to others live in China (about six million). It is estimated that each of these 'smear positive' patients may pass on the illness to ten to 15 people a year.

Vaccination of children throughout the country has reduced the risk for future generations. This is part of a six-year project launched in 1992 with a £58 million loan from the World Bank, which has already provided 340,000 people with infectious tuberculosis in twelve provinces with free medical treatment. More than 90 per cent of the treated patients have recovered.

The family of Shi Yushuang, from Tangtougou, a village in the Hebei Province, were hit by tuberculosis. Her husband, two daughters, two sons and one grandchild were ill. When the free tuberculosis treatment became available in her village in 1994, one of her daughters, both sons and the grandchild recovered. Unfortunately this came too late for her husband and her elder daughter who had already died.[17]

China's medical history

To Western visitors, this situation often comes as a shock, especially as China appears to have a wealth of knowledge of traditional treatments such as acupuncture and herbalism. To understand why China's healthcare is in such an appalling state, you have to look at the country's 'medical history'.

Before 1949, there were very few medical facilities in China. These included traditional herbalists, as well as a few Western-style hospitals in treaty ports. Both operated to high standards, but they could not offer enough healthcare for the whole country.

The communists opened new hospitals all over the country to make healthcare available to everyone. However, there were not enough doctors and nurses to staff them. During the 'great leap forward' (1958–1963), the training period for doctors was reduced to three years. When the Cultural Revolution began in 1965, hospitals were already poorly staffed, with doctors who had only basic medical knowledge. The only highly qualified doctors at the time were those who had had missionary training before the war.

However, qualifications no longer counted. During the decade of the Cultural Revolution, the red guards took over the hospital administration. Doctors with high education or qualifications, or who held responsible positions in hospitals, were regarded as intellectual, and therefore bourgeois, counter-revolutionary and suspect. They were discriminated against, harassed, dismissed from their jobs, sent to hard labour in the countryside, or imprisoned. Not all of them survived. Those who did were mostly prevented from carrying out their profession for many years. Successful practitioners of traditional medicine suffered a similar fate. Medical colleges were closed until the beginning of the 1970s and medical standards deteriorated further.

At the same time, basic medical care became more widely available. At the beginning of the Cultural Revolution, on 26 October 1965, Mao Zedong issued his famous instruction 'In medical and health work, put the stress on rural areas'.[18]

'Barefoot doctors' were quicker to train and cheaper to equip than Western doctors and surgeons. These women and men had basic paramedic skills and carried out their trade in the employment of work units or covered large areas, carrying with them an instruction manual and some basic equipment and medicines. In 1974, there were over a million barefoot doctors in China.[19]

At the beginning of the 1970s, some medical colleges re-opened, but offered only part-time studies in basic medical care, the approximate equivalent of a first aid course. It was not until 1978 that medical colleges were opened on a large scale but by then, there were not enough qualified doctors to train the students. Those who had survived the Cultural Revolution were rushed to become professors of medicine.

Like in most communist countries, medicine is a popular career for women: of the doctors I met in urban northeast China, a third were women. Some ran small clinics for work units, others worked in hospitals, but the senior doctors in hospitals appeared to be mostly men. I was not able to obtain any figures on the gender distribution in the medical profession, but I talked to a woman doctor who believed there were more male doctors in the cities and more female doctors in the countryside. She also reckoned that a woman doctor had better opportunities to achieve senior positions in the countryside because few men want to go there.[20]

Medical standards today

Since the end of the Cultural Revolution, standards and availability of healthcare have improved. The number of hospital beds throughout China has increased from 13.3 for every 10,000 people in 1970 to 23.6 in 1990. The number of medical staff (including technical staff working for medical units) rose from 17.5 per 10,000 in 1970 to 35 in 1994.[21]

Medical care is widely available. Even small villages have a clinic with a doctor or health worker, however, standards vary greatly. Hospitals can be scrupulously clean, with well-trained staff and modern equipment, especially in Shanghai, Guangzhou and Beijing. In some other areas doctors and nurses are not familiar with the most basic rules of hygiene, not only in the countryside, but in well-developed areas and industrial towns.

My experiences in some Chinese hospitals were devastating. A mother instructed her small daughter to pee in the middle of the treatment room. The nurse watched this, smiling; nobody cleaned the mess away. A patient bled heavily from an injury; three weeks later, the bloodstains were still on the floor. A nurse pointed out an old man, saying he was probably suffering from tuberculosis. She did not prevent him from spitting on the floor. Piles of blood-stained sputum remained there all day, in a room which was crowded with a dozen other patients. A doctor working in the chest department in a hospital smoked while treating patients. Another doctor had a coat which may have once been white, but had apparently not been washed for a couple of years. She had grimy brown hands with black fingernails, and when she arranged a drip in my hand she fingered the needle for a while before inserting it.

At the college, students were encouraged to donate blood. The same needle was used for about 1,000 donors. With widespread tuberculosis, hepatitis B, and an increasing risk of venereal diseases and AIDS, the risk was enormous, but nobody seemed aware of it. When I had to get a series of injections I was relieved that the college doctor washed her hands. However, she proceeded to wash a used needle and syringe with warm water from a tea kettle. I gave her several needles from my own supply. Grateful for the opportunity to increase her stock, she gave me some rice cakes in return.

A Western medical expert resident in China described the situation in 1994: 'If you find a doctor over the age of 70, he or she is probably good. A doctor over 60 is possibly good. Doctors in the age group between 35 and 60 are very badly trained. Those under 35 had the best training China could offer, which was not a lot. And if there is a young Chinese doctor who is really good, then he or she is in America.'[22]

Rural health workers often have only basic training, but some are qualified nurses, midwives, doctors or paramedics. One health worker can be responsible for a large area. Sometimes there is a clinic or health centre with several staff, and peasants from a large area attend these centres when they need help. Since 1972, the focus of rural healthcare has been mostly on family planning, antenatal care and children's health.

Women attend health centres and clinics to obtain contraceptives – usually an IUD – or for premarital health checks. The visit to the town provides a rare opportunity to get out of their villages and see the wider world. However, poor transport facilities make it difficult or impossible for some peasant women to get to the clinics.

Yinan, a poor county in the Yimeng Mountains in the Shandong Province, probably provides a typical example. Eighty per cent of its 900,000 population live in rural areas. The town of Linyi has a maternity and childcare centre with several medical staff and many villages have their own clinics.

Niu Hongxia, a 21-year-old woman doctor, works at such a village clinic. This is a room with a table, a cabinet containing medical apparatus, a small iron stove and a bed. On the wall, there are several posters explaining the human body and prenatal healthcare. Niu's father and grandfather were both village doctors. After secondary school, Niu studied for two years at the county medical school, followed by one year of gynaecology and obstetrics at the county's maternity and childcare centre, and she then became one of the 977 women village doctors. Each administrative village in Yinan County has one woman doctor.

Niu's work comprises of prenatal exams, postpartum visits, preventive inoculations for newborns and medical examinations of children. According to Niu, a woman fills in a health protection form when she is three months pregnant; she gets monthly, semi-monthly and weekly check-ups throughout her pregnancy, and is encouraged to give birth in hospital – where four doctors are working – rather than at home. A doctor visits the baby four times during its first year.[23]

Environmental pollution

Industrialisation has brought great environmental problems. Much of the pollution can be noticed easily, especially the air pollution from coal burning for domestic and industrial use, and the litter.

Most Chinese have the habit of keeping their own houses as clean as they possibly can. But what happens outside their four walls concerns them little. They dump their litter on the roadside or in streams. I have seen streams which contained more litter than water – yet they still served as the main supply of drinking water for villages. At the same time, the villagers washed their clothes in them. Litter was piled up around the outer walls of some restaurants, often two metres high at every wall, with just a gap for the door, so that it felt as if you were entering a cave inside a rubbish dump.

China's train attendants clean the trains frequently and thoroughly, sweeping the floors and the seats. I was impressed by this hourly ritual until I saw where the litter went. Every carriage has a flap opening to the outside: the attendant simply pushes the litter through the flap to dump it out of the moving train. Once I realized this, I could not watch the attendants' efforts without feeling sick. The railway tracks through China's scenic landscapes are lined with strips of red and white plastic bags and bottles.

At a company outing, my 40 colleagues searched for a picturesque picnic spot. They rejected one because 'someone's been here before' (the place was littered with coke bottles and plastic bags) and they held a picnic in a meadow. When they got ready to move on, they left behind all their plastic carrier bags, food wrapping and paper plates.

I could not bear this and asked if we could not take the rubbish home, but my Chinese friends could not see the point. 'Why? This is far away from the road, nobody sees it. Anyway, we are a developing country, you cannot expect us to worry about minor things such as nature.'

Normally, I tried to follow my Chinese colleagues' examples in every aspect of life, but in this case I insisted on tidying up. They tried to prevent me physically. Ding, a trainee editor, came to my assistance and, between us, we tidied up the place, but they would not allow us to take the litter home. The only compromise I could achieve was to dump the litter in a place where other people had dropped theirs already and seemed on the way to becoming a rubbish dump.

Other environmental problems are less visible: chloride and sulphur in the air, and toxic chemicals let into streams or leaking into the groundwater. These problems are worst in new industrial zones, but the Chinese appear to worry very little about such matters. However, health problems caused by environmental pollution are on the increase, especially itchy eyes, ear infections, asthma and catarrhal colds.

Social security, pensions and old age

In 1994, the government spent 210 billion *yuan* on social security (the per capita GNP was 2,664 *yuan* in the previous year). About 180 million employees are covered by labour insurance and welfare programmes. Old, sick, injured and disabled workers and staff receive a pension from the state, usually 75–100 per cent of their wages, depending on the length of their service. They also enjoy the same medical insurance as those who are still in employment.[24] Retirement regulation demand that women retire five to ten years earlier than men.

There are 940,000 beds in homes for the elderly and orphans, serving 730,000 current clients. However, these homes are frequently underfunded and understaffed, and reports suggest that some provide appalling conditions.

Social security networks are not available everywhere in China. By 1994, only 32 per cent of the country's townships had established rural social security networks.[25]

Unfortunately, the state cannot increase pensions to keep up with the inflation rate. Consequently, many old people find they cannot live on their pensions alone. To many Chinese who felt sure that their work unit would look after them and provide a secure old age, this comes as a shock. They have to find other sources of income; in urban areas, this is often part-time employment, for example in domestic service. In the countryside, they continue to work as farm labourers. Others rely on their adult children to provide for them. A little over forty-four per cent of men over 60 continue to work, but only 14.2 per cent of women of the same age are employed. It is more difficult for women to find post-retirement work because they have had less education and training.[26] As remarriage for widows remains a taboo in some rural areas, retired widows often live in great poverty. Those who have neither a caring family nor a job face a hard time, especially when they become ill. Chinese society does not care for them, there simply aren't the resources and other concerns are considered to be more important.

When I went shopping in the street market of Tonghua with my Chinese friends Li and Xiao, I noticed something looking like a life-size plastic doll lying in the street between the vendors' stalls. The body was crooked and bent, the clothes torn and stuffed thickly with straw. The face looked black brown and wrinkled, like a half-rotten pear, or even like burnt and molten plastic. At first I thought this was a straw doll, some kind of effigy, but then it moved: it was a human body. I was not sure if it was a woman, but I felt certain that she was dying. The Chinese ignored her. Li pulled me away, and even pretended not to have seen the body. I persisted with my questions and finally she said: 'That's someone who has no home and no children. There are many such.' But she refused to tell me more. Neither Li nor Xiao showed any sign of pity, only embarrassment.

The following day I asked my colleague Joy, a compassionate and sensitive young woman who had trained as an English teacher but secured an editorial position, and she was more forthcoming with information.

> Yes, there are many homeless people. Some of them have no adult children who could care for them; others have children who don't want to pay for their parents' upkeep, or to care for them. So as soon as they grow too frail or too ill to work, they are in a bad situation. They seek refuge in the caves and forests of the hills. They stuff their clothes with straw to keep warm because they don't have enough warm clothes.
>
> People with infectious and disfiguring diseases also seek refuge in the hills, and of course they infect the other homeless people with whom they share the caves. Some of these illnesses are so horribly disfiguring, and so infectious, that healthy people avoid any contact with the homeless.
>
> A third group of homeless people are criminals who have escaped from prison. Some of these are murderers or others who were sentenced to death or who got life imprisonment. Others escaped from concentration camps during the Cultural Revolution, more than 20 years ago.

If they survived in the hills, they are now diseased and cannot return into society even if they could be politically rehabilitated.

Some probably live on theft and raids, and some are highwaymen, but they avoid the towns. I believe the person you've seen may have come into town because she knew she was going to die and she may have been desperate for a scrap of food or some warmth, but people are afraid of her illness.

I believe there have been criminals and escapees in the mountains for a long time. But I think that desperate old people turning to the hills are a new phenomenon of recent years. Before, they always had families or work units taking care of them.[27]

Crime: most offenders are men

Women appear to be law-abiding citizens in China. They account for only 2–3 per cent of criminal offenders sentenced by the courts. Between 1986 and 1993 it was never higher than 3.2 per cent. Most criminal offenders are men, and many criminal offences are committed by men towards women, especially rape, abduction and hooliganism.

Although the figures only include criminals who were sentenced by the courts and therefore exclude unreported and undiscovered crimes, they give an idea of which crimes are most likely to be committed by women.

Looking at the 1993 statistics, it appears that bigamy is the number one crime among women: almost 40 per cent of all bigamists are female. This is followed by traffic in narcotics, kidnapping and selling people, and corruption, in each of which women account for about 10 per cent of convicted criminals.[28]

Getting rich at all costs

The average living standard has risen dramatically over the last decade and will continue to rise at a breathtaking rate, especially in the cities. Increasing migration from the countryside to the cities will be the result of this. People without jobs or qualifications will flock to the cities, and many will live there in utmost poverty, which will lead to the emergence of slums. The rich will get richer, the poor will get poorer. Corruption among officials is likely to become more frequent.

The collapse of the social security system and the government's withdrawal of funds mean that an increasing number of people will exist below the poverty line. Old and sick people, especially widowed women without children, will suffer most. It is likely that China will soon face a big problem of a growing homeless population.

The increasing unemployment rate on the other hand seems to be more of a temporary problem, although it will at first worsen as more of the formerly secure state-owned work units collapse. China's rapid economic growth may soon lead to many more jobs, and it may be only a matter of training people.

As a consequence of the increasing living standards and the constantly growing population, China is building more private housing and will have to continue for many years. This will use up more and more valuable agricultural land, sharpening the problem of supplying enough food for everyone.

In the hurry to provide housing, and in the prevailing mood of 'get rich quick at all costs', the Chinese give little thought to the environment and nature is going to be the main loser.

8 Putting on the lipstick ... fashion and beauty

The traditional women's dress

Traditionally, women in most parts of China wore a long dress called the *qipao* (or *cheongsam*), with a curved front overflap, fastened with hoops and toggles at the right. Up to the nineteenth century the *qipao* was wide to hide body contours, but at the beginning of the twentieth century it became more tight-fitting and 'sexy'.

Sleeves used to be wide and long enough to hide the woman's hands because it was considered impolite to show one's hands.

But as the gowns became tighter, the sleeves became tighter too, and shorter. In the warm south, some *qipaos* were sleeveless. In the 1930s the *qipao* presented an image of sleek sophistication: vents at the side, introduced for easier walking, were extended to slits up to the hips, and fashion conscious women wore silk stockings and high heels with their *qipao*.

The 'Mao' suit

After the Liberation, the *qipao* was considered immoral, and fewer and fewer women wore it. The government actually outlawed the wearing of *qipaos* during the Cultural Revolution.[1] The communists introduced a standard garment that was in every respect the opposite of the *qipao*; the 'Mao suit' which was made from cotton in dark muted colours, usually navy blue. It was cheap, sturdy, comfortable, practical, sensible in every climate, and it was standard for women and for men. It gave women the same freedom of movement as men and was a great contribution towards practical equality. But it suppressed individual taste and style, and did not allow for people's natural desire to be different and to be beautiful. Even the most daring Chinese would not deviate further from that standard than wearing black, dark brown or dark green colours.

Ethnic dress: bamboo earsticks and fishskin trousers

Each of the 56 ethnic minorities have their own traditional clothes, which survived the 'Mao suit' period and are encouraged today. Some sub-groups have costumes which differ from the main tribe's, and unmarried and married women may wear different dresses.

Among the Dai people in Yunnan, for example, there is a difference between 'land people' and 'water people'. The land people live on the fringe of the mountainous region, and their lifestyle is closely related to that of the Han majority. The unmarried 'land' Dai women wear short aprons over black trousers and decorate their braids with coloured threads, twisted up into a bun. Once they are married, they wear ankle-length black skirts, knot their unbraided hair into a bun and wear a black headscarf.

'Water' Dai women live near the rivers in the Xishuangbanna area and are dressed much more colourfully. They have tight-fitting narrow-sleeved tops, decorated in pastel colours which match their ankle-length sarongs. There is no difference in the style of married and unmarried women, but older women may wear headscarves. A third group of Dai are called 'floral-belt people' because they wrap a sash with a floral pattern around their waist.[2]

The Naxi in the west of the Yunnan Province wear blue trousers and blouses, and black or blue aprons. To this, they add a T-shaped sheepskin cape, fastened at the front. This cape is embroidered with a sun, a moon and stars. Each star has tassels hanging from it, representing star rays. These garments are known as 'firmament capes'. Traditionally, women wore a brimless round felt hat, but since the Liberation a cap with brim has become more popular.[3]

Women of the Yi nationality in the Yunnan Province wear decoratively carved pieces of bamboo as earrings. To wear bamboo in your pierced ears means you are beautiful and industrious. The larger the hole, the more diligent a woman is believed to be: this stems from the custom of piercing children's ears and putting bamboo sticks into the hole. Gradually, thin sticks are replaced by thicker ones, and when they reach a certain size, the time has come for the child to learn farming and housekeeping. A lazy girl who wants to avoid work therefore will keep the holes in her lobe small.[4]

The traditional outfit of Uygur women in the Xinjiang Province is a long one-piece dress with flared sleeves and a vest or waistcoat, plus an embroidered cap, and a lot of jewellery such as earrings, necklaces and bracelets. Unmarried women wear their hair in dozens of plaits, but after marriage they have only two plaits and a moon-shaped comb as decoration. Today, most women wear Western-style dress and many have given up the plaited hairstyles. But they still like wearing jewellery and they all wear their embroidered caps.[5]

The Hezhen, China's smallest minority, who live in the Heilongjiang Province, make a living from fishing. For centuries, it has been the main role of the women of the tribe to make clothing and household utensils from fishskin, while the men fished and hunted. Although the richer people among the Hezhen now wear cloth, the poorer women still make and wear fishskin clothes. They peel the skin intact from the fish, scale the fish and beat them until they are soft. Then they sew pieces of fishskin together according to their grain, using threads also made from fishskin and coated with fish liver.

Different types of fishskin are used for different purposes: for example, dog salmons are good for shoes, and carp skins are used for trousers. Buttons are made of catfish bones and shells form the decoration of women's dresses. Skill at making fishskin dresses was a major criterion by which a woman's proficiency was judged, and it made her a desirable marriage partner. Even today, Hezhen girls from poorer families are expected to make their own wedding dress from fishskins. One of the skills required of men was to catch fish by spearing the fins so as to leave the skin flawless for making clothes.[6]

When I was living in Tonghua (Jilin Province) which is predominantly the area of the Manchu people, I was stunned by the dazzling array of blazing colours whenever people dressed in their ethnic costumes. These outfits are comfortable and practical for the cold climate. Women wear long jackets with long narrow sleeves. They are made from a glossy, floral-patterned material in a bright colour, preferably pink or red. Originally, these were probably made from silk brocade, but few people can afford this material today, so they use synthetics. Most jackets are closed in the front centre with buttons, but some are cut to be wrapped diagonally across the chest; they have small stand-up collars and are decorated with contrasted braiding at the hems.

Women wear trousers in a plain colour, usually the same colour as the jacket, white gloves, and often a small black apron, embroidered with flowers and decorated with white fringe around the hem. In their hair, the Manchu women wear elaborate headdresses made from red and pink plastic flowers.

But in the Jilin Province, ethnic costume is no longer worn in everyday life. The Cultural Revolution put an end to colour and individual style, and now that both are permitted again, young people prefer to dress in Western fashion.[7]

Gina Corrigan notes in her book how old men go to a festival wearing the blue Mao suits and young men wear Western-style jackets. But the women still dress traditionally in dark embroidered silk or cotton jackets and swinging blue pleated skirts edged with white, their legs wrapped in blue braid. Some wear aprons either with geometrical patterns or depicting the creation story and other Miao legends. The dyes are not colourfast, so the clothes are worn only for festivals, and if it rains the Miao will cancel the event rather than risk spoiling the costumes.[8]

'Blue ants' like it colourful

Since the early 1980s, the restrictions in clothing style have been relaxed and today the Chinese are free to wear what they like. At first hesitant, they soon gained confidence, the first discovery being usually colour. From the extreme of navy blue, Chinese men and women move to the opposite extreme of bright colours. Students, workers and clerical staff like to mix and match colours and patterns in daring combinations. Only street sweepers, building workers and peasants can occasionally still be seen in the traditional blue. But even the paddy fields are dotted with the pink of frilly dresses.

By Western standards, the Chinese women seem to go over the top with fanciful adornments. But it is easy to understand their delight in colour and garnish after being deprived of the joys of fashion and individual styles for so many years.

Trends don't take place all over the country at the same time. Most fashions start in Shanghai, are swiftly taken up in Guangzhou and Beijing, and arrive a year or two later in the provincial capitals. Smaller towns follow at a slower pace. Few women in rural areas are followers of fashion, simply because they cannot afford new clothing before the old items are worn out.

Tonghua, an industrial town in the Jilin Province, is a typical example of how tastes change within a few years.

Phil Horton, a British teacher, taught at Tonghua Teachers' College from 1992 to 1994 and recalls:

> When I arrived, the girls were already experimenting with a variety of muted colours. But the boys were all in Mao suits. A few daring students began wearing grey Western suits. They were amazed at my red jumpers. And now look at them, wearing outfits in purple and neon green![9]

When I lived in Tonghua in 1994, everyone was wearing bright colours. To be considered truly beautiful, a garment had to be liberally decorated with fringes, embroideries, beads and sequins, and glitter like a Christmas tree. Frills were attached to every hem. Checks were in, and women who could not afford new garments sewed pieces of checked material on collars, hems and pockets to update older clothes. Bold patterns were mixed and matched in combinations which looked odd to the Western eye. It was not so much a matter of fashion as an uninhibited exploration of possibilities.

The new garments were not practical. High-heeled pumps were the latest discovery; women wobbled in the ankle-deep mixture of mud and snow in the street market, wearing tight-fitting long sequinned gowns and white stiletto pumps. They often imitated what they believed to be 'Western' fashion, seen perhaps in 1960s American action films in the cinema, and in advertisements. A 27-year-old secretary proudly showed me her new 'Western' outfit: a black and brown checked miniskirt over black leggings, a frilly white blouse and a bright red and black checked jacket, black lace gloves and white trainers.[10]

Li, a 23-year-old student told me in 1994:

> The change has occurred gradually over six or seven years. When I was a child, only three colours were possible for grown-ups: blue, green and black. Now we all love white and bright red. Many girls at the college also wear bright yellow, but really, this was last year's colour. Most students try to buy at least one new garment every year.[11]

At the same time, fashions in Beijing had moved on to batik fabrics and crocheted shawls.

Phil Horton's successor, Sarah Lewis from Scotland, already described a different picture for 1995–96:

> The young women who can afford it are very fashion conscious. The clothes have become more elegant and tasteful. Brown is considered a sophisticated colour. Checked patterns are in. People who like clothes follow fashion avidly. Flares and platforms are in just now, and it seems they will soon be followed by jodhpurs. On the other side, you have students, usually from the countryside, who care little for things they cannot ever buy. They are not materialistic simply because they cannot afford to be. These students are wonders at mixing and matching. They usually have a few tops, two pairs of trousers and one or two skirts.[12]

Student Jiao Hongyan, 21, from Baishan, a small town near Tonghua, described in 1995:

> Yes, the way people dress has changed radically over the last five years. Now people wear whatever they like, instead of what other people expect them to. In the old days, people wore just the same simple kind of clothes in dark colours. But now, even old people are experimenting with colours to make them look younger.[13]

The Chinese look to Westerners to bring fashion inspiration, and I believe they were deeply disappointed in me. Instead of high heels and sequinned miniskirts, I wore jeans and sweaters. To the chagrin of my new friends, my favourite clothing colour was navy blue. Only my skirt and jacket suit, made from a glossy synthetic fabric in bright emerald green, won their approval.

Although China has 130 dressmaking research organisations[14] and several fashion designers, as well as fashion colleges and even schools which train catwalk models, fashionable Chinese clothes still look like unsuccessful attempts at copying Western clothes.

One element of Western fashion does not seem to be popular in China, the off-the-shoulder dress. Cleavage is also taboo. But the Chinese don't hesitate to wear extremely short skirts barely covering the buttocks.

The Chinese buy their clothes in department stores or in street markets, or they have them made by tailors. Chinese tailors – many of them women who have taken up tailoring as an independent business – are skilled at copying clothes. If a woman possesses a particularly stunning Western-style dress or blouse, her friends may ask to borrow it and take it to a tailor to have it copied.

There is a minor trend towards rediscovering traditional Chinese clothes, such as the *qipao*, a long, tight dress, and silk brocade jackets. However, these are not as popular as 'Western' style clothes. This may be partly because the authentic material, silk, is beyond what most Chinese can afford. Another possible reason is that the *qipao* is a garment which was designed for the idle, quiet, graceful Chinese lady of an earlier period. It limits a woman's movements to tiny, graceful steps and minute arm movements, so a woman who wants to stride, run, work or dance will not wear a *qipao*.

Most people keep their Mao jacket in the cupboard and bring it out for political meetings. 'To show that I'm still a worker at heart,' as a secretary told me. However, agricultural workers and manual labourers still use the Mao suit because it is practical. Its great advantage, that of making women and men look equal by giving them equal freedom of movement in identical dress, has been forgotten.

Fabric: glossy drip-dry synthetics are the trend

Cotton, the most practical clothing material especially for the hotter climates of China, was rationed during most the communist period, because the national supply could not meet the demand.[15]

Today, most Chinese despise cotton. I gained the impression that there was a deliberate campaign to damage the image of cotton. Connie, a 19-year-old student from Tonghua, was ashamed of wearing a patterned cotton jacket: 'It's very poor material. All the other students have jackets which are made from better fabric. Synthetics are far superior to cotton.'[16]

Synthetics such as nylon or acrylic are popular for everything: clothes, bedspreads, pillowcases and curtains. To the Chinese the advantages of synthetics are that they are have a glossy shine, that they can drip-dry (few own an iron) and that they are fashionable.

Silk, a traditional fabric, is far too expensive for outer-wear for most Chinese. It is sold mostly in city hotels frequented by tourists. However, silk underwear is also available in northern towns, where several layers of silk are essential insulation against the cold.

Wearing brand labels on the sleeves: men's fashions

It is not only the women who have discovered fashion, men seem to have benefited from (or become victims of, depending on your viewpoint) fashion to the same extent. It is 'in' to wear a Western suit on every occasion. Chinese men can be seen climbing mountains, planting trees and repairing motor vehicles wearing Western suits – and white trainers. A suit is a status symbol. The label with the brand, designer name and material is not sewn discreetly beneath the collar, but on the outside of the right sleeve, for everyone to see and envy. And the main accessory for men is a pair of sunglasses: I met several Chinese men who would rather have limited sight through their new sunglasses than remove the prestigious sticker 'Made in America' from the lens.

Decadent but desirable: accessories and make-up

Jewellery is still uncommon – a little fake gold brooch here, some elaborate garnishment for the hair there, and of course, the wedding ring with a double rhombus which shows that a woman has found a husband and thus achieved a higher social status.

Perfumes, for many years a symbol of Western decadence, are just becoming popular. They tend to be very sweet and still unaffordable for most.

Make-up is changing gradually from something despicable to something highly desirable. In 1994, it was already considered all right in Beijing and Shanghai for women to wear lipstick for special occasions, whereas in the countryside, it was still an absolute taboo. In provincial towns like Tonghua, it was considered taboo for women under 25, except for special occasions or unless, as I have said, they worked as secretaries in a glamorous job which demands a 'modern' look. Once that magic age is achieved, they apply make-up in thick layers and bold colours. My Chinese friends did not see a contradiction in young made-up women being considered sluttish but more mature made-up women being respectable. A nurse told me how she made her 25th birthday a special occasion: 'I bought the brightest pink lipstick I could find!'[17]

In 1995, Tonghua had already embraced the idea of make-up for younger women for special occasions. Twenty-one-year-old Jiao Hongyan says:

> I have worn make-up only once. There was a discussion meeting held at the college. Three of us represented the English department. We wore the same colour clothes and looked very smart. I wore make-up not for myself, but for our department's fame. I had to look good to bring the department honour, so I used make-up. Only that one time.

(Doing it for the 'department's fame' is, for the Chinese way of thinking, an acceptable justification if there are any moral qualms or parental objections.)

Nineteen-year-old Lin Yanmei says: 'Yes, I wear make-up when I'm very happy and excited for a special occasion. For example, when I attend a party, especially a dancing party.'[18]

As women are not used to wearing make-up and choosing colours to suit their complexion, the result often appears clumsy and unflattering.

Hairstyles: from plaits to perms

Hairstyles, too, are being updated. During the Cultural Revolution, women had the choice between 'short' and 'two plaits'. Today, money is the only restriction. Those who can afford it wear their hair permed and asymmetrically cut, shoulder-length on the left, chin-length on the right, with a parting on the left, and experiment with henna or hair-dye. Blonde or red hair is considered the ultimate in fashion and beauty. In the countryside, where perms are too luxurious to even dream about, women create the asymmetrical look with little braids and plaits. These are often traditional styles which have been revived.

The Miao in central China are known for their elaborate hairstyles, which, like the costumes, vary from region to region. Hair is swept into buns and knots of various sizes and shapes, or arranged in huge structures supported with extra hair or pieces of wood. At Puding and Liuzhi, a lot of hair from dead female ancestors is wound around two wooden horns, over which the woman brushes her own hair. Girls begin to arrange their hair when they are six or seven years old. As young teenagers, they pay great attention to the style that is individual for their group. Married women of one Miao group shave off their hair. Many Miao women pluck the hair from above the forehead to achieve a 'high brow' look which is considered particularly beautiful.[19]

In the northeast, I observed many women wearing their hair in buns in a complex pattern of thin plaits. It was only when I asked one of them how they achieved this complicated pattern that she told me, giggling, that she had bought an accessory of artificial hair already made up.

When my colleague Liang from the accounts department heard about my interest in local hairstyles, she invited me to spend my *xiuxi* (break) in her office. With a comb, some rubber bands and red ribbon she created a plaited look. This was much simpler than the ones I had seen, consisting of plaits from one side of the head to the other, constantly adding more strands. It was a practical and comfortable style to wear.

Liang, delighted with my compliments, invited me to have my hair styled once a week. I was the first foreigner she had ever met, and she kept whispering 'golden hair, golden hair'. I was proud of my 'authentic' hairstyle and wore it for many weeks, until my editorial colleague, Joy, confessed that it wasn't a woman's hairstyle at all. 'It's how little girls wear their hair. Miss Liang thinks you are her baby.'[20]

To the Chinese, blonde hair is an incredible phenomenon. It was as if I had gold threads growing on my head. Even in the market, some Chinese women approached me and asked shyly if they could touch my hair. Others sneaked behind me, had a quick pull to convince themselves that the hair was real, and ran away. One old Chinese woman offered to act as a matchmaker for me: 'I can find a good husband for you. You have golden hair. Your hair is so precious, it makes you almost beautiful. With hair like this, it doesn't matter that you have an ugly big nose.'

Hairdressers in China have their own methods. The one I visited used a lot of shampoo and very little water. He spent a long time scratching my scalp with long hard fingernails, and hitting my neck in karate-style strokes, while my Chinese friends used his combs and scissors to do their own hairstyling in the shop. I was the first foreign client and he declared to the assembly of curious Chinese that my golden hair wasn't so special after all. 'Western hair is hard and doesn't feel nice,' he concluded. I noticed that the hair of all my Chinese friends was always well-cared for, soft, glossy and healthy-looking.[21]

New beauty ideals: cosmetic surgery and padded bras

The traditional image of a beautiful woman was a delicate, petite creature with white skin, a small nose, small hands and and small feet. This has been replaced by what is perceived to be 'Western' beauty: European eyes, blonde hair and big breasts. Posters and advertisements show blonde Western women, or Chinese women with Western features. These 'Western' faces are often the result of cosmetic surgery. I met several women in the cities who said they would have cosmetic surgery if only they could afford it. Most of them dreamt of 'Western' eyes, and some desired 'Western' noses and breast enlargements as well. Many women try to make their breasts look larger. Department stores sell lacy bras, heavily padded to give the look of Western-size breasts.

However, the Chinese have preserved their own preference for white skin. Rather than acquire a Western-style tan, they carry large umbrellas with them which they use as parasols to keep the sun from their skin.

Slimming is becoming more and more important. A product called Guo's Totally Nutritious Slimming Extract is heavily advertised in newspapers and magazines as 'a completely New Concept of Scientifically Reducing Fat'.[22]

Schools of etiquette have sprung up, teaching a mix of old Chinese and new Western codes of behaviour, combined with what the principals fancy as being attractively female. At the Beijing Etiquette Special Training College, for example, where courses last between ten days and two years, students must bow to their teachers when meeting them and women must wear skirts to class except in the coldest weather. Most students are female high school graduates. They learn 'feminine' skills such as how to make up and how to smile for two hours without saying a word. College president Li Ning initially selected students according to looks and height, accepting only attractive people, but she had to give in to protests from the municipal government.[23]

All these trends would have been completely unthinkable ten years ago. It did not occur to any of the women I talked to – neither in the cities nor in the countryside – that by embracing fashion to such a large extent they were making themselves slaves of fashion and objects of beauty, thus losing out on equality and individuality.

The right to be beautiful seemed more important than the right to be equal.

A few women admitted that fashion could make women 'materialistic and greedy', and that this could 'damage their character'.[24]

Fashion victims of the future?

Chinese women's wear changed from the elegant, feminine and unpractical *qipao* to the practical, unflattering unisex uniform of the Mao suit. Today, women can wear what they want and are attracted by Western fashions, bright colours and elaborate trimmings. In a few years, all Chinese will wear Western fashions, even if these are far less practical than the sturdy Mao suit.

Beauty and clothes are top priority with most Chinese women. They prefer 'fashionable' or 'beautiful' clothes to comfortable and practical clothes. They will gladly accept considerable discomfort in order to achieve a fashionable look.

There is no doubt that, because of the enormous interest of Chinese women in clothing and fashion, there will be a rapid development, and it seems likely that one or the other of the young Chinese designers will make their mark on the international fashion scene. I expect that fashion will become one of the main industries in China. Both nationally produced garments and foreign imports will boom, and Chinese women will spend a large part of their income on fashionable clothes, accessories and cosmetics.

The influence from the West seems to succeed where the Cultural Revolution failed in eradicating the ethnic dress of the minorities. The Chinese government tries to counteract this, by praising the colourful outfits, by showing them in newspapers and magazines, by encouraging the minorities to wear their outfits at national meetings and festivals and be proud of them. Ethnic clothing will probably survive as 'special occasions' dress and tourist attraction.

Within the next few years, perfume and make-up will lose their taboo, and women of all age groups will wear them if they choose to.

9 Leisure pursuits

Time use: women work more than men

The average urban woman spends her day like this: 7 hours and 3 minutes paid work, 37 minutes travel to and from work, 1 hour 28 minutes cooking, 45 minutes washing, 1 hour 32 minutes doing other housework, 38 minutes shopping, 33 minutes studying, 1 hour 40 minutes watching television, 7 hours 46 minutes sleeping, and 2 hours 37 minutes pursuing other activities such as hobbies.

Her rural counterpart has only 5 hours 46 minutes paid work and 26 minutes travel to and from work. But she spends more time cooking (1 hour 56 minutes), washing (51 minutes), and doing other housework (2 hours 3 minutes). This could be because rural families often have two or more children. She uses 11 minutes for studying, 1 hour 5 minutes for watching television, 8 hours 13 minutes sleeping, and 2 hours 27 minutes for other activities such as hobbies.

Not surprisingly, men spend a little more time in paid work, do far less cooking, washing and other housework, but find a more time for studying, watching TV and hobbies.

This information stems from a survey conducted in September 1990, and it covers the activities and time spent on the day before the survey, which was a weekday and it was not a particularly busy season for the rural respondents.[1]

I think this survey is useful as a general indicator of how the Chinese spend their days, but I doubt that it is really representative or gives the correct picture. Firstly, for some groups of respondents the time spent on all activities does not equal 24 hours, due to an admitted error in the survey. Secondly, there are not as many television sets as the Chinese government likes to believe. Many of my Chinese friends, even from urban areas, had never watched television, so I doubt that the respondents represented a typical sample. Thirdly, the working women among my friends had far

149

less spare time than the women in the survey. Their leisure consisted of watching television (if they had one) while they peeled potatoes, of supervising their daughters' homework and of occasional visits to relatives for a shared meal. Fourthly, this was an official survey and the respondents would have given the politically correct answers. I suspect that the women exaggerated the amount of time they spent studying, and the men the amount of time they helped with cooking, washing and housework.

The same survey concludes that women spend about 4 hours each day on housework, twice the time spent by men, and that women spend 1.2 hours each day more than men on paid work and housework combined. This gives over an hour more leisure time daily to the men. Again, I believe that in reality the difference is much greater than the respondents would have admitted when questioned officially.

Slow movements and quiet occupation

The Chinese, especially the women, prefer quiet leisure pursuits: playing chess or mahjongg, collecting stamps, making papercuts or folding paper, embroidery, calligraphy, painting, reading, gentle noiseless exercises, or simply hanging a birdcage on a good tree, sitting near it and listening to the bird song. Retired people like to take their caged bird to the teahouse, and I have seen several female market vendors who placed a birdcage on their stall to enjoy a bird song during their working day.

Angling is the latest craze. According to the China Anglers' Association, there are about 90 million people in China (women as well as men) who have taken up the sport because they enjoy the quiet and the number is growing.[2]

The ideal of slow movements and quiet occupation has existed throughout many centuries and applies to women much more than to men. The Chinese do enjoy loud noise with music and fireworks, but they limit it to special occasions, such as a one-off dance party, a festival or a wedding.

Comparatively new hobbies which have been taken up with great enthusiasm by those who can afford them are going to the cinema and photography. They also like going to scenic spots to have a picnic with friends or family.

Controlled leisure

Whenever I asked young women in the presence of parents, relatives, older friends, teachers or officials about their hobbies, they would say virtuously that they spend most of their free time studying. Studying is encouraged and praised by teachers, parents and society to an extent that it limits pupils and students in their freedom.

As I have pointed out, at Tonghua Teachers' College, students are not allowed to practise any hobbies in their bedrooms. Every minute is precious and must not be wasted on frivolous activities.

Wang Shulan (a pseudonym), an English student at the college, told me:

> Of course we do knit and we play mahjongg in our bedroom, although we are not allowed to. Sometimes they (the teachers) come and check on us, but then we hide our knitting quickly. We may get punished or fined but usually they just scold us. They don't check very often. If you come and play mahjongg with us and they discover us we can say that we are doing this to practise oral English, then they will not punish us. I very much like reading novels and magazines. If I can borrow English books from the library, or if you give me English novels and magazines to read, I can say that this is for studying. But I am not allowed to read Chinese novels. It makes me unhappy that in my bedroom I cannot do anything I enjoy doing except study. There is nowhere at the college for us to have fun, and we cannot afford to go elsewhere. They don't want us to have fun. They want us to study.[3]

Sports activities and games on the other hand are encouraged. Students often gather in groups to play ball games or badminton. There is also a tennis court and a site for netball and tennis. But the harsh cold climate, with minus zero temperatures from early October to April, strong wind carrying sand and dust in spring and heavy rainfalls in summer make the opportunities for games rare. The climate and regulations differ from province to province, and from college to college, but Tonghua Teachers' College can be regarded as a typical case.

After I promised the students that the results of my survey would not be shown to the college or university, students in Tonghua and Beijing described what they liked doing when they were supposed to be studying:

> I like listening to pop music and reading romantic novels. I enjoy talking with friends but I have no real close friend at college. Singing. I don't like sports. I often go to the reading room to read newspapers. I visit my uncle to eat a good meal. (Li Guoyou, 23)

> Painting, reading, sleeping, shopping, going out for a walk after a meal. Visiting foreign teachers. (Xiao Wenjun, 21)

> My main hobby is reading novels. I have read a lot of novels both foreign and Chinese. And I also like playing table-tennis and basketball. I'm interested in dancing, too. (Lin Yanmei, 19)

> Reading, dancing, eating, to be with knowledgeable persons (Jin Xuelian, 19)

Most male students of the same age group mentioned sports, stamp collecting and reading martial arts novels.[4]

Martial arts and sports

Sports are encouraged as an activity for the masses and carried out at schools, universities, work units and the armed forces. It is estimated that 300 million people participate in sports activities. In 1994, 104.36 million people met the physical training standards set by the state. Schools at all levels have full-time physical education teachers and provide sports facilities. Students who don't meet the physical education standards requested by the state are not allowed to enter higher education.[5]

Twice a year, schools and colleges hold sports meetings at which departments or individual students compete with each other for one or several days. Every four years, there are national high school games and national college games sports competitions. Promising students are sent to regular training at special sports schools in their spare time to prepare them for competitive sports events. From kindergarten to university, most educational institutions follow a compulsive programme of daily exercises, as I have outlined in Chapter 2. Pingpong is popular at primary schools.

But the popularity of sports at educational institutions is decreasing. *China Daily* mentions a survey by the Public Opinion Research Institute of the People's University, which indicates that half of the Chinese university students take no exercise at all. Many enjoy watching sports, but they don't practise it. Ball games are still popular on campuses, but running and calisthenics are ignored by students. The number of students taking daily exercise has been shrinking steadily over the last years, by 30 per cent in 1995 alone. According to the survey, women students exercise even less than their male counterparts.[6]

Employers are asked to give clerical staff and manual labourers a 15-minute break both in the morning and in the afternoon to do supervised exercises or attend other sporting activities. Government offices and large work units observe this rule and everyone gathers in the courtyard or in another suitable place. A large organization may offer a choice of exercises; small new enterprises often ignore the workers' right to exercise. The publishing house for which I was working and which had 40 staff did not provide such exercises. However, the publisher provided two badminton sets, and on the rare occasions when it was warm, sunny but not windy, he ushered us outside. Everyone played for a few minutes while colleagues looked on.

For older and retired people, similar exercise classes are held daily or weekly in parks. They may be run by the authorities or by the work units with whom they were employed before retirement. Others are held as informal exercise meetings and anyone can join in. In the early morning particularly, women and men are seen exercising in parks and other open spaces. In many cities, there is a choice of sporting activities, such as *taijiquan*, *wushu*, folk dancing, sword dance and *qigong*, or a combination of these. *Wushu* is a martial art exercise, based on self-defence movements, very popular among women and men. There are several variations of set exercises, with or without weapons. *Taijiquan* is 'shadow-boxing', with movements also based on the idea of self-defence and exercise which combines body, mind and *qi* (energy). Movements are gentle, graceful and firm. There are several forms of these set exercises, some of them using swords, and there are several different spellings. In the West, this exercise form is often known as Tai Chi Chuan. *Qigong* is a breathing and fitness exercise which aims at controlling the mind and regulating breathing to keep alert. The Chinese believe that it helps strengthen the body, overcome illness and prolong life. Women and men exercise in mixed groups, wearing everyday clothing.

In areas inhabited by minority groups, traditional forms of exercise and sports are encouraged, such as wrestling and horsemanship in Inner Mongolia, or crossbow for the Miao. These events sometimes serve as entertainment for an audience or as a competition for participants.

China is also considered to be a significant and up-and-coming women's football nation. China hosted the FIFA world championship for women in 1988, and China's women's football team came fourth at the World Championships in Sweden in 1995.[7] They were also runners-up in the inaugural women's football competition in Atlanta in 1996 and were beaten by the US team in the final. However, most Chinese regard football as a men's sport, for male players and male spectators. The women's footall team, despite its success, doesn't seem to count. An article in *China Pictorial*, entitled 'Hurray for Chinese Football', begins with 'There is no world-class football team in China ...'. Instead, it paints the picture of football fans who get so carried away by enthusiasm that they neglect their families, resulting as the same 'football widow' syndrome as in the West. It cites the example of Lui Xi from the Liaoning Province, who made a pledge that he would not marry until the China National Football Team had won a victory in Asia. His fiancée apparently persuaded him to break this football pledge, but after their marriage she found that he devoted all his affection to football rather than to his wife: she divorced him.[8]

Dancing

Dancing is an extremely popular pastime. Considered an important sports discipline, it features in school and college sports competitions.

On festival days and bank holidays, villagers or groups of townspeople dance up and down the streets, in parks and squares. These folk dances are based on peasant traditions and court dances; most of them are procession dances based on a pattern of four steps. Many groups also dance on Sundays in parks, simply as a keep fit exercise and for fun. Some of these dance meetings are open for everyone to join, others are organized by specific groups. In Tonghua, for example, the Retired Railway Workers'

Organization meets on Sunday mornings for folk dances in the town's park.

Although traditionally these dances have been performed by men and women alike, and are still performed by mixed groups, today most of the folk dancers are women. Young people scorn the traditional dances.

There are many regional dances and each ethnic group has its own dances. Most of them involve the use of 'props', usually items taken from everyday life, such as straw hats, chopsticks and lanterns.

The Han majority perform a ribbon dance which is a traditional thanksgiving dance. A brighty coloured 'ribbon', usually red, about 50cm wide and up to 10 metres long, is knotted around the waist, with one end held in each hand; however there are regional variations. Movements are large, lively and energetic. The ribbon dance is always a group dance, and the larger the group, the better the effect. They are performed with music reminiscent of German marching music, with a strong rhythm and a repetitive tune.

More delicate music is used for the Manchurian double-fan dance, which used to be a courtly dance with graceful, teasing, flirtatious movements. It is a communicative dance and every movement conveys a mood or a message. It can be danced solo or with group choreography with each dancer holding two large silk fans. Pupils learn it at kindergarten or primary school; older students usually loathe it, but still have to perform it at school events. Today, it is almost only women who perform the fan dance.

During festivals, dragon and lion dances (where several people get together to form the body of the animal) are spectacular attractions for audiences. Other folk dances include chopstick, parasol and handkerchief dances. In the Xinjiang and Ningxia areas, folk dances resemble Arabic belly dances with accentuated hip lifts and shoulder shimmies.

Some folk dances are mostly or exclusively for women: the Tujia and the Bouyei have weaving dances; Dai girls learn a peacock dance from early childhood and Uygur girls have a hand-drum dance.

Others, such as the Axitiaoyue dance of the Yi, the Duoye dance and reed-pipe dance of the Dong are danced by men and women, especially by young people, and are regarded as an opportunity to meet the opposite sex.

Young people – women and men equally – in urban areas are drawn to 'modern Western' dances, meaning ballroom dances. They adore the tango, foxtrot, waltz and chacha, and place great importance on executing every step correctly. Many colleges or universities hold a ballroom dance party once a year or more. People who are wealthy enough to own a television set spend several hours per week watching programmes with ballroom dance competitions or instructions.

Supplementing the family income with crafts

Crafts, especially paper and textile crafts, have always been considered suitable leisure occupations for women. However, a fine line was drawn between 'professional' and 'folk' arts and crafts. Professional craftsmen passed on their skills only to their sons, and never revealed techniques to their daughters, because these would marry and take the secrets with them. Women were not allowed to join crafts guilds. However, they could embroider and weave at home, and received payment for this from the local (men-owned) workshops.

Folk art was a different matter. Peasant women engaged in folk arts and crafts, such as making ceramics, weaving baskets, embroidery, papercuts, batik, paper lanterns, painting umbrellas and so on during the months when there was not much agricultural work to do. A girl's skill in a traditional craft enhanced (and still enhances today!) her marriage prospects.[9]

In towns and cities, women practise crafts as hobbies, but among the rural women crafts are either their main occupation or a sideline which helps increase the family income, or at least supplies the family's food. Bai and Miao women specialize in embroidery and batik techniques, Zhuang women in weaving brocade.

Making flowers and animals from folded paper – a technique related to Japanese origami – is a popular pastime, especially as paper is affordable for almost everyone. Family units produce colourful paper lanterns, especially for the spring festival period. Papercuts demand nimble fingers and are considered a hobby mostly for women. They are often made within the family unit and given to friends and neighbours. Some women create individual, artistic designs, but most use traditional techniques and motifs: dragons, birds, flowers or people. The tradition goes back to at least the fifth century AD. These were used as an inexpensive way to adorn homes during seasonal festivals and family celebrations, and papercuts depicting butterflies and birds often adorned the high hairstyles of noble ladies.[10] The artist may use scissors, knives, stencils or scalpels. The papercutting technique is often combined with paperfolding and painting to create works of art.

Papercuts remained popular throughout Chinese history, although the motif changed. During the Cultural Revolution, revolutionary images were encouraged. Typical papercuts surviving from this period include a proud peasant woman driving a small modern tractor (Guangdong Province, 1970) and the happy end from the approved revolutionary story, *Little Sisters of the Grasslands*, showing two girls riding home after their struggles, with the sun of the communist party shining radiantly behind them (Beijing, 1974 or 1975).[11]

In some rural areas, papercuts made by the daughters of the family are displayed in the window, to demonstrate the girls' skill and industry and attract offers for marriage. The women and children of many families still make papercuts with good luck symbols to celebrate the spring festival.

Within the context of arts and crafts, women can be creative, but most of the patterns and designs are handed down from mother to daughter, just as fathers pass their skills on to their sons. Motifs are used frequently by women for embroidery, papercuts and painting, the most popular of which is the dragon, which brings good luck, postive transformation, power and wisdom. Others include the crane, the phoenix, the fish, the peach, the peach blossom, the lotus, the chrysanthemum, the peony and the pomegranate.[12]

The media

There are many national and local newspapers in China. Most of them are published in Mandarin Chinese. The largest dailies are *People's Daily* (the official organ of the communist party), *Guangming Daily* (which reports mostly on science, art and education), *Liberation Army Daily* (the organ of the Central Military Commission), *Daily Economic News* (specializing in economic construction), *Workers' Daily, Chinese Women's News, Chinese Childrens' News, China Legal System,* and *Peasants' Daily*. Also in

Mandarin are a number of women's magazines, which are mostly fashion-led, and what appears to be a growing number of men's magazines with pornographic images of women on the cover which started being sold openly in the early 1990s.

Educational newspapers and magazines which supplement students' learning materials are on the increase. I worked for one of four publishing houses specializing in newspapers and magazines which help students of the English language, mostly by providing exercises, texts and simulated examinations.

A variety of English language publications are aimed at foreigners in China, but also at wealthy or educated Chinese for whom it is a status symbol to be seen reading an English language paper. These include *Women of China* (a colourful monthly A4-size magazine with interviews of interesting or successful individual women which was first published in 1956 but was forced to stop publication during the Cultural Revolution), *China Pictorial* (another A-4 size monthly which looks mostly at customs, traditions and tourist interest) and *Beijing Review* (a weekly which, despite its title, doesn't have a special focus on the capital but reports increasingly on matters of economy and business).

Most families can afford to subscribe to one or two publications, except in the very poor minority areas. All newspapers and magazines are ultimately controlled by the government. They can carry critical articles, but only when the government has acknowledged the existence of a problem. Surprisingly, when this is the case, articles can be surprisingly frank.

But in delicate matters, journalists tread very carefully. Some articles are phrased with so much care, emphasizing that the information was derived from state minister so-and-so, that one has to read between the lines for the journalist's unspoken different view. This was particularly the case with any article about Tibet and the Dalai Lama. As Tibet is a touchy subject, none of my Chinese friends wanted to discuss the possible hidden meanings of such articles.

News articles about Tibet compare, for example, how people used to die in the cold winter of 1956 (before the Chinese occupation), and how competently the Chinese government helps in similar situations. Tibetans are quoted as saying that they 'were taken as no better than cattle or sheep when the Dalai Lama ruled Tibet'.[13] Occasionally articles reveal recent discoveries about alleged atrocities committed in Tibet's pre-occupation past. A *China Daily* article in April 1996 refers to a request for 'a set of intestines, two heads, bowls of blood and a complete human skin' to celebrate the Dalai Lama's birthday, and to a common habit of using parts of human bodies for their religious activities 'before the region was peacefully liberated'. (Please note: the article does not give full details about who made this strange request and in which function! The impression the article wants to give is obviously that the request was made with the approval of the Dalai Lama, but it could have been a lunatic acting on his own initiative.) The article continues by saying that findings in archives show that 'slave trading was rampant' in pre-Liberation days.[14] Taking these articles at their face value, the reader will conclude that life in independent Tibet was sheer misery, whereas today they have nothing to worry about. *China Daily* quoted a Tibetan who said his only worry was now the occasional power failures which mean he can't always use an electric mixer to make the traditional buttered tea.[15] I get the impression that most of these reports and quotes are truthful (that is, they don't tell direct lies), but reflect a small, careful selection of incidents while hiding the rest of the overall picture, and sometimes deliberately manipulate the reader by witholding details. Naturally, the reporters would only quote Tibetans who are happier now than they were before the occupation – just as Western reporters seem to quote only the victims, for example the nuns, and never the people who benefited from the change, such as the peasant women who gained access to education.

I would not be surprised if in a decade or two the Chinese government was ready to admit much of the violence and cruelty involved in the occupation of Tibet, just as it is currently admitting many of the atrocities committed during the Cultural Revolution. When this change of strategy occurs, the newspapers will publish the life stories of brave old Tibetan nuns who survived injustice and abuse in the 1950s, just as they currently publicize the life stories of brave old intellectuals who survived injustice and abuse in the early 1970s.

Other examples where the Western media show predominantly one point of view and the Chinese media exclusively the other are, of course, the Tian-An-Men student rebellion in 1989, orphanages and conditions in prisons. Again, the newspapers choose only interviewees and material which serve to support the current official line. In 20 years, the Tian-An-Men students may be celebrated by the media as heroes and role models.

In the Chinese press, foreign news is almost always about kidnappings, bombs, terrorist attacks, hijacked aircraft, exposed corruption, war and starvation. The only positive news about foreign countries is the signing of trade agreements with China and very occasionally the results of a major sports event.

News about China, on the other hand, consists of 99 per cent success stories, and only about 1 per cent reports about officially acknowledged problems such as illiteracy in minority areas. The uninformed reader will inevitably get the impression that she's lucky to live in China where living standards increase all the time, where the government cares for the needy and where most people are kind-hearted, instead of in the dangerous and corrupt West.

Books, poems, short story and essay anthologies are sold in bookstores at comparatively low prices. Chinese literature can be very critical. Acknowledged writers are expected to expose weaknesses and abuse as long as they don't criticize individuals. Many short stories are about bribery, corruption, greed and so on, showing the major problems of Chinese society. But they use fictional characters, and there is always a 'good' government official who is more powerful than the 'bad' official, who comes to the hero's or heroine's aid and puts matters right. The emphasis of modern Chinese fiction is on realism, but with happy endings.

Foreign literature, available in the original languages or in Chinese translations, is still limited. While most modern literature is considered suspect, most of the classics are considered acceptable and the Chinese are encouraged to read the works of writers such as Charles Dickens and Mark Twain, who are supposed to represent the case of the proletariat.

The Chinese enjoy watching television, partly because owning a TV set is a status symbol (they will usually place it in the centre of the room for everyone to see and admire), partly because watching TV is an easy way to relax. Only the richest among my friends owned a TV, but every family aspired to have one within the next few years. A few college students wanted to make friends with me specifically to have access to the TV in my flat. The most popular programmes are historical costume dramas (*The Last Emperor* was serialized and everyone loved it), dating and matchmaking programmes and instructions in ballroom dancing. There are a lot of educational programmes, for example English language lessons. It is possible to get foreign channels, but this is frowned upon (except, of course, for the purpose of learning the foreign language).

Radio seems to have lost the importance it used to have. In the early 1980s, it had been everybody's dream to possess a shortwave radio, but this has been replaced by the TV. I believe that the radio plays a more important role in the daily lives of country people than of urban people.

Free time – an opportunity to show off status symbols

Exercise breaks during work time are becoming rarer and may soon be abolished in many work units or cut down to a few token minutes. On the other hand, the Chinese are now working only five days a week, which gives them more leisure time. However, women, who carry more than their husbands of the double burden of paid work and housework, are having less spare time than the men.

Many are having increasing amounts of money available to spend on hobbies and leisure interests; much of this will go towards fashion and beauty. It seems likely that the tendency for leisure pursuits will be the same as with fashion, in that they both follow Western examples. Western dances are already more popular than Chinese dances, and other 'Western' leisure facilities such as cinemas with Western movies are much in demand. Hobbies will, at least among the young people, become more noisy and already, discotheques are popular in the cities.

I believe that many women will not regard their newly-gained 'free time' as an opportunity to do what they really enjoy, but as an opportunity to show off their wealth and display status symbols. Traditional, low-cost hobbies such as papercutting will lose out to Western, expensive leisure pursuits such as camcorder filming, skiing, collecting music CDs.

Papercutting, embroidery and other traditional women's hobbies will survive in the countryside, where women produce crafts items in their spare time for sale as tourist souvenirs to supplement the family income. Many 'nouveau riche' women will also dedicate themselves to these traditional feminine pastimes to demonstrate that they don't have to go out to work and can afford stay at home in leisure. I expect these women will be particularly attracted to those traditional crafts for which they can use expensive materials – silk embroidery for example – to enhance their value as a status symbol.

10 Praying to Mao – religion and politics

Religious beliefs

Religion is the most difficult Chinese topic to research, because until the late 1970s it was forbidden and it is still frowned upon. Most Chinese people are embarrassed to admit to any religious belief at all, and official sources are not forthcoming with facts and figures. Indeed, this was the only subject on which the Chinese Embassy in London, otherwise generous with information, ignored my requests for data. Western sources were out of date, vague, and could not contribute substantially to the relationship between women and religion.

Over the centuries, China has embraced religious infusions from other countries, such as Christianity and Islam. The basis for Chinese faith has always been ancestor worship. Taoism, Buddhism and the teachings of Confucius especially have become so interwoven and have borrowed from each other so extensively that it is difficult to know where one belief ends and another one begins. Marxism-Leninism, together with the teachings of Mao Zedong and Deng Xiaoping, have a role similar to that of religion, to the extent that people have little private shrines dedicated to Mao (who would certainly be horrified at the thought).

During the period of the Cultural Revolution, foreign beliefs were regarded as alien, not in line with communism and therefore to be rooted out. All religions were persecuted. Tens of thousands of people were killed because of their religious beliefs and temples, mosques and churches were destroyed. Today, religious worship is tolerated and many of the old sacred places have been rebuilt.

For example, Guiyang, the capital of the Guizhou province, with a population of 1 million from 14 different ethnic groups, has three publicly used religious buildings. The Guiyang Christian Church was originally established by the China Inland Mission. It was rebuilt in 1982, and is attended every Sunday by about 1,000 people. Another 1,000 people go regularly to the Catholic church, which was reopened after the end of the Cultural Revolution in 1976 and which looks from the outside like a traditional Chinese temple. There is also a well-restored Buddhist temple where an active community meets regularly to study Buddhist texts.[1]

Officially, there are about 100 million followers of Taoism, Buddhism, Islam and Christianity. Ethnic groups have their own religious preferences. For example, among the Han majority, Buddhism, Protestantism, Catholicism and Taoism are popular. Many Tibetans, Mongolians, Lhoba, Moinba, Tu and Yugur are Lamaists. Bland, Dai and Deang people tend to be Hinayana Buddhists. The Bonan, Dongxiang, Hui, Kirgiz, Tatar, Kazak, Ozbek, Tajik and Salar mostly follow Islam.[2]

Limited religious freedom

The Chinese constitution guarantees freedom of religious belief and all normal religious activities are protected. The interpretation of what is 'normal' may vary. It seems that the Chinese are free to worship individually or in groups, but preaching and attempts to convert others may meet with obstacles.

The state has established official Buddhist, Islamic, Catholic, Protestant and Taoist organizations which are 'not subject to the direction of foreign powers'.[3] This means that as long as the believers support the state, the state supports them. Magazines such as *Beijing Review* publish illustrated reports from time to time, showing followers of the various religions at their 'independent' worship. They are widely shielded from influences of the international religious communities.

The State Religious Affairs Bureau controls all religious matters, to the extent of appointing Christian bishops and organizing the search for its own eleventh Panchen Lama in accordance with rituals of Tibetan Buddhism and historical convention. The six-year-old living Buddha was confirmed and approved by the central government of China.[4] The State Religious Affairs Bureau also promotes the official religious statements and decisions, and opposes decisions and criticisms from the outside.

Newspapers and magazines report on religious matters, but they stick strictly to non-controversial subjects, usually describing a picturesque ritual without explaining its significance. For example, on 8 April 1996, *China Daily* showed a photo on its front page, with the bishop of the Beijing Catholic diocese offering the Lord's Supper on Easter Sunday in the Xishiku Catholic Cathedral. The caption mentions that nearly 20,000 believers attended Catholic churches in and around Beijing.[5] The picture and caption were typical in their safe approach, a mere token of acceptance of religion, neither praising nor condemning the Catholic faith and its followers. But although it is nothing but a token, it has significance because it signals to other Christians that it is politically safe and socially acceptable to practise their faith these days.

Outside the big cities few religious buildings exist. Members of religious communities meet in each other's houses but these house church communities are small.

I found that my Chinese friends were more hesitant talking about religion than about any other subject. While they had trust in me to talk about such delicate matters as Mao's political errors and premarital sex, religion remained taboo. One problem was language: words such as 'religion' or 'God' are simply not taught in English.

When I brought up the subject, the Chinese were evasive, and seemed to look around carefully to make sure the discussion was not overheard. I got the impression that it takes courage to confess to a religious belief, but not as much courage as it took a few years ago.

Xiao Wenjun, a student from the Jilin Province, said: 'Now there is the freedom to believe in anything you like. Before, people were not permitted to believe. Eight years ago, I didn't know anyone who believed, or belonged to a religious group. Now I know many who say so openly. Most of them are Buddhists. More and more people are also becoming Christians.'[6] But despite my repeated requests, nobody came forward. They all 'knew someone who knew someone' and promised to introduce me but never did.

It was shortly before my departure that Shu Li (a pseudonym), a relative of one of my Chinese friends, admitted to being a Catholic Christian, shedding light on the situation.

> If you come and join our church, the government will send people to spy on us. If there is a foreigner in our midst we may lose what little freedom we have. They want to shield the Chinese churches from foreign influences and opinions. As long as we just worship and don't try to

convert, the party officials don't bother us. But when we try to spread the word of God, they make life uncomfortable. They have the power. It is difficult for us to get enough religious literature, even bibles, in the Chinese language. The state-owned printing factories won't produce them, the bookshops won't sell them, and we would not get permission to print and distribute them ourselves.[7]

I cannot judge how much of her fear is based on fact, and how much on her own perception of the situation. It is possible that believers still have a deep fear ingrained from earlier periods of persecution and that they would rather play safe than lose their newly-gained, precious but limited freedom.

A British woman who stayed in another town in the Jilin Province at the same time as me, told me she had been actively welcomed by the local Christian community and joined their worship regularly. If these Christians had the same fears of repercussions as a result of sharing worship with a foreigner, they did not admit it.

There seems to be no problem if foreigners wish to attend church services in cities which have a high number of foreign residents and where there are public religious buildings, such as Shanghai and Beijing.[8]

David Rice, author of *The Dragon's Brood*, found it equally difficult to get young Chinese to talk about religious beliefs. He got the impression that the only religion the Chinese were willing to discuss was Christianity, and that probably only out of politeness because they presumed him to be a Christian. Neither Taoism nor Buddhism was ever mentioned. Here are extracts some of the answers he finally got from women:

> It is our duty and our responsibility to go on believing in communism as ... a dream for things like justice, beauty, human goodness. Many Western intellectuals believe in God and Jesus ... I don't think [they] really think that God is a separate being somewhere in this vast universe, but perhaps in their mind God represents justice, beauty, human goodness. My belief in communism is similar – it represents a certain aspiration to goodness. (Xiahong, 37)[9]

> I wish I could believe in something ... but I can't find anything to believe in ... Since I stopped believing in

socialism, I can't believe in anything else. (Mujie, 22, bank clerk)[10]

What do I believe? I've never thought of it before. It's difficult to answer: we Chinese never think of these things. (A 32-year old doctor)[11]

God? You want to push me to God? No, what I believe in is fate ... I don't expect another life [after death]. (A 20-year-old English student)[12]

Old beliefs and superstitions

Shortly after a discussion during which my colleagues declared their atheism, we went on a company outing to Baishan (Jilin Province) where we visited a new tourist attraction, a large cave. To make the caves more impressive, stalactites and stalagmites had been taken from caves from other Chinese provinces and glued to the ceiling and the ground of this cave, making the place look bizarre and unnatural. Even with these extra adornments, the authorities obviously felt that the caves lacked something. Consequently they looked for rock formations within the cave which inspired the visitors' imagination. One lump of stone was declared to be a 'fat woman', others were supposed to be 'an eagle' and 'a dog'. Another piece of stone resembled (after a bit of extra stone carving to get it into the required shape) the statue of a sitting Buddha. To my amazement, one after the other of my colleagues prostrated themselves on the icy stone floor. They lay down or kneeled, touching the ground with their forehead, then touched their forehead with their hand; some had even brought candles to light in front of the 'statue'. They seemed to be deeply and genuinely in awe of the stone.

I imagine I must have stared at them in utter amazement. These were the people who declared they did not believe in anything, had never prayed in their lives, and thought that religion was something ridiculous from the nineteenth century. When they saw me looking at them, they reacted with an embarrassed, apologetic shrug. I bowed my head and withdrew quietly.

I visited a young married woman, who claimed to be an atheist, in her home. Next to the television set I found a little altar where incense had been burnt recently, decorated with a Buddha statue, pictures of ancestors and a photo of Mao. When I asked her about it, she was embarrassed, and mumbled something about doing it to please her mother-in-law.

When I became ill, my employer's response was to send a colleague to buy not only medicines but also a long-life charm for me, an amulet filled with herbs to be worn around the neck.

At the White Cloud temple in Beijing, a working Taoist temple, people crowded to touch the relief of their birth sign on a wall for luck. They also queued to kowtow in front of statues, and a monk hit a gong each time a visitor kowtowed. Uncertain what to do when my turn came, I bowed my head and made the sign of the cross to show my respect. The monk accepted the gesture and hit the gong. A Chinese woman who was behind me in the queue and who spoke English said I had done the right thing. 'You don't have to be a Taoist believer to benefit from a Taoist blessing. I don't believe in anything, but it is a wise move to pay your respect to various gods from various religions, just in case they do exist.'[13]

At one end of a rectangular pit there was a huge metal disc with a bell in the middle. Visitors could buy small metal disks at 2 *mao* each, and throw them. Those who hit the bell secured good luck for themselves and their families for one year. It appeared that people who were particularly skilful at throwing were bound to have more luck than others, and that wealthier people could afford to keep trying for longer, thus buying their portion of luck.

Spiritual forces in everyday life: *feng shui*

Most Chinese deny fervently that they believe in *feng shui,* but at the same time they all seem to follow it and place great importance on it in their everyday lives. *Feng shui* is a complex system of geomancy. Professional geomancers can explain every event in one's life – from birth to marriage to death, from business failure or success to illnesses and their cures – with *feng shui* influences. Spiritual forces are everywhere on earth and they influence people's fates. Wind directions, the situations of hills (the homes of dragons), the proximity of lakes and rivers, all must be considered when building or furnishing a house or an office. If there is an evil influence, for example because of a neglected window or a because the front door is on the wrong side of the house, the spirit can be appeased with sacrifices and ceremonies. Many Chinese know the basics rules of *feng shui* and follow them, but it takes a professional geomancer to give qualified advice in case of serious health or business problems.

Ancestor worship versus farming land

Funerals play an important role in the Chinese belief system of ancestor worship. People will pay as much money as they can afford for a burial plot in a favourable site for their parents and grandparents. They bury or burn paper money, paper wreaths and paper flowers, or use them to decorate the graves in place of real money and sacrifices.

In China, there is a deep conflict between long traditions of burials, connected with superstitions and belief systems, and a shortage of farming land. Traditionally, the dead were buried in auspicious sites – usually on sunny slopes, which happened to be the best farming land. As the population grows, so does ultimately the number of graves. In a country where every square metre of land is precious to help feed the population, the problem is severe.

To make matters worse, many Chinese – even the most practical, atheist people – are afraid of ghosts. They believe that the souls of people who have died recently, or of people who have died before their natural lifespan was over, hover around their graves. The living are often petrified to go near the graves, which means the whole area around a tomb may be lost to cultivation.

Having said that, necessity prevails and farmers cultivate much of the land adjoining the graves. I have seen many grave mounds standing like islands in irrigated rice fields and like hills in soybean fields, with not an inch between the cultivated soil and the grave.

Experts fear that if all dead people were buried, this would use about 660 hectares of land annually. The government encourages cremation to save agricultural land. China's cremation rate has reached 33.7 per cent in 1996; more than 2.6 million bodies were cremated in China out of a total of more than 7.8 million dead. This is a record, indicating that the government's endeavours to encourage cremation are paying off.[14]

New Year customs in disguise: Spring Festival

The Spring Festival was introduced only this century, but it is based on the old traditions of the abolished Lunar New Year.

Sun Yat-Sen became president of the new Chinese Republic on 1 January 1911 and he declared that, to mark the change, China would henceforth follow the Gregorian Calendar with its seven-day weeks and the New Year beginning on 1 January every year as in the Western world, instead of the lunar year with its ten-day periods.

However, the Chinese population was not happy about the change. In particular, they refused to give up the New Year celebrations in February and continued to hold the traditional festivities despite the Republican (and later communist) government's effort to suppress them. Over the years, governments only succeeded in renaming the event Spring Festival, but the date is still calculated according to the beginning of the lunar year.[15]

So the old customs continue under the new name. The Spring Festival, which begins on a day between 21 January and 19 February, has the same function as the Western Christmas. Festivities begin well before the festival day and last for 15 days after it.

There is at least one special meal with many courses for which extra shopping is done and preparations are made days in advance. Some families slaughter a pig for the occasion, even if it uses up all their savings. Being able to slaughter a pig for the Spring Festival is believed to maintain reasonable prosperity for the rest of the year. People give presents on the occasion, but most importantly, the Spring Festival is a time of family reunion. Even city-dwellers make their way to their ancestral villages to meet their grandparents or other relatives who still live there, causing trains to be hopelessly overcrowded.

Festivities often include public displays of lion and dragon dances, fireworks, opera and other performances. It is usually the women who produce the festive decorations, prepare the home and the food. Festive decorations include papercuts with good-luck symbols and characters, 'red couplets' (diamond-shaped pieces of red paper inscribed with good luck wishes), paper garlands and paper lanterns. People decorate their homes and their front doors with posters. These are usually red – the colour of luck – with pictures in gold, green, black and yellow. Printed posters are sold in department stores and street markets. Typical motifs include: dragons, fish, boats (for good luck), banknotes, coins, television sets (for wealth), old men with long white beards (for longevity), smiling fat baby boys (nowadays regarded as a wish for health rather than for numerous offspring). I've seen hundreds of good luck posters in China, but none of them showed an old woman or a female baby.

The Spring Festival encompasses many different beliefs. Depending on the region, different religions are combined during the 15 days: for example, on the eighth day of the last moon, the Buddhist festival of the 'Cold Eighth' is held. People eat a rice soup containing nuts, dried lotus seeds, red beans, dried dates or other locally available ingredients.

On the 24th day of the last moon, people worship the kitchen god. Once a year, the kitchen god is supposed to travel from earth to heaven and back, to report to the jade emperor on the family's activities. Families burn his picture as a symbol of his departure to heaven. They may also burn paper money for his travel expenses or smear honey on his statue's lips so that his report will be 'sweet'.

The flower fair begins on the 26th day of the old moon. The flowers and plants on sale have a symbolic relevance. The peach blossom stands for longevity and is supposed to keep demons at bay; peach blossoms are often put indoors as part of the festival decorations. The Kumquat tree stands for gold, wealth, unity and perfection. The peony is the flower of riches and honour, and a symbol of feminine beauty.

On the eve of the new lunar year, the kitchen god is welcomed back into his home and tempted with fresh fruit and incense. The head of the family – usually the oldest man – pays the family's respects to their ancestors by burning incense and paper money.

Children try to stay awake until at least midnight, because this is supposed to prolong their mothers' and fathers' lives and it is a tradition to give children money in little red paper packets.

On the first day of the New Year, women wear their new clothes for the first time. This custom makes sense in areas where most people can afford something new only once a year. In some families, the tradition is that married members of the family give money to unmarried members of the family, irrespective of their age. It can be embarrassing for an unmarried woman to be given money by a younger wife, because it reminds her and everyone else present of her failure to find a husband. As a token of self-purification and renewal, the first day of the New Year is often a vegetarian day. No lifestock must be slaughtered on this day and no housework should be done either. By sweeping the floor, the woman might accidentally sweep away good fortune. Similarly, hair must not be washed on this day either to avoid washing the good luck away.

On the second day of the New Year, the Chinese visit friends and relatives and distribute yet more money in red envelopes. On day three, visits must be avoided because they would result in arguments. Instead, many Chinese visit temples or have their fortunes told. Day seven is meant to be the birth of humankind and is celebrated with a meal.

The lantern festival takes place on the 15th day, and families make or buy paper lanterns in various shapes and sizes. Glutinous rice balls (*yuanxiao*) are a typical Spring Festival dish. Walking on stilts, lantern processions and folk dancing are common traditions. The lantern festival day used to have special significance for women: in the old days when Han women were not permitted to leave the house, this was the one day of the year when they were allowed out to walk up and down the road in the evening, carrying their lantern.[16]

A special New Year custom of the Dai people in the Yunnan Province (also observed by some other ethnic groups) celebrates the victory of women's loyalty over male brutality. The legend has it that a cruel demon king abducted twelve innocent women and forced them to become his concubines. The women worked out a way to kill him by strangling him with his own hair and chopping off his head. But whenever the head was set down, fire would break out. To protect the people from fire, the twelve women volunteered that each one would hold the head for a day before passing it on to the next woman. They splashed each other with water to wash off the demon's blood. So the Dai celebrate a water splashing festival, where people splash water on each other to commemorate the twelve women and to prevent misfortunes in the New Year.[17]

Women in politics

The Chinese government encourages women to enter politics, and it is possible for women to take powerful positions, such as Wu Yi, who is China's Minister for Foreign Trade. According to the leaflet *China's Professional Women*, published in 1993, 626 of the newly-elected deputies of the Eighth National People's Congress (that is, 20.2 per cent of the total) were female, and there were 283 women on the Eighth National Committee of the Chinese

People's Political Consultative Conference, CPPCC, (which represents 13.52 per cent of the total).

China Pictorial reported that there were more than 20 women governors, vice-governors, secretaries and deputy secretaries of provincial party committees, and more than 300 female vice-mayors. The editors estimated that there are about 500 male governors, secretaries, deputy secretaries, mayors and vice-mayors in China.[18]

Nationwide, 10.82 million female cadres account for about 20 per cent of the total number of cadres;[19] but for only 10 per cent of senior ones.[20] There is often enormous pressure from society, husbands and parents-in-law, demanding that a woman fulfil her 'more important roles' first: to serve her husband, her parents-in-law and her children.

Zhong Xiu mentions a typical case in her book *Yunnan Travelogue*. When Miyuwang, a Dai woman in the Yunnan Province, was elected deputy, everyone rejoiced, especially her husband, who immediately volunteered to take on the greater share of the housework. He offered to cook the meals and to fetch water from the stream, when most of her time was taken up with meetings and visits. However, while his wife could stand up to pressure from society, he could not. His mates made fun of him, saying he was being 'henpecked'. Gradually, he took to sabotaging his wife's double role: instead of looking after the children when his wife went to a meeting, he sent them off to be fed by another woman.

One day he went as far as hiding Miyuwang's only smart dress to prevent her from attending an important meeting. Miyuwang hesitated, then decided to wear her grubby worksuit. She turned out to be the only one among 600 delegates who was not dressed up. Many gave her curious glances, but she had the confidence to behave as if she were making a political statement. On her return, she did not reprimand her husband, but managed to change his attitude and some of his close friends' attitudes. She convinced him that by doing the greater share of the housework, he was supporting the collective as a whole. Now he helps her packing whenever she leaves for a trip, prepares her lunchbox and sees her off; he also helps her weave new bamboo baskets for the household.[21]

Another story about Miyuwang illustrates the second problem that female politicians encounter. When she returned from the Fifth National People's Congress, all commune members assembled to hear her report. But several conservative men refused to listen to a woman, even a people's deputy. They made a point of not going into the hall, but sat in a nearby hut instead and listened from there. The fragments of speech they picked up were so interesting that they soon regretted not being in the hall and able to understand every word, so when the meeting was over, they went to her and asked her to repeat everything they had missed.[22]

None of my Chinese friends were actively involved in politics. Many were uninterested in politics, probably because of disillusion with the crumbling communist system. Others seemed to feel that politics was dangerous ground and political activism would mean having your private life investigated and mistakes punished by interference in your life. Most Chinese women were very reluctant to talk about politics; they were afraid that their comments, which might be inadvertently critical of the government, could be fed to the local representative of the communist party or to their employers, and that they would suffer repercussions. Discussing politics with a foreigner was twice as dangerous.

The only political activists I met were men, and the Politics Department at Tonghua Teachers' College seemed to train more male teachers than most of the other departments. The most critical remark I ever heard from one of the students of the Politics Department was 'Mao made some mistakes', and she immediately indicated that she wished she had not said that.

The Women's Federation

Founded in April 1949, the All-China Women's Federation is the equivalent of the Women's Institutes in Britain, but has more influence of power. The mass organization consists of women from all walks of life and all ethnic groups and fights for women's emancipation. There are 90,000 professional cadres working for 56,879 branches nationwide.

The All China Women's Federation is the largest non-governmental organization in the country. Liaising closely with the government, it works for the protection of women's interests and rights, especially political rights, labour and employment rights, property rights, cultural and educational rights, marriage and family rights, and individual rights. For example, the Law of the People's Republic of China on Protection of Rights and Interests of Women, adopted at the fifth session of the seventh National

People's Congress in April 1992, was largely the work of the Women's Federation.[23]

As well as involvement in politics at governmental level, the Women's Federation and its local branches are often involved in charitable activities, such as social work or fundraising. The Women's Federation also draws public attention to specific problems and organizes campaigns, such as discrimination against girls in education. Specific tasks include: to unite and mobilize women to take part in modernization and reform; to teach and guide women to reinforce self-respect, self-confidence, self-improvement and self-support; to improve economic development and social progress; to represent women in democratic management, supervision and in making laws and regulations relevant to women and children; to upgrade female personnel; to safeguard women's legal rights and interests; to coordinate and promote social circles to do practical things for women; to communicate with women in Hong Kong, Macao, Taiwan and abroad; and to liaise with non-governmental women's organizations in other countries.[24]

Representatives of the Women's Federation will also interfere with women's private lives if they feel that it is for the best of the individual, the family or the society.

The president of the All China Women's Federation is the highest ranking woman in China. This post has been held by Chen Muhua, 72, since 1988. She has always been ambitious in her career. Aged 17, she became the first woman staff officer of the Eighth Route Army. Later she held successively the posts of Minister of Foreign Economic Relations and Trade, President of the People's Bank of China and Vice-Premier of the State Council. As well as being the president of the Women's Federation, she is currently the vice-chair of the Standing Committee of the National People's Congress. It was Chen Muhua who initiated the Spring Bud project to support girls who are otherwise unable to go to school.[25]

Despite the power of the All China Women's Federation, I never met a woman who was actively involved in it. In fact, I learnt about most of the Federation's activities only after my stay. It is possible that the Federation has a stronger impact on women's lives in some geographical areas than in others, depending on which campaigns are currently going on. For example, the campain against women's illiteracy will be noticed and talked about much more in the countryside than in an industrial town which has good primary and secondary schools and a college.

Concessions for obedience

Today, the Chinese are free to practise any faith, and the major religions are flourishing again, albeit under the strict control of the State Religious Bureau. Buddhism and Christianity (which is perceived as a 'Western' and therefore a fashionable religion) are rapidly gaining followers.

However, most Chinese are still scared to admit their religious beliefs. The fear of persecution is still deeply ingrained. The two exceptions are the Ningxia and Xinjiang Province which are governed according to Islam and where Muslim belief is the norm.

The state is likely to allow more freedom for each religion, for example, the printing of large quantities of bibles, but these will be concessions which the religious leaders have to earn by keeping their congregations calm and in line with government policies – like children are rewarded for obedience with sweets.

As the government continues to send out signals that it is acceptable to have a religion, more and more people will come out in the open about their beliefs. I expect that anyone who does not conform with the restrictions imposed by the State Religious Bureau will be imprisoned or persecuted in other ways but I don't believe that the State Religious Bureau will succeed in keeping out foreign influences. There are simply too many foreigners in China and their number is increasing. Also, more and more Chinese travel abroad on business and to study, and an exchange of ideas and views is inevitable.

There are fewer women than men in politics, but the proportion of women and men in positions of political responsibility is higher than in many other countries. The state encourages women to go into politics and the proportion of women in government organizations will continue to grow. However, pressures from society and family can make it difficult for a woman to be active in politics either as a volunteer or as a career politician.

11 Looking into the future

The World Conference on Women: a symbolic gesture

The United Nations' Fourth World Conference on Women, held in September 1995 in Beijing, drew Western attention to the situation of Chinese women. Their living conditions and women's rights were discussed in newspapers, magazines, radio programmes and television documentaries.[1]

How has the conference affected women in China? Very little. Apart from those women who found work in the jobs created specifically for the conference, such as hostesses, interpreters, guides and policewomen, the conference made little impact on the average Chinese.

Most Chinese women knew that the conference was taking place. A survey conducted among 1,100 families in central Beijing, showed that 94.7 per cent of Beijing people had heard about the conference via television and 69.5 per cent from newspapers. Half of them said that they watched the conference on TV or read about it regularly.

Over sixty-three per cent of the respondents could name the theme of the conference, which was 'Equality, Development, Peace'. Ninety-one per cent said they thought the conference was helping to advance the status of women in China and in the world, and promoting women's development. Eighty per cent thought the conference helped significantly to bring awareness of women's issues, strengthen the social consciousness of equality between the sexes. Almost ninety-two per cent believed the conference would help the world to know China better.

However, as with all official surveys conducted in China, I suggest taking the responses with a pinch of salt, because respondents would automatically give the politically correct response by demonstrating interest and approval. For example, in the open questions many women took the opportunity to praise the socialist system.[2]

Shortly after the conference I corresponded with a female university student in Beijing who said she had found television broadcasts about the conference stimulating, but that few of her acquaintances had showed similar interest and had neither the television set nor the leisure to follow the conference on TV. Some eager followers of the conference were apparently less interested in the papers presented than the fashionable clothes the foreign women wore. My correspondents in the Jilin Province knew about the conference and said they had read a newspaper article or two about it, but did not find it particularly relevant to their lives. Of course, I can't claim that my friends and their acquaintances are a representative sample of the female population in China, but I find it interesting that their response deviates from the official survey results.[3]

Nevertheless, I believe the fact that the conference took place in Beijing has enormous significance. By inviting conference participants, and with them a host of foreign investigative journalists who would inevitably research, point out and publicize human rights abuses and unfavourable conditions for women in China, the government has shown enormous courage. It has sent a signal that it is willing to expose the country to foreign criticism – something which had been unthinkable for several decades. I believe this means that the government will allow more free flow of information and ideas between China and the rest of the world, which will lead towards freedom of opinion, speech and press. Hosting the conference was a symbolic gesture of acknowledgement that China now regards itself as part of the world and no longer as a world within itself.

Looking ahead

In the past the position of women in large parts of Chinese society was lower than in most other societies, past or present, worldwide. The 1949 revolution (the 'Liberation') acknowledged women's equality and gave women equal rights in theory and to a large extent in practice. This enormous jump form 'no worth' to 'equal worth' has probably not been equalled by any other event in history worldwide. However, after the enormous improvements in the first few years after the Liberation, matters have slowed down, and hardly anything has changed over the past 30 years. Women are officially equal, but despite many official speeches, papers and campaigns, practice still doesn't keep up with the theory. Most Chinese consider women to be worth 'almost' as much as a man. The average Chinese woman desires equality, but will not fight for it. She gives higher priority to acquiring wealth, raising living standards, marital and family harmony, fashion and beauty.

I have noticed that many women and men seem to favour a reverse process and cherish the ideal of the woman as homemaker, decorative accessory, or husband's assistant and supporter. This trend is strongest among the newly-rich who regard a non-working wife as the latest status symbol, and it seems to be growing rapidly. An article in *Women of China* in 1996 points out that today more women agree with the idea that 'the husband's success is also the wife's, and therefore the wife should do all she can to support her husband' than in 1990.[4]

With no strong driving force behind women's emancipation, there will probably be no major advance over the next decade. It is likely that there will be minor improvements in some aspects, such as 1 or 2 per cent more women in government and management positions, simply because the government wants to demonstrate progress in this matter. Other improvements will be local, especially in the Muslim provinces, where women's status is currently low and where groups of determined women get together and demand their rights.

I believe that only when the first surge of consumerism is over (which will happen in the cities before the rural areas), Chinese women will again look at improving other aspects of their lives, and these may include equal opportunities and power. A strong women's movement will probably start in Shanghai (the centre of modernity), or possibly in the Guangdong Province (where people are considered the least conventional).

Several people who have, like me, lived and worked in China, used the word 'schizophrenic' to sum up their impression of the culture. For Westerners, China has always been difficult to understand, and with China's gradual opening to the West, more and more visitors have had the opportunity to see and be mystified. Some of the apparent discrepancies or oddities in Chinese culture can be explained by traditional and still ingrained ideals, such as the family's interests taking precedence over the individual's, and society's over the family's. The other point to bear in mind is that Chinese women have experienced several drastic changes from one extreme to the other (more frequent and more severe than in most other countries), and it is small wonder that they are left confused. How well they will adapt to future changes depends on the age groups to which they belong. I'm describing the typical Chinese women's response to changes, but please bear in mind that these are broad generalizations which do not apply to everyone.

Children and teenagers are used to the attention and affection of parents and grandparents, who encourage their individuality. They would almost certainly offer fierce resistance should anyone – be it government or husband – try to reduce their freedom and self-worth.

Women who are now in their late teens and early twenties grew up in a time of limited resources and limited freedom, then encountered a wealth of opportunities when they reached adulthood. They are embracing the new enthusiastically, be it the 'trendy' Christian religion or the American fashions. They lack the information and the experience to see developments in perspective and many become victims of clever marketing. The typical woman in this age group does whatever is fashionable, and if an acknowledged trendsetter tells her that the ultimate status symbol is to stay at home, pamper the husband and have her breasts enlarged, then she'll dream of the day she can afford to do these things.

Women aged 40–50 who have survived the Cultural Revolution will respond cautiously to all changes, getting involved as little as possible and not committing themselves to any viewpoint. They are afraid to be seen as leaders of any group or campaign, in case the political climate changes in an unexpected way and they suffer repercussions for past activities. Many women of this age group like the idea of supporting their husband's ideas and activities. If the husband is responsible, he's the one who will get the blame if whatever he does is denounced later. In this age group self-preservation is usually stronger than loyalty.

Older women, who experienced not only the change to market economy and the Cultural Revolution but the Liberation, the Nationalist Revolution and maybe even a childhood where starvation, bound feet and slavery were the norm, are the ones who are best able to take changes in their stride. They are calm and secure, knowing that whatever happens, they have survived worse conditions. I found the women in this age group remarkably content, self-confident, adaptable and wise, and many of them see their role as helping and encouraging their granddaughters to succeed in the changed society.

Glossary

Azhu	A temporary marriage in some matriarchal Chinese societies, whereby both partners continue to live with their mothers
Cheongsam	Long gown historically worn by men. The term is also used by Westerners when they mean the *qipao*
Cultural Revolution:	A decade of upheaval, during which Mao Zedong enouraged China's youth to destroy tradition, learning, and everything suspected to be bourgeois or foreign. It resulted in continuous violence and a huge number of fatalities. The period is usually given as 1966–1976, but according to some books it began or ended a year earlier or later
Feng shui	Geomancy
Guanxi	Connections, networking, mutual favours, bribery
Liberation	The word the Chinese use for the Communist Revolution 1949
Pinyin	The romanized written Chinese
Qi	Energy
Qigong	Breathing exercises
Qipao	Women's gown, usually long and tight-fitting
Taijiquan	Shadowboxing
Wushu	Martial arts
Xinhua	The New China News Agency, which is controlled by the government and supplies information and photos to Chinese and foreign newspapers. The head office is in Beijing
Xiuxi	Take a break
Yin	Weight measure, approximately 1lb
Yuan	Chinese currency. 1 *yuan* (or *kwai*) = 10 *jiao* (or *mao*) = 100 *fen*

References

Chapter 1: Women in China – their history

1. *Welcome to China,* China National Tourist Office, London
2. Kevin Sinclair with Iris Wong Po-yee, *Culture Shock! China,* Kuperard (London) Ltd, 1991, p. 35
3. *Welcome to China,* op. cit.
4. *Welcome to China,* ibid.
5. Zhong Xiu, *Yunnan Travelogue – 100 Days in Southwest China,* New World Press, Beijing, 1985, p. 5
6. Liu Zhonglu, *A Colourful Life – Sketches of Ethnic Minority Women,* Chinese Women Series, China Intercontinental Press, Beijing, pp. 1–2
7. David Rice, *The Dragon's Brood, Conversations with Young Chinese,* HarperCollins Publishers, London, 1992, p. 217
8. Hui Wen, 'Hani Women Gear Up for Opening', *Women of China,* July 1996, pp. 13–14
9. *Culture Shock! China,* op. cit. p. 213
10. Bobby Siu, *Women of China, Imperialism and Women's Resistance 1900–1949,* p.80
11. Edgar Snow, *Red China Today – The Other Side of the River,* Penguin Books Ltd, Harmondsworth, 1970, p. 289 (first published by Random House as *The Other Side of the River,* 1962)
12. Liying, 'The Situation of Child-wives of Min-Nam', *Funu Shenghuo,* Vol. III, No.iii, August 1936, quoted in *Women of China,* op. cit. p. 80
13. Kaari Ward (ed.), 'Famine in China', *Great Disasters,* Readers Digest, New York/Montreal, pp. 132–7
14. Jonathan D. Spence, *The Search for Modern China,* Hutchinson, London, 1990, p. 309
15. Ibid, p. 373
16. *Women of China,* op. cit. p. 80
17. Ibid, p. 125
18. Ibid, p. 127
19. Colin Mackeras, *Modern China, A Chronology from 1842 to the present,* Thames and Hudson Ltd, London, 1982, p. 220
20. *Women of China,* op. cit. pp. 124–6
21. Ibid, p. 132
22. *Modern China, A Chronology,* op. cit. p. 289

23. *Women and Men in China Facts and Figures 1995*, Department of Social Science and Technology Statistics, State Statistical Bureau, PR China, pp. 3–6
24. *The Situation of Chinese Women*, Information Office of the State Council of the People's Republic of China, Beijing, 1994, pp. 1–3
25. *Red China Today*, op. cit. pp. 249–50
26. *The Dragon's Brood*, op. cit. pp. 63–5
27. Interview with the author, spring 94
28. Based on a conversation with the author, June 1994, written from memory in April 1996
29. *The Dragon's Brood*, op. cit. pp. 69–72
30. Qin Shi (ed.), *China 1995*, New Star Publishers, Beijing 1995, pp. 79–81
31. *Women and Men in China*, op. cit. p. 12
32. *Culture Shock! China*, op. cit. pp. 13–14
33. *China 1995*, op. cit. p. 79
34. *Yunnan Travelogue*, op. cit. p. 21

Chapter 2: Too many and too few teachers: education and training

1. *Study in China: A Guide for Foreign Students*, by the Secretariat of the Chinese National Society of Universities and Colleges for Foreign Student Affairs, Beijing Language and Culture University Press, undated
2. Su Xiaohuan, *The First Step Towards Equality – Topic on Women's Education*, China Intercontinental Press, Beijing, 1995, pp. 32–3)
3. Author's diary notes of Shau Bin's speech (interpreted by Bao Tianren) at Language Education Conference, Harbin, April 1994
4. *The First Step Towards Equality*, op. cit. pp. 36–8
5. Ibid. p. 30
6. Ibid. p. 31
7. Qin Shi (ed.), *China 1995*, New Star Publishers, Beijing, 1995, p. 98
8. *The First Step Towards Equality*, ibid, p. 33
9. Interview with the author, summer 1994
10. *China 1995*, op. cit. p. 98
11. *Women and Men in China, Facts and Figures 1995*, Department of Social Science and Technology Statistics, State Statistical Bureau, PR China, p. 64
12. *China 1995*, op. cit. p. 99
13. Information supplied by the staff of *China Pictorial*, New Star Press, 1996
14. *The First Step Towards Equality*, op. cit. pp. 18–19
15. Wei Wei, 'Help wanted: Anyone that can teach music', *China Daily*, 12 May 1994

16. 'Russian language back in vogue with Chinese students', *China Daily,* 16 April 1996
17. 'Help wanted', op. cit.
18. Chen Jian, 'New College Students', *China Pictorial,* January 1996, pp. 43–5
19. Li Li, 'Who Will Be the First College Student of De'ang Nationality?', *Women of China,* March 1996, pp. 13–15
20. Ibid.
21. *The First Step Towards Equality,* op. cit. pp. 39–41
22. Cui Ning, 'Graduates decide own employment', *China Daily,* 30 March 1996
23. *China 1995,* op. cit. p. 101
24. Nu Naitao, 'The Benefits of Distance Learning', *Beijing Review,* 13–19 May 1996, pp. 11–15
25. Shi Lihong, 'Literacy efforts still require tenacity', *China Daily,* 18 April 1996
26. *China 1995,* op. cit. p. 98
27. 'Literacy efforts', op. cit.
28. *Women and Men in China,* op. cit. pp. 58–9 and 92–3
29. *The First Step Towards Equality,* op. cit. pp. 8–9
30. Ibid, pp. 11–12
31. T.H. Peng, *Fun with Chinese characters,* Straits Times Collection, Federal Publications, Singapore, 1980

Chapter 3: Careers: a bed in every office

1. *China's Professional Women,* Pictorial China leaflet no 196, New Star Press, Beijing, 1993
2. Law of the People's Republic of China on Protection of Rights and Interests of Women, 1992, chapter 4, article 22
3. *China's Professional Women,* op. cit.
4. *The Situation Of Chinese Women,* Information Office of the State Council of the People's Republic of China, Beijing, 1994 p. 18
5. *Women and Men in China, Facts and Figures 1995,* Department of Social Science and Technology Statistics, State Statistical Bureau, People's Republic of China, p. 47
6. Ibid. p. 49
7. *The Situation of Chinese Women,* op. cit. p. 12
8. Interview with the author, February 1994
9. Xie Chen, 'How Do You Spend Your Weekends', *China Pictorial,* February 1996, p. 8
10. I mislaid that newspaper and have not been able to trace the article. It was published between February and May 1996.
11. 'Dalian uses test to fill posts', *China Daily*/Xinhua, 8 April 1996
12. Kevin Sinclair with Iris Wong Po-yee *Culture Shock! China,* Kuperard (London) Ltd, 1991, pp. 124–5

13. 'Foreign firms urged to protect women's rights', *China Daily,* 14 March 1996
14. Private conversation with the author, spring 1994, with Bao Tianren as interpreter
15. Interview with Sarah Lowis on behalf of the author, 1995
16. Interview with Sarah Lowis on behalf of the author, 1995
17. Interview with the author, February 1994
18. Interview with the author, February 1994
19. Interview with Sarah Lowis on behalf of the author, 1995
20. Wang Xiuying, 'China's First Generation of Policewomen', *China Pictorial,* June 1996, p. 55
21. Interviews with the author, February 1994
22. Interview with Sarah Lowis on behalf of the author, 1995
23. Conversation with the author, summer 1994, written from memory, April 1996
24. Interview with the author and author's diary notes, April 1994
25. Interview with the author, summer 1994
26. Interview with the author, spring 1994
27. Conversations with the author, spring and summer 1994, written from diary notes
28. Interview with the author, February 1994
29. Xiao Huan, 'She Devoted Her Youth to Yimeng Mountains' *Women of China,* 3 March 1996, pp. 19–21
30. Law of the People's Republic of China on Protection of Rights and Interests of Women, Chapter 2 – Political Rights
31. Su Bo, 'Women's Marital Status: Past and Present', *Beijing Review,* 11–17 March 1996, p. 19
32. Jia Chunming, 'Deng Zaijun Brings Happiness to TV Audiences', *China Pictorial,* January 1996, p. 14
32. Xiao Ming, 'Pride of Uygur women', *Women of China,* June 1996, pp. 13–15
34. Conversation with the author, May 1994, written from memory, April 1996
35. Nicholas Kristof and Sheryl WuDunn, *China Wakes,* Nicholas Brealey Publishing, 1994, p. 193
36. Interview with Sarah Lowis on behalf of the author, 1995
37. 'Unemployed women find hope in class', *China Daily*/Xinhua, 14 March 1996
38. Liu Yinglang, 'Centre helps unemployed women train for new jobs', *China Daily,* 20 March 1996
39. *China Wakes,* op. cit. pp. 34–5
40. Ibid, pp. 193–4
41. Written interview with the author, December 1994
42. Conversation with the author, May 1994, written from memory, March 1996
43. *China Wakes,* op. cit. p. 219
44. *China Wakes,* op. cit. pp. 218–219
45. *The Situation of Chinese Women,* op. cit. p. 13

46. Conversation with the author, spring 1994
47. Fan Zhimin, 'Cai grows seeds of prosperity', *China Daily*, 11 March 1996, p. 10
48. Xiao Ming, 'Pride of Uygur Women', *Women of China*, June 1996, pp. 13–15

Chapter 4: Love, sex, relationships

1. Interview with the author in the author's flat in Tonghua, March 1994
2. Interview with Sarah Lowis on behalf of the author, 1995
3. Interview with the author, March 1994
4. Interview with Sarah Lowis on behalf of the author, 1995
5. Based on interviews and informal conversations with the author, February–May 1994
6. Private correspondence with the author, March–May 1996
7. Conversation with the author, spring 1994, written from memory, March 1996
8. Gina Corrigan, *The Odyssey Illustrated Guide to Guizhou*, The Guidebook Company Ltd, Hong Kong, 1995, p.189
9. Wu Naitao, *Mother Wife Daughter – A discussion on marriage and family*, China Intercontinental Press, 1995, p. 4
10. Ibid. p. 27
11. *The Odyssey Illustrated Guide to Guizhou*, op. cit pp. 188–9
12. *Mother Wife Daughter*, op. cit. p. 27
13. Ibid. p. 27
14. Interview with the author, April 1994
15. Conversation with the author, spring 1994, written from memory, March 1996
16. Guo Nei, 'Agency makes fine matches', *China Daily*, 29 April 1996
17. *The Odyssey Illustrated Guide to Guizhou*, op. cit. pp. 150 and 212
18. Based on interviews with the author, spring 1994, and with Sarah Lowis on behalf of the author, 1995
19. Zhong Xiu, *Yunnan Travelogue – 100 Days in Southwest China*, New World Press, Beijing, 1983, pp. 29–30
20. *The Odyssey Illustrated Guide to Guizhou*, op. cit. p. 151
21. Written (telefax) interview with the author, December 1994
22. Interview with the author by correspondence, 1995
23. Interviews with the author, spring 1994 and (by correspondence) 1995
24. Interviews with the author, spring 1994 and (by correspondence) 1995
25. Conversation with the author, spring 1994
26. Jonathan D. Spence, *The Search for Modern China*, Century Hutchinson Ltd, London, 1990, p. 708

27. Kevin Sinclair with Iris Wong Po-yee, *Culture Shock! China*, Kuperard, London, 1991, p.164

Chapter 5: Serving the mother-in-law – weddings, marriage and divorce

1. Wu Naitao, *Mother Wife Daughter*, China Intercontinental Press, Beijing, 1995, pp. 8–9
2. *Love, Marriage and the Family in Today's China*, New Star Publishers, Beijing, 1995, p. 2
3. *Women and Men in China, Facts and Figures 1995*, Department of Social Science and Technology Statistics, State Statistical Bureau, P. R. China, p. 33
4. *Mother Wife Daughter*, op. cit. p. 15
5. Correspondence with the author, March 1996
6. *Women and Men*, op. cit. p. 11
7. *Mother Wife Daughter*, op. cit. pp. 2–7
8. Jung Chang, *Wild Swans*, Flamingo, London, paperback 1993 (from HarperCollins hardback 1991), pp. 173–4
9. Teresa Poole, 'A Marriage of East and West', The *Independent*, 30 May 94
10. *Love, Marriage and the Family*, op. cit. p. 6
11. 'A Marriage of East and West', op. cit.
12. Feng Jianping, 'To Preserve Beauty Forever', *China Pictorial*, April 1996, pp. 18–19
13. Liu Zhonglu, *A Colourful Life – Sketches of Ethnic Minority Women*, China Intercontinental Press, Beijing, 1995, p. 37
14. Gina Corrigan, *The Odyssey Illustrated Guide to Guizhou*, The Guidebook Company Ltd, Hong Kong, 1995, p. 151
15. Zhong Xiu, *Yunnan Travelogue – 100 Days in Southwest China*, New World Press, Beijing, 1983, p. 11
16. *The Odyssey Illustrated Guide to Guizhou*, op. cit. p. 151
17. Interview with the author, summer 1994
18. Li Yan, 'Big is beautiful for televisions', *China Daily*, 4 March 1996
19. Liu Weiling, 'Unwanted gifts wanted by enterprising merchant', *China Daily*, Business Supplement, 15–21 May 1994
20. Kevin Sinclair with Iris Wong Po-yee, *Culture Shock! China*, Kuperard, London, 1991, p. 24
21. *Mother Wife Daughter*, op. cit. p. 9
22. Nicholas Kristof and Sheryl WuDunn, *China Wakes*, Nicholas Brealey Publishing, 1994, p. 213
23. Ibid. p. 213
24. *Mother Wife Daughter*, op. cit. p. 9
25. Cited in *Love, Marriage and the Family*, op. cit. p. 7
26. *Love, Marriage and the Family*, op. cit. p. 15

27. 'An Investigation of Chinese Women's Social Status', cited in *Love, Marriage and the Family*, op. cit. p. 16
28. Interview with the author, spring 1994
29. Xu Yuefen, 'Chinese Rural Women's Decision-Making Status in Family', *Women of China*, July 1996, pp. 4–5
30. *Yunnan Travelogue*, op. cit. p. 26
31. *Yunnan Travelogue*, op. cit. chapter 9
32. *Love, Marriage and The Family*, op. cit. p. 14
33. *Love, Marriage and The Family*, op. cit. pp. 13–14
34. *Mother Wife Daughter*, op. cit. p. 39–42
35. Interviews with the author, summer 1994
36. *Mother Wife Daughter*, op. cit. pp. 41–2
37. Chen Erkang, 'Phoenix Costumes of the She Ethnic Group', *China Pictorial*, April 1996
38. This and all previous paragraphs in the section on divorce are based on information from *Mother Wife Daughter*, op. cit. p. 10 and pp. 12–20.
39. *Mother Wife Daughter*, op. cit. p. 19
40. *Mother Wife Daughter*, op. cit. p. 20
41. Civil Affairs Ministry statistics, cited in *Mother Wife Daughter*, op. cit. p. 20
42. 'Couples opt to go it alone', *China Daily*, 11 April 1996
43. *Mother Wife Daughter*, op. cit. pp. 16–17
44. *Mother Wife Daughter*, op. cit. p. 15
45. *A Colourful Life*, op. cit. p. 37
46. *Mother Wife Daughter*, op. cit. pp. 21–4
47. *Mother Wife Daughter*, op. cit. pp. 23–4
48. 'Couples opt to go it alone', op. cit.
49. Xiao Yuan, 'Effort to Rebuild Happiness', *Women of China*, May 1996, pp. 17–18
50. Statistics Bureau figures, cited in *China Daily*, 1 April 1994
51. *Women and Men*, op. cit. pp. 24–28

Chapter 6: Family planning and motherhood

1. Delia Davin, 'China's Population Policy', *China Review*, Autumn/Winter 1996, pp. 9–11
2. Wu Naitao, *Mother Wife Daughter*, China Intercontinental Press, Beijing, 1995, p. 11
3. Interview with the author, spring 1994
4. Nicholas Kristof and Sheryl WuDunn, *China Wakes*, Nicholas Brealey Publishing, London, 1994, p. 227
5. *Women and Men in China, Facts and Figures 1995*, Department of Social Science and Technology Statistics, State Statistical Bureau, P. R. China, p. 13
6. *China Wakes*, op. cit. p. 229

7. The Law of the People's Republic of China on Protection of Rights and Interests of Women, adopted at the fifth session of the seventh National People's Congress on April 3, 1992, Chapter 6, 'Rights Relating to the Person', Article 35, cited in Elisabeth Croll, *Changing Identities of Chinese Women*, Hong Kong University Press and Zed Books, London, 1995

8. *China Wakes*, op. cit. pp. 229–30

9. *China Wakes*, op. cit. p. 231

10. *China Wakes*, op. cit. p. 229

11. *China Wakes*, op. cit. p. 224

12. Part of an information pack sent to the author by the Chinese Embassy, 1996

13. Liu Zhonglu, *A Colourful Life*, China Intercontinental Press, Beijing, 1995, p. 39

14. Kevin Sinclair with Iris Wong Po-yee, *Culture Shock! China*, Kuperard, London, 1991, p. 206

15. Xie Chen, 'A Day in the Life of an Extraordinary Primary School Student', *China Pictorial*, January 1996, p. 30

16. Conversation with the author, spring 1994, written partly from memory, partly from diary notes

17. Conversation with the author, summer 1994, written from diary notes

Chapter 7: Living conditions

1. Huang Wei, 'Charities: An Ascending Priority in China,' *Beijing Review*, 25–31 March 1996, pp. 12–15, based on State Statistical Bureau reports

2. Qin Shi, *China 1995*, New Star Publishers, Beijing, 1995, pp. 95–6

3. Yang Zingshi, 'Rocky Building Industry Targeted', *China Daily*, 12 April 1996, p. 1, (based on a blueprint approved by plenary session of National People's Congress March 1996)

4. Kevin Sinclair with Iris Wong Po-yee, *Culture Shock! China*, Kuperard, London, 1991, p. 218

5. Bao Li and Lai Yin, 'All-China Women's Federation Works to Eliminate Women's Poverty', *Women of China*, March 1996, pp. 6–7

7. For further reading on traditional Chinese architecture, I recommend the illustrated feature series by Leng Hanbing and Chen Erkan, 'Residential Houses in China, Cave Houses and Their Residents', *China Pictorial*, published in instalments in 1996

8. Author's observations of visits to families in northeast China, spring and summer 1994, written from diary notes and from memory

9. Teresa Poole, 'The cutting edge of capitalism', The *Independent on Sunday*, 22 August 1993, p. 13

10. Author's conversation with a Beijing man, February 1994, written from diary notes and from memory
11. Hong Bian, 'Fishy lifestyle of Hezhen people', *China Daily*, 6 May 1996
12. Wang Xiuying, 'Green Food in China', *China Pictorial*, June 1996, pp. 18–19
13. Cui Lili, 'Food Vendors Improve Quality', *Beijing Review*, 29 April–5 May 1996 pp. 22–4
14. Information supplied by the Chinese Embassy in London, February 1996
15. 'China reforming health care system', *China Daily*, Xinyua, 2 April 1996
16. In conversation with the author, spring and summer 1994
17. Zhu Baoxia, 'World Bank loan helps state fight tuberculosis', *China Daily*, 22 March 1996
18. Colin Mackerras, *Modern China, A Chronology from 1842 to the Present*, Thames and Hudson, 1982, p. 525
19. Jonathan D. Spence, *In Search of Modern China*, Century Hutchinson, London, 1990, p. 641
20. Interview with the author, spring 1994
21. Information supplied by the Chinese Embassy in London, February 1996
22. Conversation with the author in spring 1994, written from memory. I am not able to verify what she said or to back it up with figures
23. Xiao Huan, 'Maternity and Child Care in Yinan County', *Women of China*, March 1996
24. *China 1995*, op. cit. pp. 96–7
25. *China 1995*, op. cit. p. 96
26. Tao Liqun, 'Conditions of Elderly Chinese Women', *Women of China*, June 1996, pp. 15–18
27. Conversations with the author, 3 and 4 April 1994
28. *Women and Men in China, Facts and Figures 1995*, 'Percentage and sex distribution of total crimes 1993', p. 79, based on information from The Supreme People's Court, Department of Social Science and Technology Statistics, State Statistical Bureau

Chapter 8: Putting on the lipstick ... fashion and beauty

1. Andrew Bolton, 'Fashion in China 1910–1970', *China Review*, spring 1996, pp. 30–33
2. Zhong Xiu, *Yunnan Travelogue – 100 Days in Southwest China*, New World Press, Beijing, 1983, pp. 16–17
3. Ibid. p. 66
4. Ibid. p. 27

5. Xiao Ming, 'Pride of Uygur Women', *Women of China*, June 1996, pp. 12–13
6. Hong Bian, 'Fishy lifestyle of Hezhen people', *China Daily*, 6 May 1996
7. Author's diary notes and photographs, 1994
8. Gina Corrigan, *The Odyssey Illustrated Guide to Guizhou*, The Guidebook Company, Hong Kong, 1995, pp. 66–7 and 167–180
9. Interview with the author, April 1994
10. Author's diary notes, March 1994
11. Interview with the author, March 1994
12. Correspondence with the author, 1995–96
13. Interview by correspondence with the author, 1995
14. *China's Fashion*, Pictorial China, leaflet no. 173, New Star Press, Beijing, 1993
15. Jonathan D. Spence, *The Search for Modern China*, Century Hutchinson, London, 1990, p. 574
16. Conversation with the author, April 1994
17. Conversation with the author, April 1994
18. Interviews conducted by Sarah Lowis on behalf of the author, 1995
19. *The Odyssey Illustrated Guide to Guizhou*, op. cit. pp. 167–180
20. Author's diary notes, spring–summer 1994
21. Author's diary notes, spring–summer 1994
22. Advert in *China Pictorial*, April 1996 and other magazines
23. Jiao Yu, 'School works to improve society', *China Daily*, 20 March 1996
24. Conversations with the author, spring–summer 1994

Chapter 9: Leisure pursuits

1. 1990 Survey on the Social Status of China's Women, in *Women and Men in China, Facts and Figures 1995*, published by the Department of Social Science and Technology statistics
2. Feng Jianping, 'Angling Catches on Again as a Pastime in China', *China Pictorial*, June 1996, p. 13
3. Interview with the author, summer 1994
4. Interviews with the author, spring 1994, and with Sarah Lowis on behalf of the author, 1995
5. Qin Shi, *China 1995*, New Star Publishers, Beijing, 1995
6. 'Survey says university students shun exercise', *China Daily*, 26 April 1996, p. 3
7. Sue Lopez, *A Guide to Women's Football*, London, Scarlet Press, 1997
8. Feng Jianping, 'Hurray for Chinese Football', *China Pictorial*, September 1996, pp. 20–22.
9. Roberta Helmer Stalberg and Ruth Nesi, *China's Crafts*, pp. 19–20

10. Ruth Bottomley/Victoria & Albert Museum, *Chinese Papercuts. A Selection*, Sun Tree Publishing Limited, Singapore/London, 1994
11. See the Victoria & Albert Museum's (London) collection of Chinese papercuts, accessible on request only
12. If you are interested in motifs and symbols in Chinese customs, textiles, arts and crafts, read *China's Crafts* (ibid), *Chinese New Year Traditions and Customs*, Chinese Community Centre, London and Gina Corrigan, *The Odyssey Illustrated Guide to Guizhou*, The Guidebook Company, Hong Kong, 1995
13. 'Storm-hit Tibetans enjoy better lives', *China Daily*, 2 May 1995
14. 'Archives reveal Tibetan changes', *China Daily*/Xinhua, 6 April 1996
15. 'Electricity changes Tibetan lifestyle', *China Daily*/Xinhua, 9 April 1996

Chapter 10: Praying to Mao – religion and politics

1. Gina Corrigan, *The Odyssey Illustrated Guide to Guizhou*, The Guidebook Company Ltd, Hong Kong, 1995, p. 53
2. Qin Shi, *China 1995*, New Star Publishers, Beijing, 1995, p.31
3. Ibid. p. 32
4. 'Panchen Lama starts life's work', *China Daily*/Xinhua, 11 March 1996
5. 'Bishop of Beijing' (photo and caption), *China Daily*, 8 April 1996, p. 1
6. Interview with the author, March 1994
7. Conversation with the author, summer 1994
8. Conversations with the author, spring 1994
9. David Rice, *The Dragon's Brood, Conversations with Young Chinese*, HarperCollins Publishers, London 1992, p. 71
10. Ibid. p. 108
11. Ibid. pp. 105–106
12. Ibid, pp. 105–106
13. Private conversation with the author, February 1994
14. Liang Chao, 'Rising cremations save farmland', *China Daily*, 5 April 1996
15. For further reading about the change from New Year to Spring Festival, see Else Unterrieder, 'Neujahrsbeginn und Frühlingserwachen', *China verstehen*, Sympathie-Magazin Nr 10, and for further reading about the change from lunar to Gregorian Calendar, see Jonathan D. Spence, *The Search for Modern China*, Hutchinson, London, 1990
16. *Chinese New Year Traditions and Customs*, Chinese Community Centre, London (undated), and *China 1995*, ibid.

17. Zhong Xiu, *Yunnan Travelogue – 100 Days in Southwest China*, New World Press, Beijing, 1983, p. 15
18. Zhao Jun, 'An Interview with Chen Muhua', *China Pictorial*, March 1996, p. 8, and correspondence with the author, March 1996
19. *China's Professional Women,* Pictorial China leaflet no 176, New Star Press, Beijing, 1993
20. 'An Interview with Chen Muhua', op. cit.
21. *Yunnan Travelogue,* op. cit. pp. 12–13
22. Ibid. pp. 12–13
23. *China 1995,* op. cit. p. 47
24. *Women and Men in China, Facts and Figures 1995,* Department of Social Science and Technology Statistics, State Statistical Bureau, P. R. China, p. 87
25. 'An Interview with Chen Muhua', op. cit. p. 5

Chapter 11: Looking into the future

1. I was not in Beijing at the time of the conference
2. The survey was conducted by the All China Women's Federation Research Institute. Extracts published in 'Beijing Citizens Respond to the UN Conference', *Women of China*, pp. 4–5, March 1996, translated by Jennifer Lim
3. Private correspondence with the author, October–December 1996
4. 'Evaluation of Women's Status and Changing Ideas About The Sexes', *Women of China*, March 1996. The article gives the All China Women's Federation as its source, and does not specify percentages

Bibliography

Most of the following books give fascinating insights into the lives of Chinese women in the past; very few look at the China of the 1980s and 1990s. If you want to read more about how the Chinese live today, I recommend Nicholas Kristof & Sheryl WuDunn, *China Wakes,* as well as David Rice, *The Dragon's Brood.*

I have listed Western writers under their surnames, and Chinese writers under their first names (=family names).

It can be difficult to obtain books published in China in the West. Try the following address for mail order: China International Book Trading Corporation, 35 Chegongzhuang Xiulu, Beijing 100044, P.R. China.

Analects of Confucius, Sinolingua, Beijing, undated

Annotated Chinese Proverbs, Supplementary Readings for Elementary Chinese Readers, Sinolingua, PR China, undated

'Archives reveal Tibetan changes', *China Daily*/Xinhua, 6 April 1996

Atlas of the People's Republic of China, Foreign Languages Press, Beijing, 1989

Bai Fengxi *et al, I wish I Were a Wolf: New Voices in Chinese Women's Literature,* New World Press, China, 1994

Baker, Hugh D.R., *Chinese Family and Kinship,* Macmillan, London and Basingstoke, 1979

Bao Li and Lai Yin, 'All-China Women's Federation Works to Eliminate Women's Poverty', *Women of China,* March 1996, pp. 6–7

Belden, Jack, *China Shakes the World,* Penguin, 1973

'Bishop of Beijing' (photo and caption), *China Daily,* 8 April 1996, p. 1

Bolton, Andrew, 'Fashion in China 1910–1970', *China Review,* London, spring 1996, pp. 30–33

Bonavia, David, *The Chinese,* Penguin, London, 1980

Bottomley, Ruth (Victoria & Albert Museum), *Chinese Papercuts. A Selection,* Sun Tree Publishing Limited, Singapore & London, 1994

Brule, Jean-Pierre, *China Comes of Age,* Penguin, 1971

Bull, Geoffrey T., *When Iron Gates Yield,* Pickering & Inglis Ltd. London, 1976

Burland, Cottie A., *The Travels of Marco Polo,* Michael Joseph, London, 1971

Butterfield, Fox, *China: Alive in the Cruel Sea,* Hodder and Stoughton, London, 1983

Cammann, Schuyler, *Substance and Symbol in Chinese Toggles,* University of Pennsylvania Press, Philadelphia, 1962

Carruthers, Ian, 'Who will feed China', *China Review,* London, autumn/winter 1995, pp. 4–6

Chen, Jack, *A Year in Upper Felicity: Life in a Chinese Village During the Cultural Revolution,* London, 1973

Chen Erkang, 'Hakka Earthen Buildings in Southwestern Fujian Province', *China Pictorial,* March 1996, pp. 22–26

Chen Erkang, 'Phoenix Costumes of the She Ethnic Group', *China Pictorial,* April 1996

Chen Jian, 'New College Students', *China Pictorial,* January 1996, pp. 43–5

Chen Qide, 'Rural households see incomes climb 22 per cent from 1994' *China Daily,* Business Supplement/Shanghai & East China, 10–16 March 1996

Cheo Ying, Esther, *Black Country Girl in Red China,* Hutchinson, London, Melbourne, Sydney, Auckland, Johannesburg, 1980

'China aims for top in trade', *China Daily,* 5 March 1996

'China reforming health care system', *China Daily*/Xinhua, 2 April 1996

China's Fashion, Pictorial China no 172, New Star Press, Beijing, October 1993

China's Professional Women, Pictorial China no 176, New Star Press, Beijing, November 1993

Chinese Maxims – Golden Sayings of Chinese Thinkers, Sinolingua, PR China, undated

Chinese Papercuts, John Warner Publications, Hong Kong, 1978

Chinese Traditions and Customs, Chinese Community Centre, London, undated

Ch'u Chai and Winberg Chai, *The Changing Society of China,* New American Library, New York, 1962

Clayre, Alasdair, *The Heart of the Dragon,* Harvill Press and William Collins Sons & Co Ltd. London, 1976

Contemporary Chinese Women Writers, vol. 2, Panda Books, China, 1991

Contemporary Chinese Women Writers, vol. 3, Panda Books, China, 1993

Cooper, Elizabeth, *My Lady of The Chinese Courtyard,* Peter Davies Ltd. London, 1926

Corrigan, Gina, *Odyssey Illustrated Guide to Guizbou,* The Guidebook Company Ltd. Hong Kong, 1995

'Couples opt to go it alone', *China Daily,* 11 April 1996

Croll, Elisabeth. *Changing Identities of Chinese Women. Rhetoric, Experience and Self-Perception in Twentieth-Century China,* Hong Kong University Press, Zed Books London, 1995

Croll, Elisabeth, *Chinese Women since Mao,* Zed Books Ltd. London, 1983

Croll, Elisabeth, 'Experience and Action', *China Review*, London, summer 1995, pp. 12–15

Croll, Elisabeth, *Women and Rural Development in China: Production and Reproduction*, ILO, 1985

Cui Lili, 'Food Vendors Improve Quality', *Beijing Review*, 29 April 29–5 May 1996, pp. 22–4

Cui Ning, 'Graduates decide own employment', *China Daily*, 30 March 1996

Curtin, Katie, *Women in China*, Pathfinder Press, 1975

'Dai homes: from bamboo to brick', *China Daily*, 1 May 1996

'Dalian uses test to fill posts', *China Daily*/Xinhua, 8 April 1996

Davin, Delia, 'China's population policy: abusing or protecting human rights', *China Review*, London, autumn/winter 1995, pp. 9–11

Davis, Deborah and Harrell, Stevan (eds), *Chinese Families in the Post-Mao Era*, University of California Press, Berkeley, Los Angeles, London, 1993

Dawson, Raymond (ed.), *The Legacy of China*, Oxford University Press, Oxford, 1964

Dwyer, D.J., *China Today*, Longman, Harlow, 1975

Ecke, Tseng Yu-ho, *Chinese Folk Art*, University Press of Hawaii, Honolulu, 1977

Edwards, Louise, *Men and Women in Qing China: Gender in The Red Chamber Dream*, Sinica Leidensia S., v. 31, Brill, 1994

'Electricity changes Tibetan lifestyle', *China Daily*/Xinhua, 9 April 1996

Family Planning in China, Information Office of the State Council of the PRC, August 1995, Beijing

Family Planning in China, Pictorial China no 154, New Star Press, Beijing, November 1992

Famine in China, in *Great Disasters*, Readers' Digest Association, Inc., New York, 1989

Fan Zhimin, 'Cai grows seeds of prosperity', *China Daily*, 11 March 1996, p. 10

'Farmers worm way to wealth', *China Daily*/Xinhua, 5 March 1996

Farquharson, Ronald, *Confessions of a China Hand*, Hodder and Stoughton, 1950, London

Feng Jianping, 'Angling Catches on Again as a Pastime in China', *China Pictorial*, June 1996, p. 13

Feng Jianping, 'To Preserve Beauty Forever', *China Pictorial*, April 1996, pp. 18–19

Fessler, Loren, *China*, Time-Life International (Nederland) NV, 1965

Fitzgerald, C.P., *The Birth of Communist China*, Penguin, 1964, 1976

Fitzgerald, C. P., China: A *Short Cultural History*, Praeger, New York, 1961

'Foreign firms urged to protect women's rights', *China Daily*, 14 March 1996

Gilmartin, Christina K., Hershatter, Gail, Rofel, Lisa, and White, Tyrene (eds), *Engendering China. Women, Culture and the State*,

Harvard Contemporary China Series, Harvard University Press, Cambridge (Massachusetts) and London, 1994

Grey, Beryl, *Through the Bamboo Curtain*, Collins, London, 1965

Guisso, Richard and Johannesen, Stanley, *Women in China*, E Mellen Pr, US, 1981

Guizhou Special, China Tourism brochure no 104, Hong Kong Tourism Press, Hong Kong, 1989

Guo Nei, 'Agency makes fine matches', *China Daily*, 29 April 1996

Hall, Christine, *Chinese Dancing*, Script Ease Editorial, Cranbrook, 1995

Hall, Christine, *Living & Working in China*, How To Books Ltd. Plymouth, 1996

Han Suyin, *A Many Splendoured Thing*, The Reprint Society, London, 1954

Han Suyin, *A Mortal Flower*, Jonathan Cape, London, 1966

Hemmel, Vibeke and Sindbjerg, Pia, *Women in Rural China: Policy Towards Women Before and after the Cultural Revolution*, Curzon Press, 1984

Hong Bian, 'Fishy lifestyle of Hezhen people', *China Daily*, 6 May 1996

Hong Kong Schools Chinese Dance Team, (a colour-illustrated book published on the occasion of the 1976 International Festival of Youth Orchestras and Performing Arts, publisher unknown)

Hooper, Beverley, *Youth in China*, Penguin Books Ltd. Harmondsworth, 1985

Huang Shoubao, *Ethnic Costume from Guizhou*, Foreign Languages Press, Beijing, 1987

Huang Wei, 'Charities: An Ascending Priority in China,' *Beijing Review*, 25–31 March 1996, pp. 12–15, based on State Statistical Bureau reports

Hui Wen, 'Hani Women Gear Up for Opening', *Women of China*, July 1996, pp. 13–14

'Human rights in China and US compared', *China Daily*, 11 March 1996, p. 3

Hunter, J., *Gospel of Gentility: American Women Missionaries in Turn of the Century China*, Yale University Press, 1984, 1989

Hu Sheng (ed.), *A Concise History of the Communist Party of China*, Foreign Languages Press, Beijing, undated

Impact of Economic Development on Rural Women in China, United Nations University/HMSO, 1993

Jackson, Innes, *China Only Yesterday*, Faber and Faber, London, 1938

Jaschok, Maria and Miers, Suzanne (eds), *Women & Chinese Patriarchy. Submission, Servitude and Escape*, Hong Kong University Press, Zed Books Ltd, London, 1994

Jia Chunming, 'Deng Zaijun Brings Happiness to TV Audiences', *China Pictorial*, January 1996, p. 14

Jiao Yu, 'School works to improve society', *China Daily*, 20 March 1996

Johnson, Kay Ann, *Women, The Family and Peasant Revolution in China*, University Chicago Press, 1985

Johnson, Kay Ann, *Women, The Family and Peasant Revolution in China*, University Chicago Press, 1985

Jones, Judith, *Women in China*, Worcester College of Higher Education, Social Sciences Division, 1987

Jung Chang, *Wild Swans, Three Daughters of China*, Flamingo, HarperCollins Publishers, 1991

Ko, Dorothy, *Teachers of the Inner Chambers: Women and Culture in Seventeenth-Century China*, Stanford University Press, 1995

Kristof, Nicholas D. and WuDunn, Sheryl, *China Wakes. The Struggle for the Soul of a Rising Power*, Nicholas Brealey Publishing Limited, London, 1994

Kuhn, Anthony, 'Women revolt against Chinese harassment', *The Sunday Times,* 3 September 1995, p. 20

Law of the People's Republic of China on Protection of Rights and Interests of Women, adopted at the fifth session of the seventh National People's Congress on 3 April 1992

Leng Hanbing, 'Pink-Walled and Black-Tiled Houses in Zhenhe', *China Pictorial,* May 1996, pp. 40–41

Leng Hanbing, 'Residential Houses in China, Cave Houses and Their Residents', *China Pictorial,* February 1996, pp. 31–3

Leng Hanbing and Chen Erkang, 'Residential Houses in China, Compounds in Beijing,' *China Pictorial,* January 1996, pp. 40–44

Leys, Simon, *The Chairman's New Clothes: Mao and the Cultural Revolution*, St Martin's Press, New York, 1977

Liang Chao, Rising cremations save farmland', *China Daily,* 5 April 1996

Li Jun (ed.), *100 glimpses into China, Short stories from China*, Foreign Language Press, Beijing, 1989

Li Li, 'Who Will Be the First College Student of De'ang Nationality?', *Women of China,* March 1996 pp. 13–15

Ling, Ding *et al, China for Women: Travel and Culture,* Feminist Press of the City University of New York and Spinifex Press, Melbourne, 1995 Spinifex Press, October 1995

Liu Welling, 'Unwanted gifts wanted by enterprising merchant', *China Daily* Business Supplement, 15–21 May 1994

Liu Yinglang, '300 women honoured on day for all women', *China Daily,* 9 March 1996

Liu Yinglang, 'Centre helps unemployed women train for new jobs', *China Daily,* 20 March 1996

Liu Yinglang, 'Dirty city aiming for cleaner air', *China Daily,* 5 March 1996

Liu Zhonglu, *A Colourful Life – Sketches of Ethnic Minority Women,* Chinese Women Series, China Intercontinental Press, Beijing, 1995

Li Yan, 'Big is beautiful for televisions', *China Daily,* 4 March, 1996

Liying, 'The Situation of Child-wives of Min-Nam', *Funu Shenghuo,* Vol. III, No. iii, August 1936, cited in Siu, Bobby, *Women of China,* p. 80

Loewe, Michael, *Imperial China: The Historical Background to the Modern Age*, Praeger, New York, 1969

Love, Marriage and the Family in Today's China, China in Brief series, New Star Publishers, Beijing, 1995

Lyall, Leslie, *God Reigns in China*, Hodder and Stoughton, London, Sydney, Auckland, Toronto and The Overseas Missionary Fellowship, 1985

Mackerras, Colin, *Modern China, A Chronology from 1942 to the present*, Thames and Hudson, London, 1982

Mackerras, Colin and Hunter, Neale, *China Observed*, Nelson, Great Britain/Australia, 1967

Mai Ding, *Folk Songs of China's 56 Nationalities*, New World Press, Beijing, undated

Maitland, Derek, *The Insider's Guide to China*, Gregory's Publishing Company, Australia, 1987 (revised edition 1989)

Medley, Margaret, *A Handbook of Chinese Art*, Harper and Row, New York, 1964

Mei Lichong, Wei Huailuan and Yang Jungxuan, *The Ins and Outs of Chinese Culture*, Sinolingua, P.R. China, undated

Mende, Tibor, *China and her Shadow*, Thames and Hudson, London, 1961

Mendelssohn, Kurt, *In China Now*, Paul Hamlyn, London, 1969

Meskill, John (ed.), *An Introduction to Chinese Civilization*, D.C. Heath and Company, Lexington, MA, 1973

Min Jiayin (ed.), The Chinese Partnership Research Group: *The Chalice and The Blade in Chinese Culture. Gender Relations and Social Models*, China Social Sciences Publishing House, Beijing, 1995

Minney, R.J., *Next Stop – Peking*, George Newnes Limited, London, 1957

Muir, Kate, 'The joy luck club', *The Times Magazine*, 19 August 1995

Myrdal, Jan, *Chinese Journey*, Chatto & Windus, London, 1965

Naisbitt, John, and Aburdene, Patricia, *Megatrends 2000*, Pan Books, London, 1990

New China, Foreign Languages Press, Beijing, second edition 1995

Nien Cheng, *Life and Death in Shanghai*, Grafton Books, London, 1986

Nu Naitao, 'The Benefits of Distance Learning', *Beijing Review*, 13–19 May 1996, pp. 11–15

O'Connor, Patrick (ed.), *Buddhists Find Christ, Spiritual Quest of Thirteen Men and Women in Burma, China, Japan, Korea, Sri Lanka*, CE Tuttle Co, US, 1976

Opitz, Peter J (ed.), *China verstehen*, Sympathie-Magazin Nr. 10, Studienkreis für Tourismus e.V., Starnberg, Germany, 1989

'Panchen Lama starts life's-work', *China Daily*/Xinhua, 11 March 1996

Peck, Graham, *Through China's Wall*, William Collins, London 1945

Peng, T. H., *Fun with Chinese characters*, Straits Times Collection, Federal Publications, Singapore, 1980

Pilkington, John, *An Adventure on the Old Silk Road, From Venice to the Yellow Sea,* Century Hutchinson, London, 1989

Ping Chia Kuo, *China New Age and New Outlook,* Penguin, Harmondsworth, 1960 (enlarged edition)

Poole, Teresa, 'The cutting edge of capitalism', *Independent on Sunday,* 22 August 1993, p. 13

Qin Shi, *China 1995,* New Star Publishers, Beijing 1995

Rai, Shirin *et al, Women in the Face of Change: Soviet Union, Eastern Europe and China,* Routledge, 1992

Ran, Margaret, *Young Women in China,* Enslow, US, 1989

Rattenbury, Harold B., *Face to Face with China,* George G. Harrap & Co Ltd. London, 1945

Readings from Chinese Writers, Sinolingua, PR China, undated

Rice, David, *The Dragon's Brood, Conversations with Young Chinese,* HarperCollins Publishers, London, 1992 (out of print)

'Russian language back in vogue with Chinese students', *China Daily,* 16 April 1996

Samagalski, Alan and Buckley, Michael, *China, a travel survival kit,* Lonely Planet Publications, Victoria (Australia) 1976, 1984

Schell, Orville, *To Get Rich is Glorious,* Robin Clark, London, 1985

Schell, Orville, *Discos and Democracy,* Random House, New York, 1989

Schram, Stuart, *Mao Tse-Tung,* Penguin, 1966

Schurmann, Franz and Orville Schell (ed.), *Communist China,* Penguin, 1968

Seven Contemporary Chinese Women Writers, Chinese Literature Press, China, 1990

Sheridan, Mary and Salaff, Janet W. (eds), *Lives. Chinese Working Women,* Indiana University Press, Bloomington 1984, in cooperation with the University of Toronto/York University Joint Centre on Modern East Asia

Shi Lihong, 'Literacy efforts still require tenacity', *China Daily,* 18 April 1996

Sickman, Laurence and Soper, Alexander, *The Art and Architecture of China,* Penguin Books, New York, 1971

Sinclair, Kevin with Wong Po-yee, Iris, *Culture Shock! China,* Kuperard (London) Ltd. 1991

Siu, Bobby, *Women of China, Imperialism and Women's Resistance 1900–1949,* Zed Press, London, 1981

Smedley, Agnes, *China Fights Back,* Victor Gollancz, London, 1939

Snow, Edgar, *Red China Today. The Other Side of the River,* Penguin Books, Harmondsworth, 1970 (updated from 1961 original titled *The Other Side of the River)*

Spence, Jonathan D., *The Search for Modern China,* Hutchinson, London, Australia, New Zealand, South Africa, 1990

Spence, Jonathan, *To Change China, Western Advisers in China 1620–1960,* Penguin Books, Harmondsworth, 1969, 1980

Stalberg, Roberta Helmer and Nesi, Ruth, *China's Crafts. The Story of How They're Made and What They Mean,* George Allen & Unwin Ltd. London, 1981

Stevens, K. Mark and Wehrfritz, G. E., *Southwest China: Off the Beaten Track,* Collins, London, 1988

Stockwell, Foster, *Religion in China Today,* New World Press, Beijing, undated

'Storm-hit Tibetans enjoy better lives', *China Daily,* 2 May 1995

Study in China: A Guide for Foreign Students, by the Secretariat of the Chinese National Society of Universities and Colleges for Foreign Student Affairs, Beijing Language and Culture University Press, undated

Su Bo, 'Women's Marital Status: Past and Present', *Beijing Review,* 11–17 March 1996, p. 19

Sullivan, Michael, *The Arts of China,* University of California Press, Berkeley, 1977

'Survey says university students shun exercise', *China Daily,* 26 April 1996, p. 3

Su Xiaohuan, *The First Step Towards Equality, Topic on Women's Education,* China Intercontinental Press, Beijing, 1995

Talcott Hibbert, Eloise, *Embroidered Gauze, portraits of famous Chinese ladies,* John Lane The Bodley Head, 1938

Tao Liqun, 'Conditions of Elderly Chinese Women', *Women of China,* June 1996, pp. 15–18

Teachers of the Inner Chambers: Women and Culture in Seventeenth-century China, Stanford University Press, 1995

Terzani, Tiziano, *Behind the Forbidden Door,* Allen & Unwin, London, 1985

The Art of Dancing of China 1942–1992, The Literature and Art Publisher of Jiangeu Province, P.R. China, undated

The Directory of British Organisations with a China Interest, The Great Britain China Centre, London, 1993

The Foreign Experts' Handbook, A Guide to Living in China, New World Press, Beijing, undated

The Situation of Chinese Women, Information Office of the State Council of the PRC, June 1994, Beijing

Theroux, Paul, *Riding the Iron Rooster,* Hamish Hamilton, London, 1988

Thomson, H. C., *The Case for China,* George Allen & Unwin Ltd, 1933

Tregear, T. R., *China, A Geographical Survey,* Hodder and Stoughton, London, 1980

Tregear, T.R., *A Geography of China,* University of London Press Ltd, London, 1965

Tregear, T. R., *The Chinese, How They Live & Work,* David & Charles, Newton Abbot, 1973

Trevor-Roper, Hugh, *Hermit of Peking,* Eland, London, 1993

Ward, Kaari (ed.), 'Famine in China', *Great Disasters,* Readers Digest, New York/Montreal, 1989

'Unemployed women find hope in class', *China Daily*/Xinhua, 14 March 1996

Unterrieder, Else, 'Neujahrsbeginn und Frühlingserwachen', *China verstehen*, Sympathie-Magazin Nr 10

Wang Xiuying, 'China's First Generation of Policewomen', *China Pictorial*, June 1996, p. 55

Wang Xiuying, 'Green Food in China', *China Pictorial*, June 1996, pp. 18–19

Watt, George, *China 'Spy'*, Johnson, London, 1972

Wei, Karen T. (ed.), *Women in China: A Selected and Annotated Bibliography*. Greenwood Press, London, 1984

Wei Wei, 'Help wanted: Anyone that can teach music', *China Daily*, 12 May 1994

Weiner, Rebecca, Murphy, Margaret and Li, Albert, *Living in China. A Guide to Teaching & Studying in China including Taiwan*, China Books & Periodicals Inc. San Francisco, 1991

Welcome to China, China National Tourist Office, London, undated

Wen Hua, 'A Tale of Two Cities – in China', *China Daily*, 4 March 1996, p. 9

Weng Ronghui (ed.), *The Chinese National Culture of Costume and Adornment*, China Textile Press, Beijing, undated

Wheeler Snow, Lois, *Edgar Snow's China*, Orbis Publishing, London, 1981

White, Theodore H., *The Mountain Road*, Cassell, London, 1958

Who's Who in China: Current Leaders, Foreign Languages Press, Beijing, undated

Williams, C.A.S., *Outlines of Chinese Symbolism and Art Motives*, Dover, New York, 1976

Wilson, Dick, *A Quarter of Mankind*, Weidenfeld & Nicolson, London, 1966

Wilson, Dick, *Mao The People's Emperor*, Futura Publications Limited, London, 1980

Wilson, Dick, *The Long March 1935, The Epic of Chinese Communism*, Viking Press, New York, 1971

Wo, Harry, *Bitter Winds – A Memoir of My Years in China's Gulag*, John Wiley, USA, 1994

Women and Men in China, Facts and Figures 1995, Department of Social Sience and Technology Statistics, State Statistical Bureau of PRC

Women in China: A Selected and Annotated Bibliography, Greenwood Press, 1984

WuDunn, Sheryl, 'China's secret war against women', *Sunday Times*, 3 September 1995, p. 4

Xiao Han, 'Dai Bamboo Stilt Houses', *China Pictorial*, April 1996, pp. 46–59

Xiao Huan, 'She Devoted Her Youth to Yimeng Mountains', *Women of China*, March 1996, pp. 19–21

Xiao Huan, 'Maternity and Child Care in Yinan County', *Women of China*, March 1996

Xiao Ming, 'No difficulty haunts her', *Women of China*, Beijing, May 1996, pp. 6–8

Xiao Ming, 'Pride of Uygur Women', *Women of China*, June 1996, pp. 13–15

Xiao Ming, 'Women in Jewellery Production', *Women of China*, Beijing, May 1996, pp. 4–6

Xiao Yuan, 'Effort to Rebuild Happiness', *Women of China*, May 1996, pp. 17–18

Xie Chen, 'How Do You Spend Your Weekends?', *China Pictorial*, February 1996, p. 8

Xie Chen, 'A Day in the Life of an Extraordinary Primary School Student', *China Pictorial*, January 1996, p. 30

Xu Lang *et al*, *Guiyang*, New World Press, Beijing, 1989

Xu Yuefen, 'Chinese Rural Women's Decision-Making Status in Family', *Women of China*, July 1996, pp 4–5

Ya Hanzhang, *Biographies of the Tibetan Spiritual Leaders Panchen Erdenis*, Foreign Languages Press, Beijing, undated

Yang Zingshi, 'Rocky Building Industry Targeted', *China Daily*, 12 April 1996, p. 1

Zhao Jun. 'An Interview with Chen Muhua', *China Pictorial*, March 1996, p. 8

Zhong Xiu, *Yunnan Travelogue – 100 Days in Southwest China*, New World Press, China Spotlight Series, Beijing, 1983

Zhu Baoxia, 'World Bank loan helps State fight tuberculosis', *China Daily*, 22 March 1996

Index

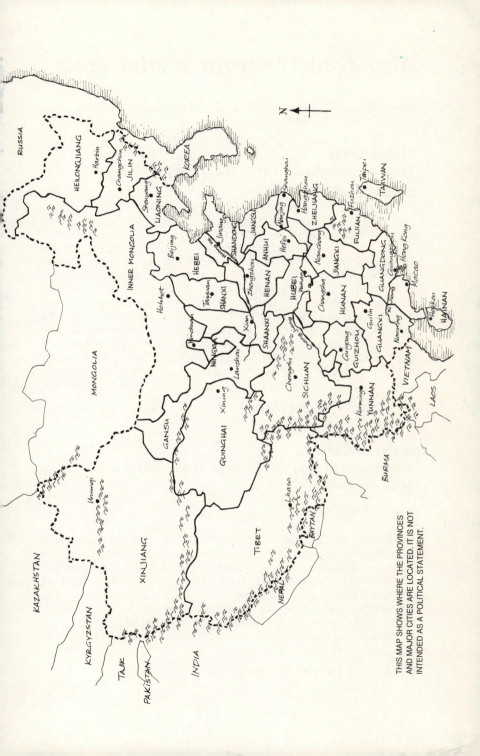

Also available from Scarlet Press

Stolen Lives
Trading women into sex and slavery
Sietske Altink

The trafficking of women for prostitution is one of the most shameful abuses of human rights. It is also a fundamental economic and development issue for Third World and East European countries. Driven by extreme poverty, women are forced to migrate in search of work which very often results in their exploitation either as prostitutes or domestic slaves. This important work reveals the way in which women are spuriously hired in their country of origin, transported, left without money or resources and are trapped into prostitution by organized crime syndicates. Sietske Altink has interviewed many women from the Far East, Latin America and the more recent recruits to the trade, women from the East European countries. Their stories tell us of their motives, the routes and methods the traffickers use and how the gangs control the women through blackmail and violence.

ISBN Paperback 1 85727 097 5

Scent of Saffron
A personal history of the lives of Iranian women in the 20th Century
Rouhi Shafii

The history of Iran in the 20th century is one of turbulent transformation. These events, have had a great socio-cultural impact on the structure of Iranian society and on the lives of ordinary people, particularly on the lives of women. Rouhi Shafii charts the impact of these changes through the experiences of three generations of women in her own family. From her grandmother's life in rural Iran in the 1920s, her mother's unhappy marriage and frustrated ambitions, to her own post-war career and final exile to London in the 1980s, she blends the personal and the political to provide a compelling social history.

ISBN Paperback 1 85727 088 6